DATE DUE

Democracy's Place

IAN SHAPIRO

Democracy's Place

Cornell University Press *Ithaca and London*

First published 1996 by Cornell University Press.

Library of Congress Cataloging-in-Publication Data
Shapiro, Ian.
    Democracy's Place / Ian Shapiro.
        p. cm.
    Includes bibliographical references and index.
    ISBN 0-8014-3309-6 (alk. paper). — ISBN 0-8014-8370-0 (pbk. :
alk. paper)
    1. Democracy. I. Title.
JC423.S465 1996
321.8—dc20

                                                96-7986

Printed in the United States of America

⊚ The paper in this book meets the minimum requirements
of the American National Standard for Information Sciences—
Permanence of Paper for Printed Library Materials, ANSI Z39.48-1984.

For Bob Dahl

Scaffolding

Masons, when they start upon a building,
Are careful to test out the scaffolding;

Make sure that planks won't slip at busy points,
Secure all ladders, tighten bolted joints.

And yet all this comes down when the job's done,
Showing off walls of sure and solid stone.

So if, my dear, there sometimes seem to be
Old bridges breaking between you and me,

Never fear. We may let the scaffolds fall,
Confident that we have built our wall.

—Seamus Heaney

Contents

Preface

Some accounts of psychological health emphasize shedding the accumulated baggage of the past; others stress coming to grips with it. It has always seemed to me that both contain sage advice. The cumulative effects of a past that we did not design and could not control have made all of us substantially what we are. Our particular histories shape our senses of ourselves, our values, aspirations, and limitations. To deny the past is to deny ourselves; at best it is fruitless, at worst a recipe for perpetual frustration. Yet, many experience a genuine lack in what the past has made of them. They resent its constraints, sense that it might have been better, and see a substantial part of the project of living as one of liberation and transformation. They are right to react in this way. Acquiescence in what the past has left denies a feature of human personality that is no more dispensable than its historical constitution: the impulse to take hold of one's destiny and reshape it in better ways. The answer is not to choose one of these views but rather to see them as mutually reinforcing. Critical owning of the past frees us from some—though not all—of its constraints, opening up the possibility of more authentic shaping of the present and future.

An underlying message of this book is that collective life exhibits analogous tensions that can be thought about similarly with profit. The account of democracy I try to render plausible and attractive treats it as a subordinate or conditioning good, intended to help reshape inherited forms of interaction in better directions as we reproduce them. It involves rejecting the idea of institutional design in favor of institutional *re*design, as more characteristic of, and appropriate to, the human condition. It takes for granted the existence of a social reality that we usually have good reasons both for embracing and for wanting to change, and it involves accepting historically constituted identities and practices without capitulating to them. It is a view in which democracy is valued without being the most important value, best realized in conjunction with—rather than instead of—other valuable goods. Hence my title, *Democracy's Place*. My central concern is with the ways in which democratic ways of doing things can be made to fit well with other human values, better to shape the ways in which people pursue their collective goals.

But why *democracy*? The answer is to be sought in the ubiquitous character of collective life. Much political theory is written as though the basic issue of politics were Whether-or-not collective life? In my view the real question is What sort of collective life? Like it or not, I argue in these pages, in the modern world this makes considerations of democracy inescapable. Because no man is an island, as Donne said, our fates are inescapably linked. Most everything we do takes for granted the existence of a panoply of collectively sustained institutions, rules, practices, and norms. These might have been ordered differently than they are, and aspects of them, at least, could be changed in the present and future. Moreover, although collective life is inescapable, every way of ordering it has effects that some will reasonably find objectionable. It is this reality, in my view, that sets the basic terms of politics. My hope is to convince readers that the understanding of democracy elaborated here offers a better response to it than do the going alternatives.

Just as individual and collective histories mold present personalities and institutions, so the history of one's thinking shapes its present form. The chapters that follow were written as free-standing essays over a ten-year period starting in the mid-1980s. They were conceived in response to discrete problems, but they have all played roles in an evolution toward the view that I describe in Chapter 8 as democratic justice. Readers will notice that much of my thinking about this subject has been shaped by political developments in my native South Africa. It would be astonishing were this not the case, given the momentous events there. No doubt my preoccupation with South African politics carries with it blindnesses and limitations. Whether the corresponding insights are of compensating value is up to the reader to judge.

In reworking the essays for this book, I have made their links with one another explicit, updated references and some of the commentary in the footnotes, and made other minor modifications. I have not, however, altered them beyond this, even though I would write some of them differently were I starting afresh today. Versions of Chapters 2 and

6 appeared in *NOMOS XXXII* (1989) and *NOMOS XXXVIII* (1996), and are reissued here with permission from New York University Press. Predecessors to Chapters 3, 5, and 8 were published, respectively, in *Political Theory*, 19, no. 1, pp. 47–72, copyright © 1991 by Sage Publications, Inc., 22, no. 1, pp. 124–51, copyright © 1994 by Sage Publications, Inc., and 24, no. 4. They are reprinted by permission of Sage Publications, Inc. An earlier incarnation of Chapter 4 appeared in *World Politics*, 46, no. 1, pp. 121–50, copyright © 1993, and is reprinted now by permission of the Johns Hopkins University Press. Chapter 7 first appeared in *Politics and Society* 23, no. 3, pp. 269–308, copyright © 1995 by Sage Publications, Inc., and is reprinted now by permission of Sage Publications, Inc. "Scaffolding" from *Poems 1965–1975* by Seamus Heaney is copyright © 1980 by Seamus Heaney and reprinted by permission of Farrar, Straus & Giroux, Inc. in the United States. Elsewhere in the world the poem appears in Heaney's *Death of a Naturalist* and is reprinted by permission of Faber & Faber Inc.

The chapters were all presented at numerous seminars and workshops, and I am indebted to a great many more discussants, colleagues, and students than it would be wise to try to enumerate. I should, however, single out my respective coauthors of Chapters 6 and 7, Richard Arneson and Courtney Jung, for kindly consenting to my including our collaborative work here. Working with Arneson reminded me that disagreements about vocabulary should never stand in the way of matters of substantive import, whereas the collaboration with Jung made it abundantly clear that professors may have as much to learn from their students as they have to teach them. Finally, I thank Ian Hurd and Graham Duncan for valiant research assistance in putting the volume together, and Roger Haydon of Cornell University Press for guiding it into print.

IAN SHAPIRO

New Haven, Connecticut

Democracy's Place

1

Finding Democracy's Place

The essays collected here were written between the mid-1980s and the mid-1990s, one of the most tumultuous political decades of our century, or any. It was an especially heady time for democrats the world over, as democratic ideals made astonishing gains in defiance of every—conventional and unconventional—wisdom. Imagine the reaction to anyone who had suggested, even as recently as 1988, that just around the corner lay the collapse of the Soviet Union and its replacement by fledgling democracies in Russia and most of the old Soviet Republics, the peaceful reunification of Germany, transitions to democracy in much of Eastern Europe and Latin America, and a negotiated demise to South African apartheid that would take Nelson Mandela from prison to the presidency, with F. W. De Klerk his elected deputy. One does not have to contemplate these developments for long to recognize that the study of politics has some distance to travel as a predictive science. Nor does one have to reflect on them much before realizing that they pose profound questions for democratic politics.

Although democracy's advances have exceeded many expectations, democrats are bound to judge the political narrative of the last decade as less than triumphalist. The new democracies are insecure at many of their moorings, as radical nationalist, neofascist, and fundamentalist ideologies vie for populist support in many of them. As was perhaps most clearly underscored by the events following the Algerian parliamentary elections of December 1991, democracy rests on fragile institutions that can easily be destroyed. In most posttransition countries it remains an open question whether meaningful competitive politics will take hold. One conventional rule of thumb in political science is that a

democracy cannot be declared established until posttransition governments have twice lost elections and given up power peacefully. By that
test the jury remains out on all the post-1989 democracies. At the end of
1995, single turnovers had occurred in Argentina, Brazil, Hungary,
Lithuania, and Poland, and the willingness of post-1989 governments to
give up power had yet to be put to any test in the remaining new
democracies. In several posttransition countries, most vividly, perhaps,
Bosnia and parts of Russia such as Chechnya, civil war remained the
threat or the reality.

The economic systems emerging in the new democracies are, if anything, less encouraging than the political arrangements. Some posttransition economies are dominated by organized-crime mafias and perhaps most aptly described as gangster capitalism. Most contain high,
and growing, levels of poverty and unemployment.[1] Perhaps they will
turn out to be viable economic orders in the medium term; it is too soon
to say. It is also unclear whether these new brands of poor capitalism
can coexist with democracy. At best, it will be difficult. At worst, the
economic reality in several of the new democracies calls to mind the
kleptocracies that developed in postcolonial Africa and Latin America
in the 1960s and 1970s. An increasingly common refrain in Western
intellectual circles in the mid-1990s is that China's potent mixture of
commu-capitalism, substantially financed by multinationals and based
on political authoritarianism and virtual slave labor in many sectors,
will prove more viable than the post-Soviet transitions. Democrats can
only hope this prognostication turns out to be as wide of the mark as so
many of the others.

The older democracies do not present a much more heartening picture. Indeed, one of the ironies of the decade is that at the same time that
democratic values have been snowballing through so much of the
world, many of the Western countries that spawned those values are
confronting major failings of democratic legitimacy. Internally, urban
decay, unemployment, cultural divisions, and generational, class, and
racial conflicts combine to put major stresses on democratic institutions.
These difficulties are aggravated by transnational forces: exponential
increases in the mobility of capital and information, unprecedented
environmental threats, new and frighteningly unmanageable diseases,
and the relentless growth of the world's population. The result is that
national political institutions confront challenges to which they are less
than equal, and political leaders appear inept. This, in turn, reinforces

[1]For data on the increases in unemployment and poverty in the ex-Soviet bloc countries, see
Peter Gowan, "Neo-liberal Theory and Practice in Eastern Europe," *New Left Review*, no. 213
(September/October 1995), pp. 16–23.

stereotypical images of politicians as preoccupied with feathering their own nests through pork barrel politics, perks, and reelection machines, while deficits soar out of control and structural problems multiply. No doubt such phenomena can be exaggerated, but there is no denying that the end-of-century global context creates new pressures for the established democracies. It drives wages down and unemployment up with a harshness many thought had been left behind in the 1960s, weakens trade unions and threatens welfare states throughout the developed West, and breeds xenophobic populism—as politicians manipulate these and other insecurities in search of electoral advantage.

Why, then, a collection of essays on the theory and practice of democracy? Part of the answer is implicit in what has already been said. For all its problems, failures, and ambiguities, democracy has won the day in the sense that it has no serious political competitor in the modern world. True, many powerful antidemocratic political forces and ideas exist, but it is striking how even fundamentalist, neofascist, and nationalist movements often find it expedient to appeal to a democratic idiom. In the United States, to give a poignant illustration, fundamentalists who attack "liberal elites" believe, no doubt, that they are acting on God's orders. Yet they seek *political* legitimacy as agents of a "moral *majority*." Such appeals reflect a grasp of what might be described as democracy's nonoptional character. Although few would openly assert that the state may require people to be liberal or conservative, or to belong to a particular (or indeed any) religion, few would deny that all are bound to accept the results of appropriately functioning democratic procedures. We are relatively free to despise democratically elected governments, but not their legitimacy as governments. This is not to dispute that different people understand different things by democracy. Nor is it to deny that every democratic order will be thought by some to be functioning not as it should, to be in the corrupt control of an illicit minority, or otherwise in need of repair. But the very terms of such objections to democracy affirm its nonoptional character, as it is the malfunction or corruption of democracy which is being objected to, rather than democracy itself.

If much contemporary politics is carried on within a democratic idiom, this does not mean that democracy rests on solid intellectual foundations. Indeed it is notable that despite democracy's unprecedented political successes of late, since the 1950s it has been subject to trenchant assaults within the academy. These have come from two principal groups that I describe as the partisans of reason and those of justice. The former question democracy's coherence as an idea, often by appeal to various findings in economics and political science about the logic of decision rules. The latter, usually writing either under the influence of or in response to John Rawls's 1971 classic *A Theory of Justice*,[2] reject democracy for its inequitable effects. Sometimes at loggerheads, sometimes in tandem, these two groups mount powerful arguments against the desirability, even feasibility, of genuinely democratic politics. Their arguments, if sound, should at least give democrats pause about the wisdom of trying to remake the global political landscape in their own image.

In my view, although the partisans of reason and justice appropriately prompt some rethinking of democracy's nature and its place in collective life, their assaults are basically wrongheaded. My wish to render this claim persuasive and explore its implications motivates these essays. In them I advance a distinctive view of democratic politics; I argue that it provides a better foundational political commitment than the going alternatives; I make the case that it is integral to persuasive arguments about justice; and I trace its implications through a variety of political contexts. As this summation indicates, my stance is not one of hostility to the claims of reason and justice. Rather, my aim is to debunk spurious appeals to both these values while articulating a view of democratic politics that can reconcile itself to their legitimate demands in a plausible and satisfying way.

Before sketching the main elements of my account, some remarks are in order about my manner of proceeding. I believe that political theory is most fruitfully developed in applied contexts. By this I do not mean to embrace a view akin to that of the old legal realists, who believed that understanding a problem in all its richness and complexity would somehow cause the right course of action to leap out as self-evident. Close-to-the-ground understanding may lead us to see a problem in a new light, or see new obstacles to—and possibilities for—its resolution; but no amount of contextual analysis will, by itself, reveal the best course of action for all concerned. We know too much today about how little uncontroversial knowledge there is in the human sciences to accept this sanguine pragmatism and contextual ethics. Furthermore, we are bound to take seriously the possibility that where people's natures and interests differ sufficiently, and alternative courses of action are open in a given situation, there may be no obvious best solution.[3]

Nor does my stance stem from the postmodern claim that political theory should be developed "without" foundations. For reasons that I

---

[2]John Rawls, *A Theory of Justice* (Cambridge: Harvard University Press, 1971).

[3]For a useful critique of legal realists' "situation sense," see Bruce Ackerman, *Reconstructing American Law* (Cambridge: Harvard University Press, 1983), pp. 93–110.

have set out in detail elsewhere, I believe that advocates of this view commit the fallacy of identifying one ill-conceived foundational enterprise, famously associated with the Cartesian and Kantian projects of providing a bedrock for knowledge that defies every skeptical doubt, with all attempts to provide adequate foundations for our beliefs.[4] Because we cannot find an indubitable basis for all knowledge in deductive introspection, so the argument goes, we should henceforth abandon the enterprise. To me, this makes about as much sense as saying that just because there is no single type of foundation on which all buildings—whatever their size, construction, purpose, or location—can be built such that they will last forever, henceforth we should build all buildings without any foundations at all. Then they would all fall over. In the fullness of time perhaps all our constructions will disappear, as will we, but this cannot concern us much. We are bound to live in the here and now, building our no doubt corrigible foundations as best we can with the materials ready to hand.

My method of proceeding is problem driven. No metaphysical or epistemological question is off limits, but I think inquiry most likely to be fruitful if we start with first-order problems and engage higher-order commitments only to the degree necessary to tackle them. If we begin with the foundational questions, the risk is that we may never reach the first-order problems or might reach them in unhelpful ways. "Better it is for philosophy to err in active participation in the living struggles and issues of its own age," John Dewey wisely urged, "than to maintain an immune monastic impeccability."[5] Such injunctions do not make Dewey an antifoundationalist, as Richard Rorty and others have contended.[6] Rather, they flow from the thought that the adequacy of general beliefs is usually tested in the realm of the particular and that we are often forced to modify and recast them in light of an unexpected or recalcitrant reality. A good deal of what passes for "ideal" political theory carries with it a whiff of irrelevance for almost everyone except those who produce it, because its links to the realm of the "second best" are often so difficult to discern or to make practical.

This is not to say that working out problems counterfactually or in the abstract is invariably without value. Such explorations can reveal contradictions and possibilities that might otherwise go unnoticed, and sometimes these may be worth knowing about. But they can also be

[4]See my *Political Criticism* (Berkeley: University of California Press, 1990).
[5]John Dewey, *Characters and Events*, ed. Joseph Ratner (New York: Holt, 1929), vol. 1, p. iii.
[6]Richard Rorty, *Consequences of Pragmatism* (Minneapolis: University of Minnesota Press, 1982), chaps. 1, 4, and 5.

artifacts of theoretical constructions with no relevance to actual problems, in which case pursuing them will be a waste of time.[7] For instance, in principle it might be useful to speculate, as neo-Kantian political theorists do, about what political institutions appropriately reflective people would unanimously have agreed upon were they designing them *tabula rasa*, even if political institutions never have been created in this way and most likely could not be thus created. If there were an answer to such a question, it might arguably provide a yardstick for political evaluation: regimes that more closely resemble the counterfactual ideal could be judged superior to those that resemble it less well. If, however, there is no compelling answer to the motivating question, as the existence of multiple pretenders to the neo-Kantian throne suggests is the case, then the enterprise is forlorn.[8] Perhaps one answer will eventually triumph over the others in debates of this kind; I remain skeptical. Accordingly, my inclination is to theorize about ideals from the standpoint of what ideal theorists think of as the realm of the second best. This is not to eschew general argument. Rather, it is to pursue it in light of more nuanced attention to the realities of politics than ideal theorists usually attempt.

The distinctive content of my account stems from democracy's historical association with opposition to unjust social arrangements. This link and its implications have been insufficiently attended to, I think, partly because of the way in which the partisans of reason and justice have defined the terms of debate. The former have operated from the presumption that the enterprise of democratic theory is to render coherent Rousseau's mind-numbing account of how to discover the "general will" in a democracy: start with "the sum of individual desires," subtract "the plusses and minuses which cancel each other out," and then "the sum of the difference is the general will."[9] Because it has been a conventional wisdom of political science since Kenneth Arrow wrote in the early 1950s that this determination cannot be achieved even in principle, democracy has too readily been rejected as an unworkable, even self-defeating, political system.[10] On my account, there is an im-

---

[7]See Donald P. Green and Ian Shapiro, *Pathologies of Rational Choice Theory: A Critique of Applications in Political Science* (New Haven: Yale University Press, 1994), esp. chaps. 3 and 8.

[8]See Robert Paul Wolff, *In Defense of Anarchism* (New York: Harper and Row, 1970), Rawls, *Theory of Justice*, Robert Nozick, *Anarchy, State, and Utopia* (Oxford: Blackwell, 1974), and Bruce Ackerman, *Social Justice in the Liberal State* (New Haven: Yale University Press, 1980).

[9]Jean-Jacques Rousseau, *The Social Contract* (Harmondsworth: Penguin, 1968), p. 72.

[10]Kenneth J. Arrow, *Social Choice and Individual Values* (New Haven: Yale University Press, 1951). For a representative example of the subsequent literature, see William H. Riker, *Liberalism against Populism: A Confrontation between the Theory of Democracy and the Theory of Social Choice* (San Francisco: W. H. Freeman, 1982).

portant democratic enterprise that does not revolve around trying to render Rousseau's project coherent. It is concerned instead with empowering the disempowered through more, rather than less, inclusive mechanisms of collective decision and through institutionalizing freedom to resist collective outcomes that one opposes.

Whereas the friends of reason often criticize democracy from the standpoint of a counterfactual of "no" collective action, the partisans of justice proceed as if what is just in the distribution of social goods and harms can be settled independently of what democracy requires. This assumption is reflected in the fact that debates about justice spawned by Rawls since the 1960s have proceeded in relative isolation from the literature on democracy. But the search for justice is more intimately linked to democracy than this mode of proceeding would suggest. In the contemporary world at least, outcomes that justice is alleged to require are unlikely to be judged persuasive unless they can be rendered compatible, in some way, with people's democratic convictions. Indeed, partly for this reason, arguments for particular theories of justice often involve tacit reliance on what theorists take these convictions to be. But because the appeals are tacit, democracy's proper place in arguments about justice remains underexplored. This is an undesirable state of affairs. It contributes to the tendency among justice theorists to focus, as one colleague recently put it, on questions that are three points to the right of the decimal. Attending to democratic considerations brings questions of institutional design and, therefore, implementability to the fore. Without that anchor, energy can all too easily be dissipated on issues that make no practical difference. This, in turn, reinforces a reality in which justice theorists write principally for one another. If the issues about which one theorizes have few, if any, consequences that can be institutionalized, it cannot be surprising that one's audience is limited to one's theoretical kin. In sum, my methodological predisposition for problem-driven argument is reinforced by the substantive account that I try to develop.

In the next two chapters I begin trying to redefine the terms of debate. Starting with the partisans of reason in Chapter 2, I debunk three common fallacies about democratic politics and majority rule which have grown out of the normative rational choice literature since the 1950s. First is the *reductionist fallacy*, proponents of which count it a defect of majority rule that it fails to "amalgamate" individual preferences in ways that parallel idealized models of the market's amalgamation of economic preferences. In effect they regard the failure of majoritarian procedures to consummate Rousseau's project as a sufficient warrant to reject majoritarian democracy. I argue, however, that this view rests on counterfactuals that should not be judged plausible. In particular, it takes for granted the implausible notion that a scheme of collective action is an alternative to a scheme of private action when in fact the latter is parasitic on the former. What ought really to be at issue is not the Rousseauist project or any ideal scheme of collective decision. Rather, it should be the going alternative decision rules and *their* comparative advantages and limitations, given the inevitability of collective interaction that is laced with inequalities of power. Viewed from that vantage point, a default presumption in favor of majority rule—or something close to it—is indeed defensible, though not for every circumstance.

The related *constitutionalist fallacy* involves the claim that because majority rule is vulnerable to manipulation, or because it can harm minorities, or both, its scope should be restricted by other institutions, such as courts. This fallacy rests on two legs, the first having to do with blindness to the limitations of the going alternative institutions, the second with ignoring one of the principal justifications for majoritarian politics. Regarding the former, many of the same analytical arguments used to attack legislatures as manipulable by agenda-setting minorities for partisan benefit can also be applied to courts, perhaps with greater force. In the American context at least, appellate courts make their decisions by majority rule, and those who control their agendas have a good deal more of the requisite knowledge about the relevant players' preferences than is often the case in larger voting contexts. With respect to the latter, it is too often forgotten that, historically, a principal justification for majority rule was that it would, indeed, lead to a diminution in the illicit power of hereditary aristocracies and the very wealthy. There are, in sum, minorities and minorities. Hostility to some of them is an appealing feature of majority rule.

Third, the *instability fallacy* involves taking it to be a defect of majority rule that it is vulnerable to what rational choice theorists describe as cycling and may fail to produce equilibrium outcomes as a result. If we lived in a world in which either perfect decision rules or a regime of pure private action were possibilities, these and related instabilities of majority rule might be troubling. Because, in fact, we live in a world of ubiquitous collective action and imperfect mechanisms of collective decision, the attractiveness of what rational choice theorists think of as stability is questionable. Building on the pluralist arguments of Robert Dahl, Nicholas Miller, and others, I make the case that we should be open to the possibility that endemic vulnerability of the status quo to disruption has its advantages, even if there are good reasons to keep the disruption within manageable institutional bounds. Permanent vulnerability of the status quo can limit the entrenchment of ossified forms of power, give those who lose in particular conflicts reasons to remain committed to a democratic order, and be conducive to institutional stability—as distinct from rational choice stability—as a result.

In Chapter 3, I turn my attention to the partisans of justice. Like the friends of reason, they suppose that there is some "bird's-eye" standpoint, existing previously to and independently of democratic procedures, by reference to which we can evaluate the outcomes they produce. In its modern formulations this perspective originates with John Locke's discussion of the workmanship ideal, the notion that rights of legitimate ownership over a thing derive from the making of it. Originally conceived as a theological account of why human beings, as God's creations, are obliged to him through natural law, the workmanship ideal supplied the basis for Locke's theory of property, the labor theory of value, and much subsequent thinking about the normative foundations of justice. I make the case that, stripped of the theological assumptions that gave the workmanship ideal its coherence, the neo-Lockean scheme confronts intractable internal difficulties. The strategies employed to deal with these difficulties all fail; as a result the workmanship ideal does not provide a normative baseline for thinking about just entitlements. No more successful are recent attempts by John Rawls, Ronald Dworkin, and others to socialize the thinking behind the workmanship ideal. Taken seriously, such attempts self-destruct as viable bases for just entitlement and even threaten the idea of personal identity. The upshot, I suggest, is that if workmanship is to be defended at all, it can only be on consequentialist grounds. The difficulty then becomes that the desirability of the consequences in question is debatable, suggesting that they should have to vie for support with other values and social policies. Like it or not, democracy thus rears its head in the very definition of justice.

If considerations of reason and justice do not dethrone democracy, neither do they coronate any particular variant of it as deserving of our first allegiance. Rather, they suggest more nuanced questions: How should we conceive of democracy? and What are its relations to the demands of justice and rationality? I begin to tackle these issues in Chapter 4 by reflecting on Joseph Schumpeter's account of democracy, arguably the most influential of the twentieth century. Acting on my rule of thumb that theoretical arguments are most fruitfully evaluated in applied contexts, I examine Schumpeterianism through the lens of South Africa's fledgling democratic institutions. What it is reasonable to expect from democracy by way of undoing historical injustice and fairly representing all pertinent interests is thrown into sharp relief there, where distributive equity has long been so manifestly lacking and no credible attempt has been made until recently to create fairly representative institutions. The message of Schumpeterianism is that the demands on democracy are prudently diminished in two ways. First, we should trade in the conceptually troublesome idea of representative government for a model in which political elites compete for voter allegiance just as—in competitive markets—firms compete for consumer allegiance. Second, as far as possible, we should divorce democracy's legitimacy from expectations that it will deliver much in the way of social justice. Given the South African reality, how should this view be evaluated?

Schumpetarianism is often criticized on the grounds that its goal of rendering democratic ideals realistic is achieved at too high a price. It might result in a model that conduces to political stability, but why should it command allegiance when it gives up so completely on representative government and abandons the link between democracy and eroding injustice? This criticism has considerable force when viewed from the standpoint of classical democratic theory or of countries that have had democratic institutions for some time. But in countries like South Africa we must consider a different and more Hobbesian question: What if the alternatives to Schumpeterianism are a continuation of an exclusionary racial oligarchy or civil war? These, arguably, are the appropriate counterfactuals to bear in mind there.

There is something to be said for Schumpeterian minimalism in such contexts, but less, I think, than its proponents do. On the one hand, viewed from an ex ante condition where they are lacking, the benefits of minimalist democracy should not be judged trivial. On the other hand, in countries with a history of injustice like South Africa's, it is difficult to imagine that democracy's legitimacy can be detached from expectations of improvement. More fundamentally, perhaps, by focusing exclusively on elite politics and national institutions, Schumpetarian writers ignore both political elites' relations with grass roots political organizations and the role of democracy within civil institutions. This result leads, ironically, to the conclusion that the goals of Schumpeterian minimalism are unrealistic. Democracy cannot be expected to sustain itself if it neither breeds democratic habits of interaction among the population nor reduces injustice within the institutions that structure everyday life.

If the upshot of Chapter 4 is that democracy cannot reasonably be divorced from considerations of justice, the argument of Chapter 5 is that justice cannot be persuasively specified without attention to democracy. In three different but related respects, I maintain, democratic considerations are appropriately implicated in arguments about social justice. The first has to do with the *metrics* of justice, the units of account by reference to which distributive principles are contended about and applied. I agree with those who, like Alasdair MacIntyre and Michael Walzer, argue that there is no single metric—such as utility or primary goods—to which social goods can all be reduced. But I advocate a more radically pluralist view of the good than they do. It rests on recognizing that in real life there is bound to be conflict and disagreement both over what the appropriate metrics of justice within different domains of social life are and over how to draw the lines that divide them. This leads me to defend the view that democratic considerations should play a role in specifying—and respecifying—the distinctions among domains and the operative values within them. People should be able to choose for themselves, within an evolving framework of democratic constraints, what their metrics of justice should be.

Democratic considerations should play a role, too, in defining the *principles* that are employed in ordering social life justly. One of the main ways in which injustice manifests itself is in the domination of some by others. Thus an essential part of the pursuit of justice should be eradicating, or at least diminishing, such domination. I make the case that although domination is not the same thing as hierarchy, it often operates through hierarchies of various kinds. For this reason, hierarchies are reasonably presumed suspect. This is not to deny that hierarchies can be valuable and efficient, but all too often they atrophy into systems of domination which impose on people unnecessarily. Democratic principles can be instrumental in limiting these corrosive effects of hierarchy, particularly if they are construed—as I argue that they ought to be—to entail a right of "loyal" opposition, a right to resist imposed solutions, within limits, and to seek to alter existing practices. It is better that collective decisions are made more, rather than less, democratically, but even when they are made as democratically as possible, this does not extinguish the right of loyal opposition on the part of those who lose. As there are no perfect decision rules, a degree of imposition attaches to all collective decisions, and those who lose may reasonably aspire to achieve a different result in the future. This is not to deny that there is a link between government and opposition in democratic theory: the more conscientiously democratic about decision making those who win in politics are, the stronger is the obligation on losers to ensure that their opposition is loyal rather than disloyal.

Essential as democratic constraints on collective interaction may be, they are not the be-all and end-all of life. They are valuable but not the most important value, best thought of as shaping the terms of collective life but not as displacing its content. Politics suffuses all dimensions of social life because power relations do; this is why rights to participate in decisions by which one is affected, and to oppose unwelcome results, are defensible and desirable. But although power relations suffuse most everything we do, they are almost never the totality of what we do. This is why democracy is best thought of as a subordinate or conditioning good. Institutional redesign and reform should be geared toward creating arrangements that nudge social practices to evolve in more rather than less democratic directions as they reproduce themselves, while remaining in a subordinate role. If doing things democratically becomes the point of the exercise, it has failed in this endeavor. The creative challenge is to promote democratic ways of doing things while avoiding this outcome. I argue that, other things being equal, this challenge is best met by bringing democratic *methods* to the project of democratic reform. The histories of vanguards, experts, and ambitious institutional blueprints reasonably prompt suspicion of all claims made on their behalf. Given the limitations of social-scientific knowledge, the appropriate course is to attend to particular impediments to democracy rather than devise grand schemes and, where possible, to find ways to induce people to democratize their interactions for themselves rather than impose democracy on them.

In Chapters 6 and 7, written with Richard Arneson and Courtney Jung respectively, democracy's appropriate role in structuring social life is explored in two applied contexts.[11] The first relates to conflicts between democracy and self-consciously undemocratic civil institutions; the second deals with democratic transitions and constitutional design. Both deal with prima facie hard cases for the view I am seeking to develop. In them, democracy finds itself in substantial conflict with widely held intuitions about the demands of reason and justice. In Chapter 6, Arneson and I take up the much debated subject of the Amish, a withdrawing Anabaptist sect that is avowedly undemocratic in its social arrangements. The Amish represent a hard case for two reasons. First, though undemocratic they are not antidemocratic; they pose no threat to the larger culture and do not even proselytize for their way of life outside the Amish community. Second, their social practices are rooted in religious convictions. Given the intensity of such convictions and the bitter history of religious conflict in so much of the West over the past four centuries, the prudent choice for democrats might

---

[11]Although, for me, these two chapters grow out of the larger concerns of this book and are vehicles for developing them, both were written as freestanding articles and neither coauthor bears responsibility for anything said elsewhere in this book.

reasonably be thought to involve navigating courses of generous toleration around them. These are among the reasons for supporting devices
such as the free exercise clause of the First Amendment, and we do not
seek to challenge them. If this were all that was at issue, the Amish
should surely be regarded as a voluntary community and left to their
own devices.

As the litigation that culminated in the 1972 United States Supreme
Court decision *Wisconsin v. Yoder* made clear, however, it is not all that is
at issue. Like all parents, the Amish exercise power and authority over
their children. But whereas most parents accept laws requiring compulsory education of children to age sixteen, Amish parents oppose it
beyond age fourteen because experience has taught them that it is in
these last two years of schooling that Amish teenagers are most likely to
develop and act on the desire to leave the community. The Supreme
Court took an accommodationist stance toward the Amish in *Yoder*,
exempting them from Wisconsin's statute requiring compulsory education to age sixteen. We argue that this was mistaken. Drawing on a
modified version of Locke's account of parental authority, we argue
that education of children to an age where critical reason is developed
and can be deployed is essential in a democracy. Children have a right
to it, and others have a right to expect it of them. This is not to say that
government appropriately guarantees every aspect of children's interests. Rather, we endorse the wisdom of a distinction between children's
basic interests and their best interests, only the former of which fall
within the province of government's fiduciary responsibility. What was
at issue in the *Yoder* litigation falls into the category of basic interests.

In Chapter 7, Jung and I explore the opposition side of the democratic
ethos and the presumption that democratization is best pursued
democratically. We attempt this in the context of a close examination of
South Africa's transition negotiations between 1990 and 1994. We
discern a profound tension between the two goals of creating an order
that facilitates effective loyal opposition, on the one hand, and negotiated transitions of the South African type, on the other. Because in such
negotiations the authoritarian government enjoys a structural advantage deriving from its control of the military, it forces its negotiating
partners to make substantial concessions during critical phases of the
negotiations. The result, when the outgoing government expects to be a
minority party in the new order, is that it manages to insist on power-
sharing arrangements that will give its representatives a guaranteed
place in the new government. A by-product of this dynamic is that
robust opposition institutions are not created because all the powerful
players are in the new government. And as Disraeli warned long ago,

"No government can long be secure without a formidable opposition."[12]

Whatever the limitations of Schumpeterian minimalism discussed in Chapter 4, in such circumstances even it cannot get off the ground. For competitive democracy to be viable, it is essential that parties compete for the right to be the government. This is why neo-Schumpeterians such as Samuel Huntington insist that before a regime can be called democratic, there must be at least two turnovers of power following elections. In constitutionally mandated power-sharing arrangements like the South African one, this dynamic is ruled out. The danger is that, as the government begins to lose popularity, those who become disaffected will fail to discern a meaningful distinction between the government of the day and the democratic political order. Instead of being expressed as loyal opposition, discontent will more readily be mobilizable in opposition to the democratic constitutional settlement, most likely by elites marginalized in the earlier transition negotiations. This is why the consociational model has been criticized by Donald Horowitz and others as unworkable in the medium term, and the evidence seems to be on their side.[13] It also brings to the surface one of the most questionable features of consociationalism: that it may produce the malady to which it is allegedly a response. If political identities are primordial givens, then institutions are appropriately shaped in response to them. If, as we suggest, political identities are to some extent shaped and mobilized by political elites in response to the institutional context, then putting consociational institutions into place will lead to the manufacture, and deepening, of ethnic division.

None of this is to deny that negotiated transitions of the South African sort may be the best way to end authoritarian government without civil war. The relevant counterfactuals are inherently unavailable, making it impossible to say definitively either way; but it seems reasonable to think that this may be so. What, then, of my contention in Chapter 5 that, ceteris paribus, democracy is best pursued democratically? Two considerations emerge from this examination of the South African transition which are pertinent to reflecting on the limits to the ceteris paribus clause. First, we note that it is really a misnomer to describe negotiated transitions like the South African one as "democratic." The two attempts at inclusive round-table negotiations to end apartheid were notable failures, largely because participating groups whose leaders believed that they stood to lose from a transition to democracy had no

[12]*The Oxford Dictionary of Quotations*, 3d ed. (Oxford: Oxford University Press, 1979), p. 185.
[13]See Donald L. Horowitz, *A Democratic South Africa? Constitutional Engineering in a Divided Society* (Berkeley: University of California Press, 1991), pp. 142–43.

incentive for the negotiations to succeed. The actual agreement was negotiated in secret between the National Party government and the moderate leadership of the African National Congress, and its terms were imposed, by force (or the threat thereof), on those who showed signs of resisting. To say that the transition was not in fact achieved democratically is not, of course, to say that it ought not to have been. But "ought" entails "can," and we argue, second, that because democratic constitutions are public goods, it may be inevitable that they be imposed. When the goal is to create a democratic constitutional order where previously one did not exist, there may be no democratic way to do it. This in turn suggests that, as South Africa moves into the phase of democratic consolidation, those responsible for institutional redesign would be wise to move in the direction of a more competitive model.[14]

My task in the final chapter is to sketch the main elements of a democratic conception of justice that builds on the preceding arguments. I explore, more fully than previously, both the foundations and the implications of the dual democratic commitment to inclusive participation and loyal opposition. I discuss the ways in which this commitment should shape a variety of institutions and relationships, including aspects of public institutions, domestic arrangements, work, and organized religious life. In anticipation of various objections, I discuss three types of tensions confronting the view that I defend. These are tensions arising from the internal complexities of my democratic account of justice, tensions between it and other valuable goods, and tensions—such as those explored in the South African context in Chapter 7—between means and ends in achieving democratic reform. In the course of exploring these issues, I fill in some of the main contours of the picture of the state suggested by my account. This leads to a deepening of my discussion of the presumption against vanguardism first put forward in Chapter 5, by way of an argument that this presumption should bow to certain exceptions where cumulative social injustice or public goods are concerned. In the course of discussing the institutional implications of this argument, I make the case for a constrained type of judicial review geared toward harmonizing the tensions within democratic justice and those between it and other social goods. This is a preliminary statement of a view that will be more fully developed elsewhere. However, I hope that it suffices as a constructive response, on democracy's behalf, to the partisans of reason and justice. If so, it will have moved us closer to the goal of finding democracy's place.

[14]This book went to press in February 1996. On reviewing final proofs in early May, I was heartened to note that a more competitive constitutional model had been adopted and that the National Party was planning to go into opposition.

2

Three Fallacies concerning Minorities, Majorities, and Democratic Politics

Minorities and majority rule, that is our subject. It is famously an American one. The tricky task for this constitutional democracy is to devise "ways of protecting minorities from majority tyranny that are not a flagrant contradiction of the principle of majority rule." The terms of the problem are set, John Hart Ely elaborates, by the fact that "a majority with untrammeled power to set governmental policy is in a position to deal itself benefits at the expense of the remaining minority." In Bruce Ackerman's words, "No modern contractarian has succeeded in vindicating majority rule without, at the same time, undermining the foundation of individual rights." As William Riker and Barry Weingast reiterate, majority rule "affords no protection against arbitrary actions or against actions directed at benefiting the temporary majority at some minority's expense."[1]

Yet at other times and in other places it was just this property of majority rule that made it simultaneously attractive to the disenfranchised and frightening to entrenched elites. For the English Chartists in the 1830s and 1840s, majority rule under conditions of universal suffrage was an oppositional ideal. In a society based on

[1]John Hart Ely, *Democracy and Distrust: A Theory of Judicial Review* (Cambridge: Harvard University Press, 1980), pp. 7–8; Bruce Ackerman, *Social Justice in the Liberal State* (New Haven: Yale University Press, 1980), p. 323; William H. Riker and Barry R. Weingast, "Constitutional Regulation of Legislative Choice: The Political Consequences of Judicial Deference to Legislatures," Hoover Institution Working Paper Series (Stanford, Calif., December 1986), p. 25.

hereditary accumulations of wealth and political privilege, majority rule was desired precisely to dispossess a minority of ill-gotten gains; and nineteenth-century liberals such as John Stuart Mill and Alexis de Tocqueville, who endorsed expansion of the franchise, were for this reason ambivalent about it.[2]

From the beginning the American preoccupation with majority rule was different. The problem was to domesticate and institutionalize an idea whose historical purpose had been to destabilize institutions. In the context of a society that, if not fully pluralist, appeared to lack one fundamental socioeconomic cleavage characteristic of nations with a feudal past,[3] Americans would be first to confront the fact that the minority harmed by the workings of majoritarian process need not be a rich and powerful elite; it could be a dispossessed racial or religious minority. American democratic theorists continue to be preoccupied with the logical properties of majority rule and its fairness from a neutral or "bird's-eye" standpoint, and they are often deeply troubled by discoveries that it can generate arbitrary outcomes as a result of cyclical majorities, strategic voting, and control of the voting agenda. Yet my central contention here is that a great deal of this concern is misplaced. Specifically, my goal is to debunk the three fallacies that dominate contemporary discussions of majority rule, minorities and democratic politics.

I. The Reductionist Fallacy

The origins of the reductionist fallacy lie in the economic modeling of political processes, specifically in the influential attempt by James Buchanan and Gordon Tullock—canonized in 1987 by Buchanan's receipt of the Nobel prize for economics—to analyze decision rules from the standpoint of a set of political analogues of neoclassical economic theory. Prefiguring a style of theoretical argument that would later be made famous by John Rawls, they asked the question What decision rules would mutually disinterested citizens choose at a constitutional convention when everyone is uncertain "as to what his own precise role

[2]Mill, for example, argued for a second vote for the intellectual classes, to temper the influence of the new majorities on bastions of privilege and autonomy; and Tocqueville argued to the reactionary Ultras in the 1830s that they should accept the inevitable expansion of democracy so as to have some hope of influencing its future direction. John Stuart Mill, *Utilitarianism, On Liberty, and Considerations on Representative Government* (London: Dent, 1972), pp. 276–92; Alexis de Tocqueville, *Democracy in America* (New York: Doubleday, Anchor, 1969), pp. 12–13.

[3]See Louis Hartz, *The Liberal Tradition in America: An Interpretation of American Political Thought since the Revolution* (New York: Harcourt, Brace, 1955), pp. 35–86.

will be in any one of the whole chain of later collective choices that will actually have to be made?" Whether selfish or altruistic, each agent is forced by the circumstances "to act, from self-interest, *as if* he were choosing the best set of rules for the social group."[4] Thus considered, they argued, there is no reason to prefer majority rule to the possible alternatives. Collective decision making invariably has costs and benefits for any individual, and an optimal decision rule would minimize the sum of "external costs" (the costs to an individual of the legal but harmful actions of third parties) and "decision-making costs" (those of negotiating agreement on collective action). The external costs of collective action diminish as increasingly large majorities are required; in the limiting case of unanimity rule, every individual is absolutely protected because anyone can veto a proposed action. Conversely, decision-making costs typically increase with the proportion required, as the costs of negotiation increase. The choice problem at the constitutional stage is to determine the point at which the combined costs are smallest for different types of collective action and then to agree on a range of decision rules to be applied in different future circumstances.[5]

At least three kinds of collective action can be distinguished requiring different decision rules. First is the initial decision rule that must prevail for other decision rules to be decided on. Buchanan and Tullock "assume, without elaboration, that at this ultimate stage . . . the rule of unanimity holds." Next come "those possible collective or public decisions which modify or restrict the structure of individual human or property rights after these have once been defined and generally accepted by the community." Foreseeing that collective action may "impose very severe costs on him," the individual will tend "to place a high value on the attainment of his consent, and he may be quite willing to undergo substantial decision-making costs in order to insure that he will, in fact, be reasonably protected against confiscation." He will thus require a decision rule approaching unanimity. Last is the class of collective actions characteristically undertaken by governments. For these "the individual will recognize that private organization will impose some interdependence costs on him, perhaps in significant amount, and he will, by hypothesis, have supported a shift of such activities to the public sector." Examples include provision of public education, enforcement of building and fire codes, and maintenance of adequate police forces. For such "general legislation" an individual at the con-

[4]James Buchanan and Gordon Tullock, *The Calculus of Consent: Logical Foundations of Constitutional Democracy* (Ann Arbor: University of Michigan Press, 1962), pp. 78, 96. Unless otherwise indicated all italics in quotations follow the original.
[5]Ibid., pp. 63–77.

stitutional stage will support less inclusive decision rules, though not necessarily simple majority rule, and indeed within this class different majorities might be agreed on as optimal for different purposes. "The number of categories, and the number of decision-making rules chosen, will depend on the situation which the individual expects to prevail and the 'returns to scale' expected to result from using the same rule over many activities."[6]

In that class of potential collective actions not covered by unanimity rule, there is an important sense in which the particular majority or minority is unimportant, because Buchanan and Tullock envisage a regime in which logrolling and vote trading are ubiquitous. While prevailing norms prohibit open buying and selling of votes, subtler forms of vote trading go on in democratic systems all the time, and they produce more efficient results in the literal Paretian sense that more people end up higher on their utility functions than would otherwise be so. If logrolling is disallowed, they argue, this can only be based on the assumption that all voters have equal, interpersonally comparable, utility scales on all issues, an assumption that is "wholly different from that which is employed in economic analysis."[7]

What makes this reductionist argument defective? To see this we must attend to the role played in it by unanimity. Unanimity as a decision rule has the unique property, Buchanan and Tullock argue, that if decision-making costs are zero, it is the only rational decision rule for all proposed collective action.[8] This argument confuses unanimity qua decision rule with unanimity qua social state. From the standpoint of the constitutional convention we have to assume that we are as likely to be ill disposed toward any future status quo as well disposed toward it, and in cases where we are ill disposed, a decision rule requiring unanimity will frustrate our preferences. Buchanan and Tullock assume throughout that it is departures from the status quo that need to be justified, but as Douglas Rae has shown, this is not warranted. Externalities over time, or "utility drift" (Rae's term), may change our eval-

[6]Ibid., pp. 77, 73, 73–74, 75, 75–76.
[7]Ibid., p. 126.
[8]This is not strictly true if vote trading is allowed. Under that assumption, and assuming also no decision-making costs, there is no optimal decision rule for the same reason as R. H. Coase showed: that, in the absence of information costs, wealth effects, external effects, and other blockages to exchange such as free riding, no system of tort liability rules is more efficient than any other. Whatever the system, people will then make exchanges to produce Pareto-optimal results. R. H. Coase, "The Problem of Social Cost," *Journal of Law and Economics* 3 (1960), pp. 1–44. Assuming, however, that a pure market in votes does not exist, and Buchanan and Tullock acknowledge that some constraints on it are inevitable, they maintain that unanimity would uniquely be chosen in the absence of decision-making costs. Buchanan and Tullock, *Calculus of Consent*, pp. 270–74.

uations of the status quo. We may feel in certain circumstances that failures to act collectively, rather than collective action itself, should shoulder the burden of proof.[9] We may change our minds for other reasons, foreseen or unforeseen, or a status quo that I reject might have been the product of unanimous agreement of a previous generation, by which I do not wish to be bound. Indeed Rae has shown formally that if we assume we are as likely to be against any proposal as for it, which the condition of uncertainty at the constitutional convention would seem to require, then majority rule or something very close to it[10] is the unique solution to Buchanan and Tullock's choice problem.[11]

Here I am concerned less with these analytical weaknesses than with unanimity's appeal as an ideal for Buchanan and Tullock. Notice first what it says about their expectations from decision rules. By arguing that decision-making costs are the only obstacles to unanimity, they take a quite benign view of political differences, such that if enough time *is* spent on negotiation, unanimity is assumed to be attainable. Although it is characteristic for economists to assume all disutilities to be compensable—so that at some price every individual will want a policy she did not previously want, some exchange that will leave her on as high an indifference curve as before enactment of the policy—in politics we cannot assume this. Even in strict interest-group politics, the narrowness of the interest being protected or advanced may mean that there are no substitution equivalents that make compensation, and hence unanimity, in principle possible. The substitution equivalent for those who opposed desegregation probably did not exist. Where votes are judgments about what public policy ought to be, the theory will often fare poorly. Involvement in a war in the Persian Gulf or Central America, or the teaching of religion in public schools, are generally embraced or rejected as matters of principle. To hold by assumption that unanimity in such cases is always possible through negotiation requires either a whiggish rationalism, a belief that if only we all talked

[9]See Douglas W. Rae, "The Limits of Consensual Decision," *American Political Science Review* 69, no. 4 (1975), pp. 1270–94. See also James S. Fishkin, *Tyranny and Legitimacy: A Critique of Political Theories* (Baltimore: Johns Hopkins University Press, 1979), p. 69.

[10]When the number of voters is odd the optimal decision rule is majority rule, n over 2, plus $1/2$; when n is even, the optimal decision rule is either majority rule (n over 2 plus 1) or majority rule minus one (simply n over 2). Douglas W. Rae, "Decision-Rules and Individual Values in Constitutional Choice," *American Political Science Review* 63, no. 1 (1969), pp. 40–56, 51.

[11]Barry Nalebuff has pointed out to me that there are other ways of tackling the problem of bias toward the status quo. For instance, our decision rule might be: adopt the policy that commands the largest majority among all proposals, including the status quo, in pairwise comparisons. Note, however, that this is empirically unrealistic (collective decisions are seldom presented in this form), and it ignores the organization costs of mobilizing to displace a status quo that will presumably be positive.

long enough all our disagreements would vanish, or a reductionist economism in which all politics is simply individual utility maximization.

The whiggish rationalism is well illustrated by Robert Paul Wolff, who also argues that only unanimous direct democracy can ensure that the autonomy of no individual is ever violated.[12] Wolff's argument is vulnerable analytically for exactly the same reasons as is Buchanan and Tullock's,[13] but he makes his expectations from social decision rules more explicit. He distinguishes the natural world, which is "irreducibly other," which stands apart from man, "against him, independent of his will and indifferent to his desires," from the social world, which often appears to be but ultimately is not. The natural world "really does exist independently of man's beliefs or desires, and therefore exercises a constraint on his will which can at best be mitigated or combated." The social world "is nothing in itself, and consists merely of the totality of the habits, expectations, beliefs and behavior patterns" of the individuals who live in it. For this reason, "it ought to be in principle possible for a society of rational men of good will to eliminate the domination of society . . . It *must* be possible for them to create a form of association which accomplishes that end [the 'general good'] without depriving some of their moral autonomy. The state, in contrast to nature, cannot be ineradicably other."[14] Yet there are many aspects of the natural world which we may be able to control despite their "otherness," from the temperature of our bath water to the genetic structure of our beings. Conversely, we may be confident that some features of human behavior, such as ethnic hatred, are learned or "socially constructed," yet we may have no idea how to alter them.

The other strategy, of economistic reduction, confronts different difficulties. First, as we saw, it may be that as a normative matter people regard their preferences as non-negotiable. The limiting case of this is Robert Nozick's problem with his "independents," those anarchists who refuse to join any state under any circumstances. Although Nozick devoted plenty of ink to arguing that these people could forcibly be included, if adequately compensated, and still be said to have consented, I have shown elsewhere that his arguments fail.[15] This kind of example might be thought a little tendentious, as the hard-boiled anar-

---

[12]Robert Paul Wolff, *In Defense of Anarchism* (New York: Harper and Row, 1970), p. 27.

[13]See my *The Evolution of Rights in Liberal Theory* (Cambridge: Cambridge University Press, 1986), pp. 163–64.

[14]Wolff, *In Defense of Anarchism*, pp. 72, 76–78.

[15]Robert Nozick, *Anarchy, State, and Utopia* (New York: Basic Books, 1974), pp. 54–87; I. Shapiro, *Evolution of Rights*, pp. 165–78.

chist presents difficulties for any contractarian theory; but it is useful analytically because it reveals that the primary value enshrined in compensation arguments is utilitarian efficiency, not consent or individual autonomy. Such arguments do not, therefore, establish unanimity as the optimal decision rule from the standpoint of individual rationality. Only if one assumes, implausibly, that every preference of every voter has its price can we say that enough negotiation would lead to consensus.

Plausibility aside, that assumption runs into serious difficulties deriving from different capacities to negotiate. Buchanan and Tullock never confront this issue, because they defend unqualified unanimity rule only in the theoretical case where decision-making costs are zero. This assumption, however, runs together the mere costs of doing business with the substantive compensation that would have to occur if such business was done. Peoples' expressed preferences are, to a degree, a function of their resources. One must anticipate that no matter how much time is spent negotiating, the bag lady from Manhattan may not have the resources to compensate the millionaire businessman and "buy off" his potential opposition to a welfare program. She may have nothing that he wants.

This example illustrates some of the analytical difficulties that arise from modeling political decision making on the Pareto system. The central purpose of microeconomic theory is to predict prices, and from this standpoint it is reasonable to be indifferent to the moral meaning of the choices being made in a market system. If our question is simply whether the businessman and the bag lady will trade, and if so at what price, we can see why it makes sense to say that voluntary action (and hence unanimity rule) dictates that no transaction will occur. But to suppose that this amounts to a justification for not departing from the status quo, on the ground that there is no way to do so under unanimous agreement, is obviously quite different and not persuasive in the absence of independent argument.

As with Wolff's argument, the Pareto system in its pure form also fails to speak to the question of externalities. If Buchanan and Tullock's political use of it is to be salvaged, it must be argued that despite the existence of externalities (which undermine the significance of voluntary transactions even from the standpoint of pure efficiency), the burden of persuasion remains on those who advocate collective action. Buchanan and Tullock try to establish a theoretical preference for private externalities over those generated by collective action, on the grounds that the former can be internalized through the market. "The fact that collective action, under most decision-making rules, involves external costs," they argue, creates a prima facie presumption against it:

> The private operation of the neighborhood plant with the smoking chimney may impose external costs on the individual by soiling his laundry, but this cost is no more external to the individual's own private calculus than the tax cost imposed on him unwillingly in order to finance the provision of public services to his fellow citizen in another area . . . [T]he initial definition of property rights places some effective limits on the external effects that private people may impose on each other. By contrast, the individual rights to property against damaging state or collective action are not nearly so sharply defined in existing legal systems. The external costs that may be imposed on the individual through the collective-choice process may be much larger than those which could ever be expected to result from purely private behavior within any accepted legal framework.[16]

So, although "[t]he continuation of private action, within the restriction of property ownership as defined, may impose certain spillover costs" on him, in the absence of "the protection of something approaching the unanimity rule," he "may rationally choose to bear the continued costs of private decision making." Here we see the rationale for Buchanan and Tullock's claim that individual rights should get special protective treatment in the choosing of decision rules:

> The individual will anticipate greater possible damage from collective action the more closely this action amounts to the creation and confiscation of human and property rights . . . This implication is not without relevance to an interpretation of the economic and social history of many Western countries. Constitutional prohibitions against many forms of collective intervention in the market economy have been abolished within the last three decades. As a result, legislative action may now produce severe capital losses or lucrative capital gains to separate individuals and groups. For the rational individual, unable to predict his future position, the imposition of some additional and renewed restraints on the exercise of such legislative power may be desirable.[17]

We have seen that unanimity as a decision rule does not in fact ensure the assent of all once omissions, Rae's "utility drift," and other unfore-

---

[16]Buchanan and Tullock, *Calculus of Consent*, pp. 65–66, italics added.
[17]Ibid., pp. 74, 82.

seen eventualities are taken into account. But what of this more general argument that collective action is particularly dubious in the area of property rights, because it creates more severe externalities than private action? Assuming that the unanimity test for collective action is an analytic parallel of compensation in welfare economics (for compensation can be interpreted "as that payment, negative or positive, which is required to secure agreement"), Buchanan and Tullock argue by reference to Pigou's classical smoking chimney that noncollective action allows for the internalization of external costs. In that example smoke from an industrial plant fouls the air and imposes external costs on the residents of surrounding areas. "If this represents a genuine externality," they assert, "either voluntary arrangements will emerge to eliminate it or collective action with unanimous support can be implemented." If the externality is real,

> some collectively imposed scheme through which the damaged property owners are taxed and the firm's owners are subsidized for capital losses incurred in putting in a smoke-abatement machine can command the assent of all the parties. If no such compensation scheme is possible (organization costs neglected), the externality is only apparent and not real. The same conclusion applies to the possibility of voluntary arrangements being worked out. Suppose that the owners of the residential property claim smoke damage, however slight. If this claim is real, the opportunity will always be open for them to combine forces and buy out the firm in order to induce smoke-abatemant devices.[18]

In the case of a real externality, then, organization costs aside, it would make no difference whether unanimous collective action was undertaken or whether the costs of the externalities were internalized through market transactions. A privatized system and a purely voluntary collectivized system (unanimity rule) have the advantage of enabling us to distinguish real from apparent diseconomies, but once we move into the realm of "coercive" collective action, this disappears.

Here we can see the deep implausibilities attending the reductionist fallacy. Again, as a set of analytic assumptions merely to predict the conditions under which compensation through side payments will occur, there is nothing morally objectionable about Pigou's chimney. But once it is treated as a normative model for the requirements of collective action, it becomes clear that it is doubly misleading. First, it creates the impression that the "scientific" or morally neutral way of dealing with

[18]Ibid., p. 91.

externalities collectively is to approximate the outcomes of a well-functioning competitive market. Second, the assumptions about the market themselves rest on a series of fictions that are never present in actual markets.

To begin with the distinction between "real" and "apparent" externalities, there is a neat theoretical simplicity to the claim that if the transaction does not occur voluntarily, that is decisive evidence that the externality was not real. But things are seldom so simple. Consider the claim that if the working classes did not like capitalism, they would get together and buy the capitalists' factories from them; and since they do not, we know that they do not really dislike it. If this reasoning seems disingenuous, it is: for its willful disregard of the resources problem and for its concomitant insensitivity to distributive questions. This disingenuousness is inherent in the compensation tests to which Buchanan and Tullock refer. The early welfare economists devised their hypothetical tests to find a way of discussing Pareto-noncomparable outcomes that increased overall welfare. They were wholly insensitive to distributive questions, holding only that transactions that increase net social product are to be preferred, whether or not they involve redistribution.[19] As Buchanan and Tullock employ the compensation argument, it depends critically on revealed preferences, because externalities that are not internalized in private transactions are declared not to be real. To reveal a preference in a competitive system, one must have the resources to reveal it; the market is sensitive only to preferences backed up by dollars. But it seems a little much to maintain that residents around a major airport who claim to find the noise intolerable cannot really find it so, else they would have bought the airport, and then to treat this standard as the model that collective action should try to emulate.

Second, just as unanimity qua decision rule can give a single individual veto power in decisions for or against collective action, the same thing can occur in private markets. Buchanan and Tullock's a priori preference for private action rests on the presumption that "[m]ore often, the external costs imposed by private action will be concentrated on a minority group of the total population, and other individuals in the group will receive some external benefits as a result of these external costs."[20] Yet as their own example of Pigou's chimney makes clear, there is no theoretical reason to believe either of these empirical claims. It may well be a minority, even a monopolist, who imposes externalities

[19]For a fuller discussion of these tests, see my *Evolution of Rights*, pp. 169–76.
[20]Buchanan and Tullock, *Calculus of Consent*, p. 91.

on a majority. Instead of localized smoke creating in one neighborhood, suppose that it is toxic chemicals that are damaging the ozone layer, the destruction of tropical forests at a rate that is affecting critically the production of gases essential for long-term human survival, or the local externalities of the actions of multinational corporations in the third world, of which the activities of Union Carbide in Bhopal, India, are a paradigm case. In such circumstances it may be that only collective action can prevent a minority from imposing external costs on a majority; under a private regime the majority will be powerless to prevent the external effect. As for the collateral benefits to third parties, unless we make a leap of Mandevillean faith that individual profit maximization will typically have positive external effects, there is no special reason to believe that these effects are any more likely to be positive than negative.

A third difficulty concerns the failure of Buchanan and Tullock's analysis to grapple with voluntary collective action problems other than those connected to decision-making costs. Consider circumstances where the benefits to the victims of negative externalities from potential preventative collective action, minus total decision-making costs, exceed the current benefit of the action to the perpetrator, but no change from the status quo will occur voluntarily. There are many game-theoretical reasons why this can happen, the commonest having to do with the prisoner's dilemma and free riding. It is by no means clear that the structure of choice situations will always permit the incentives of self-interested individual rationality to work to the mutual benefit of those who would benefit from voluntary collective action. Here again, "coercive" collective action may actually be superior, even in terms of individual rationality, to unregulated private action.

Buchanan and Tullock's use of the Pareto principle in evaluating decision rules reinforces the reductionist fallacy at a subtler level. This is most obvious in their discussion of intensity of preference, which is integral to their critique of majority rule. Strict majority rule, they claim, imputes to every voter equal intensity of preference, but there is no reason to take this step of "imputing to each individual . . . [this] . . . most restrictive utility function . . . To the modern economist this approach to individual calculus seems anachronistic and sterile." Their defense of logrolling and vote trading also turns on this claim; it is just because of the presence of different intensities that these devices can produce superior results. "Applying the strict Pareto rules for determining whether one social situation represents an improvement over another, almost any system of voting that allows some such exchange to take place would be superior to that system which weights all preferences equally on each issue."[21]

But what is really being argued here? Note for one thing that this reasoning again ignores the resources problem. Thus it is entirely compatible with a system in which landowners require tenants to vote as directed or be thrown off the land. The tenant who complies, when otherwise she would not have done, merely reveals a more intense preference to stay on the land than to vote the other way. In terms of the "strict Pareto rules" the outcome is superior. Once logrolling and vote trading are permitted on the grounds that they produce Pareto-superior results, it is hard to see any reason to limit the existence of a "free" market in votes. Even if we keep money and actual buying and selling of votes out of it, many will find counterintuitive the notion that if you desire that the United States goes to war in Central America more intensely than I desire that it does not, the world will be a better place if for that reason a way could be found for the war to be fought.[22]

In sum, Buchanan and Tullock's claim that unanimity rule has unique properties that would make it the rule of choice, absent decision-making costs, at the constitutional stage, is misleading and romanticizes the ideal of unanimity in the Pareto system in two different ways. It is misleading because it rests on a theory of action that takes no account of omissions as actions, and it illicitly assumes that market actions that have resulted in a given status quo will correspond to the preferences of all relevant agents at any given time. The defense of unanimity is romantic first in that it is thought to imply that if we allow only those collective actions that mimic what the market would produce, this will somehow produce efficient collective action. We saw that this relies on assumptions about intensity of preference that, while obviously useful in the prediction of price behavior in a market economy, have no necessary place in other rules of collective decision. We saw also that, through their evasion of the resources problem, Buchanan and Tullock exhibit an indifference to distributive questions that cannot amount to a justification for unanimity rule without some as yet unsupplied argument. The commitment to unanimity is romantic in a deeper sense in that it relies on a benign model of competitive economies which we have no good reason to believe realistic. Just as unanim-

---

[21]Ibid., pp. 126, 132–33, italics deleted.

[22]As Rawls has noted, those who have greater confidence and stronger feelings on an issue are no more likely to be right, and indeed they are often less sensitive to its complexities than are others. John Rawls, *A Theory of Justice* (Cambridge: Harvard University Press, 1971), pp. 230–31, 361.

ity as a rule of collective decision can permit minorities to tyrannize over majorities, the same can happen in the realm of private action, unless we make unwarranted assumptions about the ease of organizing collective action privately and about the collateral benefits to third parties of self-interested private action.

A second sense of unanimity, which contributes to the reductionist fallacy in a different way, concerns its use in the construction of the choice problem itself. At the constitutional stage, where future decision rules are chosen, the need for unanimity is taken for granted.[23] This is a common move in contractarian argument.[24] But the great difficulty with the contractarian approach, encapsulated in Rousseau's remark that Hobbes included in his account of natural man "a multitude of passions which are the product of [his] society,"[25] is that it assumes what it needs to establish. So for Hobbes a savage natural man makes political absolutism unavoidable; for Nozick a congenial but comparatively inefficient state of nature legitimates minimal government; and for Rawls risk-averse agents design a welfare principle to protect the interests of the most disadvantaged. For Buchanan and Tullock, contractarian argument is doubly problematic. First, they do not escape the basic problem of theoretical arbitrariness: while operating at the constitutional stage, they assume the existence of institutions that obviously postdate the constitution—a regime of private property rights and a market economy. Indeed their whole analysis of rules by reference to their comparative external costs assumes the existence of a legal system, because an external cost is defined as a reduction in an individual's "net worth" which is "not specifically recognized by the existing legal structure to be an expropriation of a defensible human or property right. The damaged individual has no recourse; he can neither prevent the action from occurring nor can he claim compensation after it has occurred . . . [I]t is the existence of such external costs that rationally explains the origin of either voluntarily organized, co-operative, contractual rearrangements or collective (governmental) activity."[26] This

[23]Buchanan and Tullock, *Calculus of Consent*, p. 77.

[24]Thus Rae argues that because majority rule has unique properties that make it preferable to unanimity rule, it would most probably be chosen by every individual under conditions of uncertainty. Rae, "Decision-Rules," pp. 40–56. And if we move backward in the contractarian tradition to Locke, or forward to Rawls and Nozick, the problem is typically construed as devising a set of institutional rules or structures which did or would command unanimity for the basic societal charter. It merits attention that here we expect less from reality than from theory; for no historical constitution has ever commanded anything approaching full unanimity.

[25]Jean-Jacques Rousseau, *The First and Second Discourses*, ed. R. D. Masters, trans. J. R. Masters (New York: St. Martin's, 1964), p. 129.

[26]Buchanan and Tullock, *Calculus of Consent*, p. 71.

logic is circular. If an external cost is defined as a legal but harmful by-product of the actions of another, the concept cannot be invoked to evaluate the different rules that might be employed in the design of the legal system. The only way to avoid absurdity here would be to invoke a notion of natural property rights and externalities, which Buchanan and Tullock never do. Indeed they explicitly define property rights as conventional.[27]

Their contractrarian method undermines Buchanan and Tullock's substantive argument in a different and more serious way, because it rests on assumptions about the primacy of politics and collective choice which are incompatible with their view of these same phenomena as resulting from market failure. The problem is cast as defining the conditions under which it is legitimate to depart from a regime of private action. So they speak of the "continuation of private action" as comparatively desirable, and they defend unanimity because it allegedly requires everyone to agree "prior to" collective action, claiming that "the individual will not rationally choose to collectivize an activity" under other conditions.[28] Yet the contractarian ideal implies the theoretical primacy of collective action, for which it is sometimes criticized. "Competitive markets require stable property rights and the absence of force, fraud, transaction costs and externalities," as Jules Coleman has reminded us. This amounts to saying that "[a] scheme of secure property rights is a collective good for those who have it."[29] From the standpoint of contractarian theory this collective good and its scope have to be agreed on at the constitutional stage or later; certainly they cannot be agreed on beforehand. Far from a presumption against collective action, the burden of proof would seem from this standpoint to rest with those who advocate the creation of that particular collective good (assuming it is a good) of a competitive market system. The only way to be a contractarian and at the same time avoid committing to the theoretical primacy of politics is also to commit to a theory of natural private rights, which Buchanan and Tullock are loath to do. Yet in the absence of such a theory, it is hard to discern a viable basis for their reification of legal rights that are both conventional and precontractual and that can in turn sustain their presumption against collective action.

---

[27]Thus human and property rights qualify for strong protection against majoritarian processes "after these have once been defined and generally accepted by the community. Property rights especially can never be defined once and for all." Ibid., p. 73.

[28]Ibid., pp. 74, 88, 93.

[29]Jules Coleman, "Competition and Cooperation: Some Thoughts on Frank Knight and the Market," *Ethics* 98, no. 1 (1987), p. 82.

II. THE CONSTITUTIONALIST FALLACY

Perhaps out of an awareness that unanimity as a decision rule has no special advantages for the preservation of individual rights, that it "distorts" preferences and, like any other decision rule, is manipulable through such devices as agenda control, democratic theorists have sought alternative bases for protecting minority rights from the potential devastations of majority rule. The argument can be made from several points of view: from a natural rights standpoint as embodied in the Declaration of Independence; from a utilitarian standpoint, where the argument is that the protection of certain individual rights from collective process best conduces to human welfare; or from a republican standpoint, where the separation of powers and concomitant limitations on majoritarian legislatures prevent corruption and promote political stability. The constitutionalist argument that concerns me here differs from all of these in that it purports to rest solely on findings about the defects of legislatures in the public choice literature of the past four decades—on the claim, that is, that enhanced judicial scrutiny is an appropriate democratic remedy for the analytic defects of majority rule.

Among others, Riker and Weingast have forcefully defended the view that ubiquitous voting cycles in legislatures warrant greater judicial scrutiny of their actions to protect individual rights. This is the view that Riker has characterized as "liberal," in opposition to "populist," arguing that "in the populist interpretation of voting, the opinions of the majority must be right and must be respected because the will of the people is the liberty of the people." In Riker's "liberal" view, by contrast, "there is no such magical identification. The outcome of voting is just a decision, and has no special moral character."[30]

Riker and Weingast recognize the powerful American constitutional tradition of courts protecting individual rights from the legislative process, but they argue that in recent decades an indefensible preference has been afforded civil over property rights. Since the New Deal, they argue, the Supreme Court has tended increasingly to view the economic rights of minorities as "no longer in need [of] protection above and beyond that provided by legislatures." They recognize that the tradition of judicial deference in matters of economic regulation is much older than the New Deal, traceable at least to the Court's proclamation in *Munn v. Illinois*, 94 US 113 (1877), that even when legislative power in

---

[30]William H. Riker, *Liberalism against Populism: A Confrontation between the Theory of Democracy and the Theory of Social Choice* (San Francisco: W. H. Freeman, 1982), p. 14.

this area is abused, "people should resort to the polls not the courts." Nonetheless, they argue that minimal scrutiny has given way to "complete and abject" abdication of judicial responsibility in the economic realm.[31] Decisions such as *Nebbia v. New York,* 291 US 502 (1934), which held courts without authority to declare economic policy or to override the decisions of legislatures to adopt "whatever economic policy may be deemed reasonable to promote public welfare," affirmed a quite limited role for judicial scrutiny. This decision was reinforced by *United States v. Carolene Products Co.,* 304 US 144 (1938), which sustained socio-economic regulation so long as a state of facts, either known or reasonably inferable, afforded support for the legislative judgment, and by *Ferguson v. Skrupa,* 372 US 726 (1963), which apparently abandoned even this requirement.[32] And this in stark contrast both to the strict scrutiny of the *Lochner* era and to the increasing attention, which reached its zenith in the Warren Court, to legislative abuses of the civil rights of minorities. Indeed *Carolene Products* is usually taken to have set the terms of Riker and Weingast's problem; at the same time as the Court there affirmed broad deference to legislative judgment in the area of economic regulation, Justice Stone penned his famous "footnote four,"[33] which would later be used to support greater judicial intervention in non-economic affairs. Yet, in Riker and Weingast's view,

> neither the court nor legal scholarship has provided the theoretical underpinnings for the presumption of the adequacy of legislative judgment [in the economic sphere] and, indeed, neither has even asked whether legislative judgment really works. Fundamental questions remain unanswered: What protection is there against members of today's majority from providing private, redistributive benefits to

[31]Riker and Weingast, "Constitutional Regulation," pp. 3–7, 26.

[32]For more extensive analysis of these and related decisions, see Lawrence H. Tribe, *American Constitutional Law* (Mineola, N.Y.: Foundation Press, 1978), pp. 450–55.

[33]"There may be a narrower scope for operation of the presumption of constitutionality when legislation appears on its face to be within a specific prohibition of the Constitution, such as those of the first ten Amendments, which are deemed equally specific when held to be embraced within the Fourteenth . . . It is unnecessary to consider now whether legislation which restricts those political processes which can ordinarily be expected to bring about repeal of undesirable legislation, is to be subjected to more exacting judicial scrutiny under the general prohibitions of the Fourteenth Amendment than are most other types of legislation . . . Nor need we inquire whether similar considerations enter into the review of statutes directed at particular religious . . . or racial minorities . . . whether prejudice against discrete and insular minorities may be a special condition, which tends seriously to curtail the operation of those political processes ordinarily to be relied upon to protect minorities, and which may call for a correspondingly more searching judicial inquiry." *United States v. Carolene Products Co.,* 304 US 144, 152 n. 4 (1938), citations omitted.

themselves under the guise of public purposes and at the expense of some minority of owners and the efficiency of production? Why is the abridgement of a minority's economic rights less troubling than an abridgement of the same minority's political rights?[34]

What, then, is the sense in which the legislative process can be said not to "work" in the economic realm? What, precisely, are the findings of social choice theory that render decisions of legislatures literally devoid of moral meaning and, at the same time, tools for the illegitimate appropriation of minorities' economic assets? "Social choice theory," Riker and Weingast tell us, is concerned with "the way that tastes, wants, values etc. of individual members are amalgamated into a statement of the choices for a group." Beginning from Condorcet's insight that a fairly small degree of complexity among preferences and voters can produce perpetual cyclical majorities,[35] they argue that the very idea of representative government is deeply flawed. Although individual preferences may be rational and transitive, Arrow and others have proved that resulting social rankings are fundamentally arbitrary as well as strictly irrational in that they may not even be transitive.[36] Majority rule is thus an "unfair" method of preference aggregation that results in a "forced order."[37]

From this perspective, the problem with majority rule is not simply that it harms minorities. It is more serious. The result of any pairwise vote that produces a majority outcome does not even necessarily embody "the will of the people" in the restricted majoritarian sense. There may be members of a winning majority who would have voted differently had the alternatives been presented in a different order. Majority rule can "wander anywhere"; there is nothing in it that "inherently limits voting bodies from choosing undesirable policies."[38] This means that in any legislative body those who control the voting agenda and the order of voting can decisively influence the results. What appears to be majority rule may quite often be de facto minority rule.

---

[34]Riker and Weingast, "Constitutional Regulation," p. 6.

[35]Condorcet noticed that if there are at least three voters and at least three issues, certain rankings of those preferences can produce a potential for endless cycles of majority preference, making the order in which issues are voted on the key determinant of the outcome. For instance, if voter 1 prefers policy a to b and b to c, voter 2 prefers b to c and c to a, and voter 3 prefers c to a and a to b, there is no stable result. That is, there is a majority for a over b (voters 1 and 3), a majority for b over c (voters 1 and 2) and a majority for c over a (voters 2 and 3).

[36]As in the example in the preceding footnote, where society prefers a to b, b to c, and c to a.

[37]Riker and Weingast, "Constitutional Regulation," pp. 8–9, 9–10.

[38]Ibid., p. 13.

There is considerable disagreement in the public choice literature on the empirical likelihood of cycles, but it is evident that they may occur.[39] This means, Riker and Weingast argue, that the "fundamental properties of majority rule" bring a "fundamental arbitrariness to social choices" made under it:

> When there exists a modest diversity of preference (itself, the bare necessity for political controversy), there are too many majorities. The particular majority that forms on one occasion is subject to manipulation within the legislature, and people in the position to manipulate (e.g., committee leaders) are not subject to majority rule competition. Moreover, it should be apparent that if different interests (e.g., different committees) have control over the agenda in different areas, then there need be no logical relationship between the majority that forms to support one piece of legislation and the majority that forms for another.[40]

To the extent that there can be said to be a "view of Congress" at all, then, it is likely to be internally contradictory and easily altered by strategically powerful committees, even minorities on committees.

These problems are worsened by a second phenomenon that has preoccupied public choice theorists in recent decades, strategic voting. Allan Gibbard, and others have revealed a wide variety of circumstances in which committee members can manipulate outcomes by voting for something other than their actual preferences if they know how others are likely to vote. It is exceedingly difficult to trace this kind of strategic voting, as it leaves no evidence, so that "even if an equilibrium of tastes might legitimately be called the will of the people, we would be forced, in our ignorance, to discount it entirely as a probable product of strategic voting or agenda control."[41] Indeed, representation is strategic to the core. Political scientists have shown that the legislator is "a placeholder opportunistically building up an ad hoc majority for the next election." The effect on legislation is that

> legislators do not mechanistically transmit majority opinion. Rather, they calculate the intensity of opinion, choosing their positions in such a way as to maximize the probability of successfully garnering

[39]See Riker, *Liberalism against Populism,* pp. 119–23, 186, and Donald P. Green and Ian Shapiro, *Pathologies of Rational Choice Theory: A Critique of Applications in Political Science* (New Haven: Yale University Press, 1994), pp. 98–146.

[40]Ibid., p. 19.

[41]Ibid., p. 25.

citizens' votes. By and large, legislators build coalitions of minorities, each one of which is especially concerned with a particular set of issues . . . One momentary majority of legislators finds that each one's electoral coalition would be strengthened by a particular regulation, often a small cartel. Another, possibly overlapping, later majority, also momentary, finds another regulation electorally helpful. Such legislation, of course, endures long after the electoral occasion. This has built up a cartelized society in which abridgments of property rights deter entrepreneurship and restrain economic growth.[42]

The logical defects of majority rule, the problems presented by strategic voting and opportunistic legislators, and their failure to represent anything that may confidently be termed majority opinion, combine to demolish the populist view of democratic government as embodying the will of the people. Recognizing these defects, these proponents of the liberal or Madisonian view argue that popular election can at most provide a popular veto on recent legislative action. Accordingly, majoritarian process cannot be expected to protect constitutional rights, and judicial scrutiny provides a needed "veto of another kind." Particularly in the area of property rights, where legislators typically operate as if the populist view legitimates their actions, the courts should scrutinize, and if necessary invalidate, legislation if it impinges on economic constitutional rights. Riker and Weingast explicitly deny that they are calling for a revival of the substantive due process of *Lochner*, which allowed judges to "substitute their own logic for that of the legislature." This, they note, "merely transfers the problem of unpredictability and insecurity of economic rights . . . to the judicial stage." Yet they conclude that "[w]hile we cannot fully explicate the rationale here, we do point out that judicial review, as developed in the seventeenth and eighteenth centuries, did render property rights more secure."[43]

Two major classes of difficulties confront Riker and Weingast's argument. First, if the claim that the presence of cycles and strategic voting produces outcomes that are often, perhaps even typically, arbitrary with respect to the preferences of committee members is valid, then they have proved too much. There is every reason to believe that courts are just as vulnerable to cycles in theory and in practice, not least because they also employ majority rule, and this has been shown in the public choice literature.[44] In fact the problems generated by strategic

---

[42]Ibid., p. 22, footnotes omitted.
[43]Ibid., pp. 23, 24, 26.
[44]See Frank H. Easterbrook, "Ways of Criticizing the Court," *Harvard Law Review* 95 (1982), pp. 802–32. For an earlier argument, see Walter Murphy, *Elements of Judicial Strategy* (Chicago:

voting might be expected to be worse in courts, where the numbers are sufficiently small and the votes of others sufficiently predictable to make strategic voting a more realistic option.[45] Furthermore, Riker and Weingast assume that the "constitutional rights" they defend but nowhere define have a special status that is somehow anterior to legislation. But the Constitution is, ultimately, one more piece of legislation, and Riker has himself documented the existence of some vote trading at the Constitutional Convention.[46] Certainly there is no a priori reason to suppose that there were not cyclical majorities and strategic voting there, or in the passing of the Bill of Rights and the other amendments.

Riker and Weingast operate with an implicit notion of certain preferred individual rights with a superior moral status, in need of protection from an interest-group politics that generates encroachment on them from multiple origins. The "hodge podge of regulation" has "significantly encroached on property rights," creating a "cartelized society in which abridgments of property rights deter entrepreneurship and restrain economic growth."[47] Here we detect the same unwarranted assumptions about collective action as we did in our discussion of Buchanan and Tullock. While failure to regulate (or, one must suppose, a collective decision to "deregulate" property rights) functions neutrally to the general benefit of society, decisions *to* regulate invariably benefit some well-organized pressure group at the expense of the general interest. Kenneth Shepsle and Weingast have gone further, arguing that even in circumstances of demonstrable market failure, the difficulties with collective action we have been discussing may warrant its rejection.[48] Whether they would go so far as to say that a court could strike down such legislation (which would be a literal return to the *Lochner* rule) is unclear. Yet to hold, as Riker and Weingast do, that there is a class of preferred rights that courts should enforce because their

University of Chicago Press, 1964), pp. 37–122. For a more general argument that if voting really is as meaningless as Riker claims, this undermines his "liberalism" at least as much as it does the "populism" he attacks, see Jules Coleman and John Ferejohn, "Democracy and Social Choice," *Ethics* 97, no. 1 (1986), pp. 11–22.

[45]Of course this will not invariably be so, as when the preferences of judges are limited by precedent, as Lea Brilmayer has pointed out to me. But when precedents are ambiguous or conflicting in their applications, judicial decisions become vulnerable to problems of collective decision. There is also the fact that when a precedent was initially created, it may have resulted from agenda manipulation in the presence of cyclical preferences, strategic voting, or some other theoretically arbitrary collective decision.

[46]William H. Riker, "Vote-Trading at the Constitutional Convention," in William H. Riker, *The Art of Political Manipulation* (New Haven: Yale University Press, 1986), pp. 89–102.

[47]Riker and Weingast, "Constitutional Regulation," p. 22.

[48]Kenneth A. Shepsle and Barry R. Weingast, "Political Solutions to Market Problems," *American Political Science Review* 78, no. 2 (1984), pp. 417–34.

abridgment will "deter entrepreneurship and restrain economic growth" comes uncomfortably close to this position. In short, they appear to want it both ways: while regulatory economic policies enacted by legislatures are inherently suspect as the product of cyclical majorities and opportunistic legislators, collective judicial acts to enforce constitutional rights that may be vulnerable in the same ways—when enacted as well as during two centuries of continuing Court reinterpretation as to meaning and scope—somehow escape the problem.

If the argument regarding cyclical and strategic voting proves too much, undercutting the notion of a general or public interest so completely as to render all forms of majoritarian collective action literally meaningless, it proves too little in restricting the problematic implications of majority rule. Arrow's impossibility theorem was a landmark in the public choice literature not because of his findings about majority rule. He showed more generally that there is no social welfare function that will prevent cycling if a few minimal conditions are assumed and preferences are sufficiently diverse.[49] A good deal of the voting theory literature since Arrow has been concerned with relaxing his assumptions or introducing constraints on the heterogeneity of preferences to save majority rule from the possibility of cycles.[50] But it is clear that if the findings Riker and Weingast invoke apply to majority rule, they certainly apply to some, perhaps all, other decision rules.[51] Because the possibility of cycling is partly a function of heterogeneity of preferences, not just of the properties of decision rules (except to the extent that any decision rule requires us actually to reach a decision at least for a time), it is likely that control of the agenda will confer decisive power whatever the decision rule.[52] Sophisticated voting, too, plays no special role in majority rule. If I know the preferences of others and am willing to gamble on their strategic decisions with respect to my vote, the "honest" result that should be reached by any decision rule may be undermined, sometimes to the detriment of all concerned, as the game theorists have shown.

[49]See Kenneth J. Arrow, *Social Choice and Individual Values*, 2d ed. (New Haven: Yale University Press, 1963), pp. 51–60.

[50]See ibid., 61–120, and Dennis Mueller, *Public Choice: II* (New York: Cambridge University Press, 1989), pp. 384–407, for discussion.

[51]There are some exceptions. For example Caplan and Nalebuff have shown that a "supermajority" rule of 64 percent will under certain conditions avoid cycles, although this requires some constraints on the diversity of preferences. Andrew Caplan and Barry Nalebuff, "On 64% Majority Rule," *Econometrica* 56, no. 4 (July 1988), pp. 787–814.

[52]For a useful summary account of the public choice findings on the significance of agenda control, see Mueller, *Public Choice: II*, pp. 58–95.

If Riker and Weingast's arguments reveal nothing special about majority rule but instead are instances of more general findings that have been shown to undermine all known procedures of collective decision, their significance is cast in a different light. Were it possible somehow for society to "not undertake" collective action, as their comments about economic regulation by legislatures might be taken to imply, this might amount to a prima facie argument against all collective action.[53] But, as we saw when discussing Buchanan and Tullock, the creation and maintenance of a system of legal rights and rules which makes possible what they think of as unregulated private action is itself the provision of a public good, financed by implicit taxes on those who would prefer some alternative system. Once this is conceded, the question must inevitably arise Why have this rather than some alternative system? The problem of collective action is then seen to be inescapable. Riker and Weingast limit their concern (as do Wolff and Buchanan and Tullock) to the coercive acts performed by the state. If this turns out to be an implausibly narrow view of the problems of power and collective action, then the dimensions of social life along which we are bound to think of collective action as inevitable will necessarily expand.

These theoretical difficulties aside, what of the implications of Riker and Weingast's arguments in the actual world of American politics? Should we be persuaded that the actions of legislatures are wholly arbitrary and morally bankrupt as a result, necessitating stricter scrutiny on all fronts by the federal courts? Assuming away, for now, the problems of collective decision within courts, as well as the difficulty that the norms courts try to enforce can themselves be argued to be theoretically arbitrary, it seems clear that Riker and Weingast's proposals would encounter intractable difficulties in the real world of American constitutional law. Their practical argument turns on the different constitutional treatments of economic and political rights, but the Constitution itself treats these differently. Riker and Weingast indicate some awareness of these issues when they remark that "[i]t is one thing to argue that some rights are 'preferred' and should therefore receive greater scrutiny and wholly another to argue that some rights require and deserve no scrutiny."[54] But this is to wave misleadingly at the complexities of different tiers of judicial scrutiny.

To begin with, it is not obviously true that there is so radical a disjunction between the Court's treatment of economic and civil rights as they

[53]For a useful discussion of the practical implications of conflating neutrality and inaction in the context of *Lochner*, see Cass Sunstein, "*Lochner's* Legacy," *Columbia Law Review* 87 (1987), pp. 201–47.

[54]Riker and Weingast, "Constitutional Regulation," p. 26.

assert. The cases Riker and Weingast cite deal explicitly with the institutional incapacity of courts to fashion economic policies, but they do not declare the courts to be without power to defend economic rights. We may not go all the way with Ronald Dworkin in holding that questions of "principle" are entirely separate from those of "policy,"[55] recognizing that policies always embody principles and that choices of principles invariably restrict the range of possible policies. But it will still be the case that a range of economic policies may be consistent with basic constitutional protections, so that the claim that the courts are incompetent to make economic policy but competent to protect economic rights is by no means vacuous. Certainly it has been the presumption behind a great deal of American constitutional law. In the realm of protecting economic rights, the courts have not been nearly so inactive as Riker and Weingast suggest, as has recently been shown by Martin Shapiro.[56] More generally, the distinction between civil and property rights has become a good deal harder to draw in recent decades. Civil rights lawyers, in response to the strong protection afforded property rights in the *Lochner* era, invoked the language of C. A. Reich's "The New Property"[57] to argue with some success that what had traditionally been thought of in civil rights terms were in fact property rights.[58] Riker and Weingast offer no account of what is to count as a property right, and it is therefore difficult to evaluate their claim that property rights have received inferior protection.

With regard to the Court's alleged activism in the civil rights area, there are good reasons for thinking that this and its effects have been considerably exaggerated in much of the literature. Charles Black has usefully pointed out an important artificiality to much of the debate on the countermajoritarian problem, in that the overwhelming majority of the activities of federal courts, even when engaged in judicial review, have nothing to do with the *Marbury v. Madison* problem of the authority of the Court to review the actions of Congress. Between 1937 and 1967 the Court annulled acts of Congress only twelve times. By far the

[55]See Ronald Dworkin, *A Matter of Principle* (Cambridge: Harvard University Press, 1985), pp. 81–89.

[56]Martin Shapiro, "The Supreme Court's 'Return' to Economic Regulation," in *Studies in American Political Development*, ed. Karen Orren and Stephen Skowronek, vol. 1 (New Haven: Yale University Press, 1986), pp. 91–141.

[57]C. A. Reich, "The New Property," *Yale Law Journal* 73, no. 5, (1964), pp. 733–87.

[58]Thus, for example, in *Goldberg v. Kelly*, 397 US 254, 261–62 (1969), the Court was persuaded that welfare recipients' benefits are statutory entitlements and that due process therefore required that they could not be terminated by state officials without a hearing. It was just this assimilation of property rights with welfare benefits that outraged Justice Black in dissent, who argued that welfare recipients' benefits should not be raised to the status of a property right and so gain the due process protections property rights enjoy. Ibid., p. 275.

greater part of federal judicial review is of the actions of state courts for federal constitutionality as provided for in Article VI, geared toward bringing the states into line with national law.[59] It is not because the actions of state or municipal institutions are acts of legislatures (when they are) that they are subject to review but rather because they are the actions of subordinate institutions in the national federal structure; it is a supremacy clause issue. This has nothing to do with the counterma-joritarian difficulty as Riker and Weingast conceive of it. Further, whether the constitutionality of state or federal law is involved, the typical case of federal judicial review[60] is not of the actions of a legisla-tive branch at all; rather it is review of the actions of a federal or state official, a policeman, an investigator, a prison warden, or a prosecutor. When we think of judicial activism in the civil rights area we are accus-tomed to think of the Court usurping legislative functions, but typically the problem is administrative action where the legislative branch of the national government has not spoken,[61] or actions of questionable legal-ity because undertaken by parts of legislative bodies rather than being the product of the full deliberations of lawmaking bodies as provided for in the Constitution.[62] Furthermore, much of the Court's alleged activism in the civil rights area has been in furtherance of congressional mandates such as the Civil Rights Act of 1964; it has had nothing to do with protecting minority rights from the actions of a rampant legislative branch.[63]

In the economic realm, too, the Court is bound to enforce federal law, and its actions are limited by those provisions of the Constitution ex-plicitly conferring on Congress the power to legislate in the national economic interest.[64] Riker and Weingast's position seems to require a

[59]Charles L. Black, Jr., *Structure and Relationship in Constitutional Law* (Baton Rouge: Louisiana State University Press, 1969), pp. 67–76.

[60]Excluding the review of interpretations of federal law by state courts, which clearly is of no interest to the issues at hand here, and which no one doubts is properly the work of federal courts. *Martin v. Hunter's Lessee*, 1 Wheaton 304 (1816), upheld the power of Congress to direct the Supreme Court to hear writs of error of state court judgments denying federal claims under a jurisdictional statute that treated federal constitutional claims with other claims. Black, *Structure and Relationship*, p. 74.

[61]As in *Miranda v. Arizona*, 384 US 436 (1966).

[62]As in *Barenblatt v. United States*, 360 US 109 (1959). Black, *Structure and Relationship*, pp. 88–91, 83.

[63]Indeed there are scholars who tell us that even in the famed area of school desegregation since *Brown*, the role of the courts has been greatly exaggerated; the critical changes came about as a result of legislative action. Donald L. Horowitz, *The Courts and Social Policy* (Washington, D.C.: Brookings, 1977), pp. 255–98; Gerald N. Rosenberg, *The Hollow Hope* (Chicago: University of Chicago Press, 1992).

[64]The Constitution gives Congress the power to tax (Art. 1, sec. 8 [1], sec. 10, [1, 2], borrow (Art. 1, sec. 8 [2]), to regulate international and interstate commerce (Art. 1, sec. 8 [3], sec. 9 [5,

return to *Lochner* not only for the analytic reasons already noted but also for historical ones. The history they lamentingly describe is really the history of the Supreme Court's retreat (to the extent that it has retreated) from the doctrine of substantive due process. Lawrence Tribe points out that during the New Deal and subsequently, the Court never entirely accepted the pluralist interest-group theory of the political process, remaining wedded to the notion that legislatures, "at least in their regulatory capacity, must always act in furtherance of public goals transcending the shifting summation of private interests through the political process." But as a matter of institutional competence it retreated to the view that "even if the public good or social justice could be defined apart from the aggregation of political interests, and even if particular legislative restraints on liberty were profoundly unjust according to some cognizable standard or principle, legislative choices among conflicting values were beyond judicial competence to criticize and hence beyond judicial authority to strike down."[65] It may be that this "democratic relativism" was not entirely coherent within its own terms, as Tribe, Rogers Smith, and others have argued,[66] because some set of substantive values is immanent in even the most minimal standards of judicial scrutiny. But if this is so, it cannot be argued that rights (property or any other) should be defended by the Court against the actions of legislatures, however unrepresentative these latter might actually be, unless some theory is supplied to explain which rights are desirable, and why. This is the kind of task commentators such as Tribe and Smith set for themselves. Whatever the difficulties confronting such enterprises, Riker and Weingast appear not even to notice that they are required. Instead they take it for granted that property rights should be protected by the Court because their abridgments "deter entrepreneurship and restrain economic growth."[67] For this wealth-maximizing theory of constitutional scrutiny to be defended, an empirical theory would presumably have to be supplied establishing that it is in fact true. Riker and Weingast would then have to square the circle by arguing simultaneously that they are not violating Oliver Wendell Holmes's

---

6]), bankruptcy (Art. 1, sec. 8 [4]), money (Art. 1, sec. 8 [5]), and to prevent fraud (Art. 1, sec. 8 [6]) and issue patents and copyrights (Art. 1, sec. 8 [8]). The takings clause of the Fifth Amendment requires only "just compensation," it does not otherwise limit the power of eminent domain, and Congress is explicitly authorized, in section 5 of the Fourteenth Amendment, to "enforce, by appropriate legislation," the requirement of section 1 that no person be deprived of "life, liberty, or property, without due process of law."

[65]Tribe, *American Constitutional Law*, pp. 451, 452.

[66]Ibid., pp. 452–55; Rogers M. Smith, *Liberalism and American Constitutional Law* (Cambridge: Harvard University Press, 1985), pp. 114–16. The term "democratic relativism" is Smith's.

[67]Riker and Weingast, "Constitutional Regulation," p. 22.

dictum in criticizing the *Lochner* rule, namely that "the Fourteenth Amendment does not enact Mr. Spencer's *Social Statics.*"[68]

Squaring this circle would require more than a theory of the deficiencies of majority rule. All that the latter can generate on its own in the way of justification for judicial scrutiny of congressional action is a footnote four justification for intervention in the specific circumstances where power is abused by corrupt incumbents to the point where the system of majority rule fails to operate (in the traditional sense of violating its own procedural rules, not the public choice sense of failing to produce "socially rational" outcomes), or some "discrete and insular minority" is systematically excluded from participation.[69] Such a rationale would not, however, generate a wealth-maximizing jurisprudence. Nor would it generate a utilitarian one geared to defend or maximize "equal concern and respect" as Ely would have us believe. The public choice theorists have taught us that to expect majority rule to produce that, even in principle, is to expect too much. One is bound to be likewise skeptical of the claims of such commentators as Charles Beitz, who note that the mere quantitative fairness of equal voting power will never ensure substantively democratic outcomes. In his view, a truly democratic system of "qualitative fairness" requires a prior system of "just legislation," because mere equal voting power can never be guaranteed to produce fair outcomes. Lacking here the space to deal with this argument in detail, I simply note that the large number of competing theories of justice we have seen in recent years, none without serious difficulties that have been much commented upon in the journals, inevitably makes one skeptical that a theory of just legislation agreeable to all is around the corner.[70]

A footnote four justification, then, can at most legitimate intervention to make majority rule operate; it cannot posit some outcome that is alleged to be substantively democratic and intervene on its basis. Nor does it result in a general defense of "economic" or of "political" rights. Only if they were the rights of dispossessed groups, excluded from participation in the political process, would they merit judicial protection from legislatures. These would include some "economic" and some "political" rights, but not, one suspects, those Riker and Weingast are

[68]*Lochner v. New York*, 198 US 45, 74 (1905).

[69]For a powerful critique of even this narrow interpretation of footnote four, see Lea Brilmayer, "*Carolene*, Conflicts, and the Fate of the 'Insider-Outsider,'" *University of Pennsylvania Law Review* 134, no. 6 (July 1986), pp. 1291–1334.

[70]Ely, *Democracy and Distrust*, pp. 76–77, 82; Charles Beitz, "Equal Opportunity in Political Representation," in *Equal Opportunity*, ed. Norman E. Bowie (Boulder: Westview, 1988), pp. 155–74.

most concerned to protect.[71] Indeed, a footnote four justification would be properly indifferent to the vulnerabilities of the wealthy, propertied, and powerful at the hands of majority rule, minorities though these latter well may be.

III. The Instability Fallacy

Aside from their constitutional implications, what are the more general political ramifications of the public choice findings on the instability of majority rule? "Equilibrium," Peter Ordeshook and Kenneth Shepsle tell us, "is the pivotal concept of analytical political science."[72] Yet Condorcet, Arrow, Duncan Black, Charles Plott, and their progeny established that equilibrium under majority rule can be predicted only in highly restricted circumstances. If there is some disagreement on the extent of political disequilibrium in the actual world,[73] and if theorists like Ordeshook continue to have faith that equilibrium might be redefined in ways that make it attainable,[74] this latter has yet to be achieved without the addition of substantial constraints on preferences, bias toward the status quo, or both. For the moment one has to be persuaded by Riker that "politics is *the* dismal science because we have learned from it that there are no fundamental equilibria to predict. In the absence of such equilibria we cannot know much about the future at all, whether it is likely to be palatable or unpalatable, and in that sense our future is subject to the tricks and accidents of the way in which questions are posed and alternatives are offered and eliminated."[75]

Preoccupation with the relations between democratic procedures and stability is, of course, much older than the discipline of public choice, and different commentators have understood markedly different things by the term *stability* and thought it desirable for different reasons. Pluralist theorists such as Robert Dahl made the Hobbesian assumption that the alternative would be chaos. Indeed Dahl went so far as to argue

[71]For a useful account of footnote four and its purposes, see Robert Cover, "The Origins of Judicial Activism in the Protection of Minorities," *Yale Law Journal* 91, no. 7 (1982), pp. 1287–1316. For a critical discussion of Ely's attempt to base an entire substantive jurisprudence on it, see Smith, *Liberalism and American Constitutional Law*, pp. 90–91, 170.

[72]Peter C. Ordeshook and Kenneth A. Shepsle, eds., *Political Equilibrium* (Boston: Kluwer-Nijhoff, 1982), p. xii.

[73]See Green and Shapiro, *Pathologies of Rational Choice Theory*, pp. 98–146.

[74]Peter C. Ordeshook, "Political Disequilibrium and Scientific Inquiry: A Comment on William H. Riker's 'Implications from the Disequilibrium of Majority Rule for the Study of Institutions,'" in Ordeshook and Shepsle, *Political Equilibrium*, pp. 25–31.

[75]William H. Riker, "Implications from the Disequilibrium of Majority Rule for the Study of Institutions," in Ordeshook and Shepsle, *Political Equilibrium*, pp. 3–24, 19.

that it would be desirable in principle to devise a voting system that took some account of intensity of preference, in part because this would engender political stability.[76] Although the public choice theorists differ among themselves concerning the meaning of the term *equilibrium* (and hence of stability and instability),[77] they are united in approaching the problem from a quite different standpoint.

Far from assuming the alternative to government to be anarchic chaos, we have seen that the implicit counterfactual in this tradition is that private action is essentially benign, that collective action becomes necessary paradigmatically in circumstances of market failure, and that the problems then get generated because there is no rational way of organizing collective action. Stability, then, has nothing to do with social states. It is treated as a property of collective rationality and desired for that reason. Thus although Ordeshook concedes that governmental action is sometimes necessary to "break" what are really negative equilibria in the private sphere—like prisoners' dilemma situations—the use of government in this way

> engender[s] new kinds of dilemmas. With a government's usual powers to expropriate wealth, interest groups form to lobby for particularized private benefits. Economic efficiency becomes the new undersupplied public good, and, while all groups might agree jointly not to use the coercive powers of government for their particularized ends, none has any incentive unilaterally to choose another course. There is now, in fact, a growing belief that governments, in the grip of this dilemma, have grown too large and unwieldy, and that new constitutional rules such as spending limits are required to control the prisoners' dilemmas among interest groups and constituencies that governments engender.[78]

The problem with instability in this public choice sense, then, is that it makes possible, perhaps inevitable, constant cycles where new coalitions of interest groups form, which always have incentives to overturn

---

[76]Robert A. Dahl, *A Preface to Democratic Theory* (Chicago: University of Chicago Press, 1956), pp. 92–102.

[77]Two of the most common definitions, as formulated by Ordeshook, are (1) in situations when people are essentially acting alone, "an equilibrium corresponds to an outcome in which, ex post, no one person has any incentive to change his or her decisions unilaterally and to do something else" and (2) in "situations in which people can act in concert, with various subsets of people coordinating their actions to form 'coalitions,' an equilibrium corresponds to an outcome in which no coalition has the incentive or the means for unilaterally insuring an improvement in the welfare of all its members." Ordeshook, "Political Disequilibrium," p. 26.

[78]Ibid., pp. 28–29.

the status quo for their individual benefit by adding taxes that directly or indirectly benefit them, to the overall detriment of society.

In a brilliant little essay Nicholas Miller has shown that the traditional pluralist sense of political stability and the technical sense employed in the public choice literature contradict each other. Traditionally a pluralist society was thought to be the polar opposite of a single-cleavage (e.g., feudal) society. The early pluralists worked with a model of multiple cross-cutting cleavages; society was thought of as "ridden by a dozen oppositions along different lines running in every direction."[79] One's allies in one context might become one's adversaries in another, so that society, as E. A. Ross put it, is "sown together by its inner conflicts."[80] According to Miller, theorists treated this "pluralism of cleavages" as conducive to stability for four different but mutually reinforcing reasons. First, it was thought to moderate political preferences; the "cross-pressure" mechanisms that result from the fact that not all socialization forces operate in the same direction allegedly meant that political commitments are many sided and less extreme. Second, pluralism was assumed to moderate behavior because, in contrast to a polarized society in which "an individual or group has permanent friends" and "little incentive to behave moderately toward permanent enemies," future alliances are uncertain, and the possibility that a present opponent may become a future ally tends to moderate present behavior. Third, pluralism was thought to distribute political satisfaction more widely. No one wins all the time, making it simultaneously less likely that the same majority will systematically invade the rights of the same minority and that any particular group will lose so often as to have no commitment to the system and nothing to lose but its proverbial chains. Finally, the very fact that pluralist politics invites political "strategems" of negotiation, coalition building and splitting, agenda manipulation, strategic voting, patronage and pork barrel politics was assumed to promote commitment to the system rather than extrapolitical action, inasmuch as present losers know there is some realistic probability of becoming future winners.[81]

Yet these same factors undermine stability in the public choice sense of collective rationality. This can be seen from the theoretical strategies employed in the public choice literature to avoid cycles and produce stable equilibria. Exclusion conditions (which limit the admissible arrays of preferences, like Black's single-peakedness and Amartya Sen's

---

[79]Nicholas R. Miller, "Pluralism and Social Choice," *American Political Science Review* 77, no. 3 (1983), pp. 735.

[80]E. A. Ross, *The Principles of Sociology* (New York: Century, 1920), pp. 164–65.

[81]Ibid., 736–68, 743.

value restriction); popularity conditions (postulating a high degree of consensus among voters, even where exclusion conditions are violated); and balance conditions (such as Plott's condition requiring symmetry of disagreement) all share this in common: they attempt to combat the fact that as the number of preferences increases and becomes more heterogeneous, so does the likelihood of cycles. So they try to limit heterogeneity in a variety of ways, at the cost of undermining those factors that make for pluralist stability. Although pluralist theorists have not explicitly argued that cycling is desirable (they have tended to ignore it), "they have argued that certain preference patterns promote, and others threaten, political stability, and it turns out that the former typically entail, whereas the latter preclude, majority cycling."[82]

Miller distances himself from the early pluralists such as Earl Latham, who, while arguing that public policy is "actually the equilibrium reached in the group struggle at any given moment,"[83] had ignored those who lack the resources to form groups. Differences in size and resources and the failure of some "potential groups" ever to organize effectively means, as E. E. Schattschneider and others have noted, that even where equilibrium among organized groups exists and determines public outcomes, it "merits no particular approbation as fair public policy."[84] Miller wants, however, to rescue a version of pluralist theory that is not vulnerable in the ways that the early group theories were vulnerable and to argue that pluralist stability in this new sense should be chosen over the public choice stability qua rational social equilibrium. He argues not just that cyclical majority preference is an "otherwise undesirable phenomenon that happens to come along with pluralistic preference patterns and that we must accept [it] as the unavoidable cost of achieving the great benefit of political stability." Rather, he goes further, maintaining that the instability of the political process is itself desirable because it moderates attitudes and behavior, distributes political satisfaction more widely, and engenders political participation. He even toys with the notion that this kind of instability may actually play a causal role in creating a pluralist society.[85]

Miller's argument that stability in the public choice sense is undesirable is persuasive. Apart from the potential Stalinist implications that would attend any attempt to enforce limitations on preferences institutionally, we saw in our discussion of Riker and Weingast that the prob-

[82]Ibid., 739–40.
[83]Earl Latham, "The Group Basis of Politics: Notes for a Theory," *American Political Science Review* 46, no. 2 (1952), p. 390.
[84]Miller, "Pluralism and Social Choice," p. 735.
[85]Ibid., 742, 736.

lem of cycling is practically insurmountable. Any solution to it turns out also to be vulnerable to cycling (as are courts and procedures for determining "constitutional" rights) or to be arbitrary. Ordeshook's suggestion that there should be new constitutional constraints on spending because of the problem of cycling under majority rule can be shown to be similarly vulnerable. Just as there is no way to increase public spending neutrally, there is no way to cut it neutrally, as the Reagan tax cuts of the 1980s revealed all too well. One cannot assert that there is no public good when criticizing majority rule and then wheel out the same idea to limit its operation. When Ordeshook says that under majority rule economic efficiency becomes an "undersupplied" public good,[86] like Buchanan and Tullock before him, he is disguising in neutral language a claim that by its nature cannot be neutral—unless we implausibly solve the resources and externalities problems by definition. Given that the option of literally no government of any kind is unavailable, the inescapable fact is that different amounts and kinds of taxation and spending will benefit different groups differently, and there is no theoretical reason to expect—indeed there is every theoretical reason to doubt—that there is any mode of taxing and spending that can be said to be neutral in that it benefits everyone, let alone that it benefits everyone equally or proportionately.

Miller's argument that promoting public choice stability undermines pluralist stability, by reducing incentives for the already dispossessed to participate and by reinforcing (and perhaps even tending to create) small numbers of deep cleavages that are pervasive over time and space, is plausible so far as it goes. His picture of a pluralist culture is, however, too sanguine for our circumstances. First, his attempt to separate himself from the naïve assumptions about power and resources of the early group pluralists is less than persuasive. Miller distinguishes their group pluralism from his own "pluralism as dispersed preferences," but this does not dispose of the problem that individuals have vastly different resources for making their preferences effective, different amounts, that is, of social and economic power. Whether applied to individuals or to groups and organizations, the happy pluralist story can be true only if there are not radical inequalities in capacity to influence the political process, and Miller's tangential remarks about power fail to persuade that this is so.[87] Second, Miller contends that a stable (pluralist sense) majoritarian political process actually creates

---

[86] Ordeshook, "Political Disequilibrium," pp. 28–29.
[87] "I assume here that political power relations are simple, probably majoritarian—i.e., any majority coalition can bring about any outcome." Miller, "Pluralism and Social Choice," p. 735.

pluralism, on the grounds that "if an effective constitutional consensus prevails, members of society are free to pursue their own more particular preferences (for government outputs, rather than for forms of government), which are more likely to be pluralistically distributed."[88] This is implausible in the absence of a good deal of further argument that is not supplied. One does not have to go all the way with the Marxists to be skeptical of the claim that the existence of majority rule and competitive parties is sufficient to create a genuine social "pluralism of dispersed preferences," to the point where jettisoning the model of fundamental cleavages is warranted. For the pluralist case to be plausible we have to assume, as Miller more or less concedes,[89] and as the early pluralists certainly assumed, that the causal arrows run in the opposite direction, that we already have a society that is fundamentally pluralist.

This assumption seems unwarranted for two reasons. First, we know that there are vast inequalities of wealth that inevitably bring with them unequal influence in the political process. Congress attempted to reduce this inequality of influence by limiting political expenditures on behalf of candidates, but the Supreme Court held such limitations unconstitutional abridgments of the First Amendment; Congress may limit only contributions to political parties and political action committees, not expenditures.[90] Even in countries like Britain, where political expenditures and advertising are far more strictly regulated, it is common knowledge that the amounts spent on behalf of Conservative Party candidates always greatly exceed those spent on behalf of the Labour Party.

Second, a thoroughgoing pluralism of "dispersed preferences" has to come to terms with the problem of political elites (leaving aside, to make it an independent point, the relation in which they may stand to social and economic elites). Pluralists like Dahl developed their theories partly in reaction to the elite theories of Robert Michels and others, but if they argued that there was no "iron law of oligarchy" such that a single elite would find a way to get control of any political system however organized, they did acknowledge that in the world of mass

---

[88]Ibid., p. 736.

[89]Ibid.

[90]*Buckley v. Valeo*, 424 US 1 (1976). See also *First National Bank of Boston v. Bellotti*, 435 US 765 (1978), extending the Buckley protection of unlimited expenditures to corporations as well as individuals, and *Federal Election Commission v. NCPAC*, 105 S Ct 1459 (1985), holding it to be an unconstitutional limitation on political speech for Congress to limit expenditures of political action committees on behalf of candidates, as a condition for the receipt of public funds by those candidates during election campaigns.

politics and widespread political apathy, the most one could real-istically hope for was a circulation of elites.[91] Cycling majorities may remove incumbents from power on a fairly regular basis,[92] but we should not delude ourselves that what is at work here is a "pluralism of dispersed preferences" where everyone gets her turn.

If the public choice theorists have taught us that elected representa-tives seldom represent majorities and that interest-group politics bene-fits coalitions of minorities at best, we might welcome cyclical major-ities for a different reason than Miller's. If we remain unpersuaded by the public choice theorists' other claim—that there can be some morally and distributively neutral devices (whether courts, constitutional spending limits, or unanimity voting) for limiting interest-group poli-tics in the public interest—it follows that a degree of illegitimacy will invariably attach to incumbents. If politics is inevitable but political power holders invariably illegitimate in that they derive disproportio-nate benefits for themselves and minority constituents, we might wel-come a system that makes incumbents perpetually vulnerable. We would do so not out of any belief that a system that turns out incum-bents reflects (let alone creates) a substantively democratic culture (whatever that might be) but simply because they should be gotten out. In the classic example from the public choice literature, if there are a hundred dollars in possible benefits to be distributed by majority rule, and three or more people voting on its allocation, whatever self-interested coalition forms to distribute it to its members (or their con-stituents), that coalition will be vulnerable to an alternative majority coalition that might form containing some present winners and some present losers.[93] Yet if no group can really claim legitimate title to the benefits, and, pace Buchanan and Tullock, Riker and Weingast, and Ordeshook, "not having" the benefits is not an option because collective inaction turns out in particular cases always to amount to an implicit tax on some interest group or individual, then the perpetual vulnerability of current beneficiaries may be desirable. Everyone should always be gotten out because the politics of distribution can never be neutral and the gains of present beneficiaries are therefore to some extent ill gotten; but the paradoxical reality is that someone always has to be in. The best solution to this paradox may be cyclical majorities.

---

[91]Dahl, *Preface to Democratic Theory*, p. 131.

[92]Although, as Miller notes, the relations among changing preferences, voting, and outcome are likely to be considerably more complex than this formulation suggests. Miller, "Pluralism and Social Choice," p. 743.

[93]For further discussion of these kinds of examples, see Mueller, *Public Choice: II*, pp. 58–111.

IV. Democracy and Political Power

It is remarkable that so little of the literature in democratic theory attends to the question of what politics is about. Yet any evaluation of majority rule as a decision-making mechanism must surely be parasitic on a view of politics, else we are without criteria to judge its success or failure. Every democratic theory operates, of course, with implicit assumptions and expectations about the nature of politics, and a little digging can usually bring them to light. We saw that the public choice theorists' explicit position is that the business of politics is preference amalgamation, although they often operate with implicit utilitarian commitments. Traditional pluralists such as Dahl and their latter-day progeny such as Miller see politics as about something quite different, the circulation of groups through the political process to provide as much representation as it is realistic to expect in a post-Schumpeterian era, while maintaining social stability. Conventional Marxists see bourgeois politics in purely instrumental terms, to be employed tactically as a harbinger of a future of superabundance that will render it redundant. Communitarian democrats such as Benjamin Barber believe that politics can be, and can be experienced as, a joint enterprise of common interests without such extravagant assumptions about socio-economic transformation.[94] Utilitarians such as John Harsanyi employ end-state principles to argue that leaving things to political experts will produce more desirable outcomes than enhancing participation.[95]

My own view is that politics is fundamentally about the possession and dispossession of power and that there are three inescapable truths about power which must shape our theoretical argument. The first is that power relations are ubiquitous; this much we have learned from Michel Foucault (some would say Plato). They are ubiquitous both in that they emerge in virtually every facet of social and economic life and in that attempts to eradicate power relations invariably fail.[96] This is not to deny (as Foucault may have done) that some ways of managing power relations are preferable to others; it is only to say that there are no extrapolitical solutions to many of the struggles that drive political conflict.

[94]See Benjamin Barber, *Strong Democracy: Participatory Politics for a New Age* (Berkeley: University of California Press, 1984).

[95]See John Harsanyi, "Democracy, Equality, and Popular Consent," in *Power, Inequality, and Democratic Politics: Essays in Honor of Robert Dahl*, ed. Ian Shapiro and Grant Reeher (Boulder: Westview, 1988), pp. 276–83. For criticism of this view see my "A Comment on John Harsanyi's 'Democracy, Equality, and Popular Consent,'" in ibid., pp. 284–90.

[96]For my account of why power relations are ineradicable in principle, see my "Gross Concepts in Political Argument," *Political Theory* 17, no. 1 (1989), pp. 51–76.

A second truth about political power is that possession of it is always potentially corrupting. I do not mean to suggest that all forms of power are corrupting. Power is sometimes simply an enabling condition for an individual without reference to anyone else; the empowerment that comes from conquering a neurosis may be unambiguously liberating. But that is not political power; for political power is inherently other-regarding, it is power over others.[97] Indeed, I propose to define political power in this way, because it avoids restricting political power to power exercised by or through state agencies. That limiting assumption, we saw, played a large part in driving both the reductionist and constitutionalist fallacies. Whenever power over others is exercised, it is political in my view—though whether it is politicized (seen as political by the relevant agents) is another matter. Thus rape of a wife was always a political action, but it only became politicized when the common law presumption of its impossibility was displaced by statutes defining it as a crime.[98]

If power relations are ubiquitous and the possession of political power may tend to corrupt, a third truth about power which we cannot afford to ignore is that lack of power in a world of ubiquitous power relations is demeaning and destructive for the powerless. Powerlessness is not a happy state. When we see those without power rebel they tend to arouse our sympathy, if not empathy, and when victims of power fail to rebel we find it troubling. Consider the amazed consternation in public debate and scholarship alike at evidence of Jewish complicity in the Holocaust. We find such phenomena troubling just because they conflict with our sense that the downtrodden should fight back.

From the understanding that politics is fundamentally about power thus conceived, we are now in a position to sum up the defects behind the fallacies discussed in this chapter. The central misconception that buttresses the reductionist fallacy grows out of the failure to deal with the problem of resources, and we can now see that in so doing it ignores most of what politics is really about. For the sense of powerlessness that sometimes motivates political action, and at other times motivates our intuition that political action is warranted, is exactly the lack of resources of individuals and groups to achieve goods and limit harms on

[97]I take this understanding of the nature of political power to be behind MacIntyre's poignant observation that as Marxists approach power they tend to become Weberians; see Alasdair MacIntyre, *After Virtue*, 2d ed.(Notre Dame, Ind.: University of Notre Dame Press, 1984), pp. i-ix, 261–62.

[98]See "To Have and to Hold: The Marital Rape Exception to the Fourteenth Amendment," note, *Harvard Law Review* 99 (1986), pp. 1255–73.

their own. The constitutionalist fallacy also results largely from ignoring problems of power. Although the public choice theorists are persuasive that there is no reason to expect majority rule to produce fair or just outcomes, this does not supply a rationale for what is often an unacknowledged utilitarian jurisprudence. Rather, real differences in resources can legitimate a judicial activism intended only to weed out manifest corruption of public officials and to protect the politically excluded in terms of footnote four, a jurisprudence of permanent sympathy for the underdog but no more. Some will find this an insufficiently robust basis for judicial activism, particularly if we disallow expansionist readings of footnote four such as Ely's, which attempted to incorporate much of the Warren Court's judicial action. I am not foreclosing the possibility that there might be grounds for judicial activism other than ensuring the actual operation of majority rule, though these cannot be derived from democratic theory alone. Whatever their additional premises, proponents of broad latitude for the Court in interpreting and enforcing constitutional values[99] must live with the risk that whereas broad latitude can give us the Warren Court, it can also give us *Lochner* and what we are likely to get from the Court in the next several decades. Gone is the time when we can live on a Bickelian act of faith that the Court will "represent" public attitudes but simply change more slowly than frequently reelected legislatures. Nor is it reasonable to believe that there is a secular trend toward the triumph of more enlightened views; our own circumstances belie this.

The stability fallacy ignores power in another way, in that the public choice theorists fail to see that their sense of stability is the very enemy of the democratic aspiration. Democracy is an ideology of opposition as much as it is one of government. It is about displacing entrenched elites, undermining the powerful, and empowering the powerless. If the public choice theorists have shown us that there is no way of translating this ideal into a fair system of government, of domesticating it, not only should we not be surprised but we should welcome the perpetual instability of dominant coalitions. Although we do not share Miller's faith that *this* instability will create or promote a pluralist stability of equitably circulating interest groups—we know too much about the ubiquity of power and inequality to believe that—at least the dominant coalitions with their ill-gotten gains will from time to time be displaced. In saying this we should avoid the characteristic liberal trap of assuming

[99]For a defense of the view that there are objective constitutional values (against the conventionalist arguments of Stanley Fish and others) deriving from the "interpretive community" of federal judges, see Owen Fiss, "Objectivity and Interpretation," *Stanford Law Review* 34 (1982), pp. 739–63, and "Conventionalism," *Southern California Law Review* 58, no. 1 (1985), pp. 177–97.

that it is only the power of government that we need to be afraid of, even to be most afraid of. Government is one major source of organized power, but there are many others. And it is just because politics is fundamentally about power, and only incidentally about governmental power, that democracy as an effective ideology of opposition, of disruption, can be brought to bear in the many different dimensions of social life that are structured by power relations. Thus have we seen strong democratic rationales in recent years for the politicization of employment and family relations. No doubt the democratic ideal will, in the future, provide the impetus to politicize relations that we today take for granted as wholly without political significance.

Yet we are bound to conclude with a view more complex than that instability is always and everywhere desirable. There are too many moral ambiguities surrounding the power that, through politics, we seek to manipulate, control, escape, and possess. In a world of ubiquitous power relations, where the possession of power is frequently as corrupting as the lack of it is demeaning, it may be that although the democratic aspiration of empowering the powerless and undermining the powerful is indispensable, it remains a troubled philosophic ideal.

3

Justice and Workmanship
in a Democracy

> Though the Earth, and all inferior Creatures be common to all
> Men, yet every Man has a *Property* in his own *Person*. This no
> Body has any Right to but himself. The *Labour* of his Body, and
> the *Work* of his hands, we may say, are properly his. Whatsoever
> then he removes out of the State that Nature hath provided, and
> left it in, he hath mixed his *Labour* with, and joyned it to some-
> thing that is his own, and thereby makes it his *Property*. It being
> by him removed from the common state Nature placed it in, hath
> by his *labour* something annexed to it, that excludes the common
> right of other Men. For this *Labour* being the unquestionable
> Property of the Labourer, no Man but he can have a right to what
> that is once joyned to, at least where there is enough, and as good
> left in common for others.
>
> —JOHN LOCKE, *Second Treatise of Government*

Human beings generate much of what they want and need by mixing
their productive capacities with other resources, producing objects and
services of value. This fact about human creativity has been incorporated into Western thinking about distributive justice through the workmanship ideal of ownership. That ideal revolves around the conviction
that, so long as people justly acquire the resources with which they mix
their productive capacities, they may legitimately own the product of
the conjunction. Just how to organize things so that the caveat embedded in the workmanship ideal is not violated has been subject to vi-

tuperative debate for centuries, as have the meaning of and justification for the premise that people may be said to own their productive capacities in the first place. In a number of idioms both intellectual and political, the workmanship ideal sets the terms of debate about the just distribution, ownership, and even definition of property.[1]

The enduring intensity of arguments about this ideal signifies that it retains a powerful hold on the Western political imagination, and it is the hold as much as the ideal that concerns me in this chapter. In a deconstructionist spirit I try to account for our collective inability to let go of the ideal, despite major conceptual difficulties it confronts. In a constructive spirit I try to adduce support for the view that partly because of its internal tensions, the workmanship ideal can defensibly be part of our thinking about distributive justice only in a limited and conditional way; we must not expect too much from it, and nor should we attribute to the rights it spawns a necessary trumping power with respect to competing requirements of social justice.

In section I, I argue that the workmanship ideal formulated by Locke was part of an internally cohesive view of just ownership which derived part of its intellectual appeal from the fact that it situated the rights of workmanship in a complex moral scheme that left room for other demands of social justice. I also argue, however, that the attractiveness and coherence of Locke's view depended on theological assumptions long since jettisoned in the dominant intellectual traditions of the West. Yet because of the powerful appeal of the intuitions that drive the workmanship ideal, many have tried to formulate secular variants of it; they have sought historical linking strategies that can be used to tether legitimate property rights to the work of productive agents. Sections II and III are devoted to analysis of the two main variants of such strategies which have grown out of the Marxist and neoclassical traditions of political economy. This leads to a discussion, in section IV, of why historical linking strategies invariably fail, running into insuperable problems of overdetermination and threatening perpetually to swamp the competing values with which property regimes are bound to coexist in any intellectually compelling account of social justice. This conclusion seems naturally to counsel abandoning historical linking strategies altogether, a possibility I examine in section V through a discussion of recent attempts by John Rawls and Ronald Dworkin to displace them with socialized views of human productive capacities. But the proposal that we should abandon the workmanship

[1] I take the term *workmanship ideal* from James Tully, *A Discourse concerning Property* (Cambridge: Cambridge University Press, 1980).

ideal turns out to be as troublesome as are the difficulties that result from embracing secular variants of it. In section VI, I discuss two possible ways out of the conundrum thus generated; one involves embracing a variant of the workmanship ideal on consequentialist grounds while conceding that it rests partly on causal and moral fictions. The second, which need not be inconsistent with the first, requires us to treat the workmanship ideal as part of a democratic conception of distributive justice. This, I suggest, is the better course.

I. THEOLOGICAL FOUNDATIONS OF THE CLASSICAL WORKMANSHIP IDEAL

Locke's theory of property was elegant, coherent, and—if one accepts the premises to which he was committed—compelling.[2] He thought human labor the main source of value, but he believed that natural resources make an independent—if comparatively minor—contribution to the value of produced goods and services.[3] Against Sir Robert Filmer (who had insisted that God gave the world to Adam and his heirs according to an hierarchical system of inheritance), Locke contended that God gave the world to mankind in common, subject to two constraints: that it not be wasted and that any individual's use of the common to produce his own property was subject to the restriction that "enough, and as good" remain available to others to use in common.[4]

[2]The following discussion of Locke incorporates and builds on aspects of my account in *The Evolution of Rights in Liberal Theory* (Cambridge: Cambridge University Press, 1986), pp. 86–118.

[3]Locke minimizes the independent contribution of resources by arguing that the world that has been given us in common is God's "waste" and insisting that "*labour makes* the far greater part," although he is famously vague about the precise relative contributions of labor and nature. John Locke, *Two Treatises of Government* (Cambridge: Cambridge University Press, 1970), pp. 331, 337, 338, 341, 330.

[4]Ibid., p. 329. To this moral theory Locke added two dubious empirical claims that combined to get him from the theory of use-rights to the common to something like the view of property that twentieth-century libertarians often wrongly designate as Lockean. First was the claim that, with the introduction of money, the injunction against waste, although not in principle transcended, for practical purposes became obsolete. Locke believed that, as well as itself not being subject to physical decay, money made possible the comparatively more productive use of natural resources through trade and productive work. See Richard Ashcraft, *Locke's Two Treatises of Government* (London: Allen and Unwin, 1987), pp. 123–50, and *Revolutionary Politics and Locke's Two Treatises of Government* (Princeton: Princeton University Press, 1986), pp. 270–85, and, for the view (which Ashcraft criticizes) that Locke considered the proviso transcended with the introduction of money, C. B. Macpherson, *The Political Theory of Possessive Individualism* (London: Oxford University Press, 1962), pp. 203–21. Second was the claim that the productivity effects of enclosing common land would be so great that the "enough, and as good" proviso could in practice also be dispensed with (thereby legitimating private ownership). It is possible

Locke's treatment of human capacities was linked to his theology in a different way; it rested on his categorial distinction between natural right and natural law which explained human autonomy. Natural law, Locke tells us, "ought to be distinguished from natural right: for right is grounded in the fact that we have the free use of a thing, whereas law enjoins or forbids the doing of a thing." Right, then, is a different kind of thing from law, the former indicating a capacity for autonomous action, and the latter, externally imposed obligatory constraints.[5] It is through acts of autonomous making that rights over what is created come into being: making entails ownership so that natural law is, at bottom, God's natural right over his creation.[6] Locke's frequent appeals to metaphors of workmanship and watchmaking in the *Two Treatises* and elsewhere make it fundamental that men are obliged to God because of his purposes in making them. Men are "the Workmanship of one Omnipotent, and infinitely wise Maker. . . . They are his Property, whose Workmanship they are, made to last during his, not one another's pleasure."[7] For Locke, human beings are unique among God's creations because he gave them the capacity to make, to create rights of their own. Natural law may dictate that humans are subject to divine imperatives to live in certain ways, but within the limits set by the law of nature, men can act, as Tully notes, in a Godlike fashion: "[m]an as maker. . . . has analogous maker's knowledge of, and a natural right in his intentional actions." Provided we do not violate natural law, we stand in the same relation to the objects we create as God stands in to us; we own them just as he owns us.[8] This is not to say that, for Locke, all our capacities are God given or that their development is uninfluenced by social arrangements; he thought that productive capacities could be bought and sold

---

to reject either or both of the empirical claims without rejecting Locke's basic moral argument, although any such move would jeopardize his defenses of unlimited accumulation and private property.

[5]By following Hobbes and Samuel Pufendorf in this formulation of the distinction, Locke was embracing an important departure from the Thomist tradition, rooted in Grotius's revival of the Roman law conception of a right as one's *suum*, a kind of moral power or *facultas* that every man has and that has its conceptual roots, as Quentin Skinner has established, in the writings of Francisco Suárez and ultimately Jean de Gerson and the conciliarist tradition. Quentin Skinner, *The Foundations of Modern Political Thought* (Cambridge: Cambridge University Press, 1978), 2:117, 176–78. See also Richard Tuck, *Natural Rights Theories* (Cambridge: Cambridge University Press, 1979), and John Finnis, *Natural Law and Natural Right* (Oxford: Clarendon, 1980), pp. 207–8.

[6]John Locke, *Essays on the Law of Nature*, ed. William Von Leiden (Oxford: Clarendon, 1958), pp. 111, 187.

[7]Locke, *Two Treatises of Government*, pp. 311, 347. For further discussion, see Tully, *Discourse concerning Property*, pp. 35–38, and John Dunn, *The Political Thought of John Locke* (Cambridge: Cambridge University Press, 1969), p. 95.

[8]Tully, *Discourse concerning Property*, pp. 109–10, 121.

in ways that increased productivity, and there is some evidence that he believed workers' productivity to be influenced by mercantile workhouse discipline.[9] Certainly there was potential for tension between these causal beliefs and the workmanship ideal; we will see later that arguments that human activity and organization shape productive capacities would eventually be pressed into the service of an explosive critique of that ideal.[10] But so long as human creative power was seen as a gift from God, this possibility could be staved off; even if productive capacities are influenced by human agency, this agency finds its genesis and limits in the will of a beneficent deity.

Locke conceived of the range of human activities free of God's sanctions quite broadly; certainly it included most of what is conventionally thought of as the realm of the production and consumption of goods.[11] But the existence of natural law constraints on human autonomy meant that there were circumstances in which the exercise of otherwise legitimate rights of appropriation would be curtailed. If Locke's provisos were violated, for instance, the right to appropriate from nature would be limited. Likewise someone starving and disabled would have the right to another's plenty based on the natural law requirements of the right of preservation, and someone starving and able bodied would have the right to the means of preservation—the right to materials to work on to preserve oneself—whether by means of the workhouse system or coerced labor for a landowner. In addition, there were limits, for Locke, to the reparations a conqueror could legitimately demand in wartime, limits having to do with the subsistence rights of the wives and children of defeated soldiers.[12]

The existence of Locke's natural law constraints thus meant that not all rights were of the same kind; property rights occupied a cir-

[9]Evidence that capacities may be bought and sold can be found in Locke's insistence that "the turfs my servant has cut . . . become my property" and in his account of wage labor, which states that "a free man makes himself a servant to another, by selling him for a certain time, the service he undertakes to do, in exchange for wages he is to receive." That Locke thought wage labor enhanced productivity is evident from his defense of enclosure partly on the grounds that this would replace less efficient forms of subsistence production. Locke, *Two Treatises of Government: Second Treatise*, pp. 330, 365–66, 90–97, 290, 292–93. On Locke on discipline and productivity, see James Tully, "Governing Conduct," in *Conscience and Causistry in Early Modern Europe*, ed. Edmund Leites (Cambridge: Cambridge University Press, 1988), pp. 12–71.

[10]On the implicit tensions between the causal argument and the workmanship ideal in Locke's formulation, see David Ellerman, "On the Labor Theory of Property," *Philosophical Forum* 16, no. 4 (summer 1985), pp. 318–22.

[11]For further discussion, see Patrick Riley, *Will and Political Legitimacy* (Cambridge: Harvard University Press, 1982), pp. 64–69, and my *Evolution of Rights*, pp. 105–7.

[12]On the role of the provisos in the theory of individual appropriation, see Locke, *Two Treatises*, pp. 327–44; on charity, ibid., p. 206; and on the natural law limits to conquerors' rights to just reparations, ibid., p. 438.

cumscribed space in an hierarchical system. Productive human actions issue in rights and obligations that are binding on human beings, but these are not the only types of moral claims to which Locke believed us subject. Although not independent of the workmanship model (natural law was argued to be valid as God's workmanship), these other moral claims were conceived of as prior to claims of human workmanship.[13] To be sure, there would be disputes about when and how the natural law requirements are triggered and about the degree to which they limit property rights in particular instances which the natural law theory could not by itself resolve. As Richard Ashcraft has shown with respect to eighteenth-century English debates about poor relief, the scope of what subsistence requires could be expanded and pressed into the service of a radical Lockean critique of the claims of capital.[14] But if the theory left balancing the claims of the competing requirements of natural law and human workmanship open to interpretation and political argument, at least at the margins, it also undermined the presumption that rights of human appropriation supersede competing just claims.

II. SECULARIZING THE WORKMANSHIP IDEAL: MARXISM

In many respects, Marx's labor theory of value was more sophisticated than Locke's. Marx famously distinguished labor from labor power, developed the concepts of abstract human labor and socially necessary labor time, and from them the theory of exploitation of labor by capital. Yet Marx held onto the basic logic of the workmanship ideal, even though he transformed it radically by secularizing it and locating it in a dynamic theory of historical change.[15]

Because Locke's treatment of both resources and capacities had been linked to his theology, both would now have to be handled differently. For Marx, resources cease to be of independent moral significance; the value of a natural resource is determined by the socially necessary labor time required for its appropriation from nature. God is no longer needed as the giver of natural resources when they are, by definition, without value apart from the human capacities needed for their appro-

---

[13]On the hierarchical priority of Locke's natural law requirements, see Ashcraft, *Locke's Two Treatises*, pp. 123–50.

[14]See Richard Ashcraft, "Lockean Ideas, Poverty, and the Development of Liberal Political Theory," in *Early Modern Conceptions of Property*, ed. John Brewer and Susan Staves (New York: Routledge, 1995), pp. 43–61.

[15]I skirt the question, not relevant here, of the degree to which Marx's labor theory of value was influenced by Smith's and Ricardo's.

priation. Not until the marginalists' rejection of the labor theory of value in the late nineteenth century would natural resources reenter the explanatory and moral calculus as an independent unit of value, and by then the theory of markets would offer different conceptual tools for dealing with them.

If resources are secularized by being reconceptualized as moral proxies for capacities, what of the treatment of capacities themselves? Are we still the ultimate owners of our capacities for Marx, and if so, why? In *The Critique of the Gotha Program*, in the course of a discussion of fair socialist distribution, Marx offers his most elaborate discussion of his views about the ultimate basis of entitlements. Defining the cooperative proceeds of labor as the "total social product," he argues that after various deductions have been made by the state (for the provision of public goods, welfare for indigents, and financing new production), the balance of the surplus becomes available for consumption.[16] Because distribution in the early stages of communism is "still stamped with the birth marks of the old society from whose womb it emerges," it will continue to be based on work. The individual producer receives back from society, after the deductions have been made, "exactly what he gives to it." In these circumstances "the same principle prevails as that which regulates the exchange of commodities," but it is nonetheless an advance on capitalism because "under the altered circumstances no one can give anything except his labour," and "nothing can pass into the ownership of individuals except individual means of consumption." Thus although "equal right" continues to mean "bourgeois right" under socialism, "principle and practice are no longer at loggerheads."[17]

Marx concedes that this principle will generate inequalities by virtue of the fact that actual work becomes the basic metric of equality. Because labor must be defined either by duration or intensity to function as a measure at all, and because people differ from one another in physical and mental capacities, the right to each according to his work is unavoidably "an unequal right for unequal labour." He also notes that these inequalities will be exacerbated by differing social circumstances. Such defects are inevitable through the early stages of communism, but in a "higher phase," "after the enslaving subordination of the individual to the division of labour, and with it also the antithesis between mental and physical labour, has vanished" and the "springs of co-operative wealth flow more abundantly," then the "narrow horizon of bourgeois right" can be "crossed in its entirety" and distribution can

[16]Karl Marx, *The Critique of the Gotha Program*, in Karl Marx and Frederick Engels, *Selected Works* (Moscow: Progress, 1970), 3:15–17.
[17]Ibid., pp. 17, 18.

be based on needs. The transcendence of every regime of right is seen as necessary for the triumph of genuine equality; the work-based regime of socialism is not special in this regard; it is "a right of inequality, in its content, like every right."[18]

The workmanship ideal plays a role throughout Marx's account, but it should not be confused with his formulation of the labor theory of value. This latter is the causal thesis that only living human labor power creates exchange value (which determines prices in a capitalist economy). Marx believed this thesis explained the phenomenon of exploitation under capitalism by generating an account of how exchange value accrues to the capitalist as a by-product of the difference between the value of wages he pays his workers and the value of the products those workers produce. In Marx's hands, the labor theory of value thus became a vehicle for incorporating the moral appeal of the workmanship ideal into arguments about the production and distribution of wealth in a different way than had been the case with Locke; it rested on a different variant of the labor theory of value. Yet in neither case is the workmanship ideal part of or reducible to the labor theory of value. The ideal rests on the moral thesis that the legitimate basis of entitlement lies in productive action, and it is only because of the intuitive moral appeal of this thesis that the labor theory of value was thought to be pregnant with moral significance.

It is not surprising, therefore, that Marxists who have abandoned the labor theory of value nonetheless affirm variants of the workmanship ideal. G. A. Cohen argues that exploitation under capitalism derives not from the problematical thesis that the workers alone produce value, only from the fact that the workers alone produce the product.[19] Conceding that capitalists may *act productively* by investing, he distinguishes this from *producing goods*, which, he reasons, is exclusively done by workers. Whether Cohen is right about this we need not settle now; that he makes the argument at all exhibits his reliance on the intuitive moral pull of the workmanship ideal.[20] This reliance be-

---

[18]Ibid., pp. 19, 18.

[19]G. A. Cohen, "The Labor Theory of Value and the Concept of Exploitation," *Philosophy and Public Affairs* 8, no. 4 (1979), p. 354, Cohen's italics.

[20]Ibid., pp. 355–56. Cohen does concede that in some circumstances capitalists may also work productively, but not in their prototypical roles as capitalists. I do not mean to suggest that Cohen believes that the workmanship ideal is the only or most important basis for distributive entitlements. Indeed, his recent advocacy of equality of "access to advantage" suggests a different basis for distributive justice: that people should not be held responsible for unchosen disadvantages. It is not yet possible to assess how the imperatives generated by this injunction should affect other rights, including rights of workmanship, in Cohen's view, because he defends equality of access to advantage only as what he dubs a weak form of egalitarianism: he explicitly refrains from saying to what extent we should equalize in his sense, or even how

comes explicit in two essays on the relations between self-ownership and world ownership where Cohen advances criticisms of Robert Nozick which rely on affirming the idea that we own our productive capacities and, in certain circumstances, the goods they are instrumental in generating.[21]

Likewise, John Roemer assumes that people own their productive capacities, and he defines exploitation and unfairness (for him these two are not the same) in terms of distributions of the alienable means of production that force or supply incentives to workers to produce goods that become the property of capitalists.[22] To pack any moral punch, such arguments must rest on the claim that such class monopoly is unjustifiable, and when we ask why, the answer turns out to rest on either the claim that the monopoly was achieved by illicit appropriation of the proceeds of the work of others or the argument that the class monopoly prevents workers' realizing at least some of the potential fruits of their own labor, or both. Thus Roemer resists, on historical or probabilistic grounds, the possibility that the class monopoly might have come about as a result of differences in natural abilities or propensities toward risk, and he defines unfairness and exploitation by reference to counterfactuals in which individuals or classes would produce more goods by as much or less work than is the case when the class monopoly obtains.[23]

---

conflicts between his kind of equalization and other kinds that egalitarians might prize should be settled. G. A. Cohen, "On the Currency of Egalitarian Justice," *Ethics* 99, no. 4 (1989), pp. 906–44, and "Equality of What? On Welfare, Goods, and Capabilities," forthcoming in a volume of papers presented at the WIDER Symposium on the Quality of Life and referred to here in manuscript form. Some of these issues are taken up briefly in my *Political Criticism* (Berkeley: University of California Press, 1990), pp. 217–19.

[21]G. A. Cohen, "Self-ownership, World Ownership, and Equality: I," in *Justice and Equality Here and Now,* ed. Frank Lucash (Cornell University Press, 1986), pp. 108–35, and "Self-ownership, World Ownership, and Equality: II," *Social Philosophy and Policy* 3, no. 2 (spring 1986), pp. 77–96. In "Self-ownership: I," Cohen appeals to the idea that "value adders merit reward" to attack Nozick's defense of private ownership of external resources. Cohen demonstrates (ingeniously) that different forms of ownership of external resources may in some circumstances reward value adders more often or more accurately than a private property regime of the sort Nozick advocates; see esp. pp. 128–30. In fairness to Cohen it should be noted that in these essays he professes some discomfort with the self-ownership thesis (deriving from the inequalities the thesis must inevitably generate given that some people are more productive than others), and he promises at a future time to show how and why the self-ownership thesis should be undermined. To say that one owns oneself is to say something broader than that one owns one's productive capacities, and it may be that both Cohen and I would eventually want to say that productive capacities should be distinguished from other dimensions of personal identity and given less, or at any rate different kinds of, protection.

[22]John Roemer, "Property Relations versus Surplus Value in Marxian Exploitation," *Philosophy and Public Affairs* 11, no. 4 (fall 1982), pp. 281–313. More generally, see his "Should Marxists Be Interested in Exploitation?" *Philosophy and Public Affairs* 14, no. 1 (winter 1985), pp. 30–65, and *A General Theory of Class and Exploitation* (Cambridge: Harvard University Press, 1982).

[23]Roemer, "Property Relations," pp. 284–92, 305–10, 310. Roemer also insists that even when

If the workmanship ideal is implicated in Marxist critiques of capitalist exploitation whether or not these rest on the labor theory of value, what is its role in Marx's positive argument for the superiority of socialism over capitalism and of communism over socialism? His appeal to the workmanship ideal might be interpreted merely as a polemical charge that socialism is an advance on capitalism because under it those who actually do the work are rewarded as bourgeois ideology requires. Yet to claim that what is wrong with capitalism is that it fails to live up to a standard that cannot, anyhow, be independently justified is to say less than Marx wanted or needed to say. One only has to think of other systems to which he objected—notably feudalism—which were not subject to the particular defect of hypocrisy as capitalism allegedly is, to realize that Marx's critical arguments were intended to have more far-reaching moral impact.[24] Throughout his writings human beings are described as productive creatures, creating their means of subsistence in ways that decisively shape other aspects of their lives and identities as persons.[25] Even a communist society, where the existence of a superabundance of wealth frees people from necessity, is described by the mature Marx as a society of free *producers*.[26] The workmanship ideal thus captured something in Marx's positive conception of the human condition which motivated his attack on modes of production that alienate people from their productive natures. To be sure, the ideal was much changed in his hands; it took on a dynamic character deriving from the romantic expressivist notion that human beings produce not only the means for their subsistence but also, and as a result of that fact, themselves. This meant that the distributive implications of the ideal were more complex than in Locke's mechanistic view of the relation between the producer and his product, more complex—as becomes plain in section IV—than even Marx realized. But the workmanship ideal remained, nonetheless, the basic legitimating ideal of human ownership.[27]

---

differential ownership is necessary for reasons of productivity, if it is the differential distribution of assets as such, "rather than the skills of capitalists, which brings about incentives, competition, innovation, and increased labor productivity which benefit even the workers, then the capitalists do not deserve their returns." By its terms, this reasoning concedes the moral force of the workmanship ideal: were it, by contrary hypothesis, the differences in skill, rather than the distribution of assets as such, that accounted for greater productivity, and so forth, presumably the capitalist would deserve the differential benefit. Roemer does not face this possibility because he assumes equality of skill and propensity toward risk.

[24] See Jürgen Habermas, "Technology as Science and Ideology," in *Toward a Rational Society* (Boston: Beacon, 1970), pp. 62–80.

[25] Marx and Engels, *Selected Works*, 1:20, 26–30, 38–50, 62–73.

[26] See Karl Marx, *Capital* (London: Lawrence and Wishart, 1974), 1:82–83.

[27] The difficulties inherent in trying to pin down just what work has been done by which worker in a given cycle of production have been well explored in Cohen, "Labor Theory of Value," and Roemer, "Property Relations," and "Should Marxists Be Interested in Exploitation?"

Workmanship diminishes in significance for Marx when we turn attention to the argument that socialism is merely transitional to a needs-based communist regime of superabundance, although even here it retains a residual influence on his view. First there is the negative pole in Marx's implicit justificatory argument. A communist utopia is conceived of as the only possible regime in which there is no exploitation of one class by another. By thus requiring its own negation, the theory of exploitation leaves an indelible stamp on the depiction of communism, and so, inevitably, does the workmanship ideal that gives the theory of exploitation its critical bite. Second there is the assumption driving Marx's defense of collective allocation of the productive surplus in *The Critique of the Gotha Program* and elsewhere, namely that under conditions of advanced division of labor, private allocation is not defensible, and collective allocation is, on the grounds that—appearances to the contrary notwithstanding—the surplus is collectively produced.[28] This assumption has only to be stated for its reliance on the workmanship ideal to become plain. Unless we interpret superabundance to mean that a situation could arise in which no distributive choices of any kind would ever have to be made (because everyone could always have everything she needed or wanted), Marx would presumably continue to embrace some variant of this workmanship-based defense of collective allocation.[29] In this way Marx's speculations about the postcapitalist future affirm the justificatory power of the workmanship ideal, even if he often relies on a mixture of ad hoc argument and intuitionist appeal—rather than principled justification—in its defense.

III. SECULARIZING THE WORKMANSHIP IDEAL: NEOCLASSICAL VIEWS

Like most Marxists, neoclassical political and economic theorists exhibit an abiding commitment to the workmanship ideal which has long survived the marginalists' abandonment of the labor theory of value. Indeed, the labor theory was rejected partly on the grounds that, since

[28]Marx and Engels, *Selected Works*, 3:17–19; Marx, *Capital*, 1:83.

[29]For reasons elaborated elsewhere I do not regard Marx's notion of a superabundance that transcends scarcity as coherent or even consistent with his own account of human needs, and nor do I regard as plausible attempts by Cohen and others to reason about distribution, without taking account of endemic scarcity, by referring to the idea of "relative abundance." If I am right, those who continue to insist that the moral force of Marx's critique of capitalism depends on the possibility of a communist economy of superabundance are committed to the view that it has no force at all. See my *Political Criticism*, pp. 217–19.

the causal story it tells was thought by the marginalists to be false, attempts to use it as a basic yardstick for thinking about distributive fairness violate the ideal; such attempts were thought not to take into account the productive contributions of capitalists. Modern neoclassicists thus retain a commitment to the notion that the act of working creates entitlements in the object or service produced by the relevant work; indeed they typically defend acquisition of goods through exchange by reference to the claim that an agent is entitled to dispose of what she has produced however she likes. It is no accident that Nozick's critique of redistributive taxation reduces to the claim that it is "forced labor."[30]

The principal neoclassical strategy for secularizing the workmanship ideal replaces the Lockean theology with a foundational appeal to the value of individual autonomy, whether for more or less Kantian reasons. Its proponents link property rights over the products of one's productive capacities to the preservation of autonomy, as in Nozick's claim that everyone has an inviolable right to what he has himself produced or freely been given. It is an open secret that where these rights come from is never fully accounted for in such arguments and that the freedoms they preserve are purely formal.[31] Typically, as in Nozick's case, there is some appeal to Locke, but without grappling with the issues inevitably raised once his limited defense of private appropriation is detached from its theological moorings. Thus Richard Posner embraces a variant of the Kantian claim when arguing that no injustice results from the fact that in a market system "people who lack sufficient earning power to support even a minimally decent standard of living are entitled to no say in the allocation of resources unless they are part of the utility function of someone who has wealth." He resists the Rawlsian critique of this view (taken up in section V below), insisting that treating the more and less well endowed as equally entitled to valuable resources "does not take seriously the differences between persons" and indeed that any redistributive taxation policy "impairs the autonomy of those from whom redistribution is made."

Posner concedes that this procedure implies that "if an individual happens to be born feeble-minded and his net social product is negative, he would have no right to the means of support even though there was nothing blameworthy in his inability to support himself." Yet he insists that although this conclusion might be judged to violate the

[30]Robert Nozick, *Anarchy, State, and Utopia* (New York: Basic Books, 1974), pp. 169–72, 265–68.

[31]Cohen usefully points out that despite the much-trumpeted commitment to freedom behind libertarian thinking, in philosophies like Nozick's, freedom is derivative of self-ownership. Cohen, "Self-ownership: II," p. 77.

autonomy of the feeble-minded, there is no escape from it "consistent with any of the major ethical systems." This is a view he shares with John Harsanyi, who asserts against Rawls and without argument that our abilities "are parts of our own inner selves and belong to us as a matter of sheer natural fact." That such declarations are deemed sufficient to bridge the fact/value gap and legitimate secular variants of the workmanship ideal is testimony to its captivating power; no principled argument is thought to be needed in their defense.[32]

IV. DIFFICULTIES CONFRONTING SECULAR VARIANTS OF THE WORKMANSHIP IDEAL

In both Marxist and neoclassical traditions, then, the workmanship ideal has exhibited a staying power that has long outlived both its theological origins and the labor theories of value to which it was initially linked. Yet, in its secular form, the workmanship ideal confronts two major types of conceptual difficulty. These combine to throw into sharp relief the difficulties of determining the nature of, and limits to, human-produced entitlements once we are without Locke's natural law constraints such as the provisos, the requirements of charity, and the legitimate demands of dependents.

First, luck in the genetic pool and in the circumstances into which one happens to be born plays a substantial role in what kinds of productive capacities people develop and are able to develop. The resulting inequalities seem to be deeply at odds with what is attractive in the logic of the workmanship ideal, inasmuch as these are only the proximate result of the work of the relevant producing agent. If two people work equally hard but one is twice as productive because of her more effective natural capacities or her better-nurtured capacities, it seems that in a deeper sense it is not her work but her superior genetic or nutritional luck that is the basis of her relative advantage. If differences deriving from natural capacity or social condition were traceable ultimately to the will of God, they need not seem unjustifiable and nor need it be the responsi-

---

[32]Richard Posner, *The Economics of Justice* (Cambridge: Harvard University Press, 1981), pp. 76–87; John Harsanyi, "Democracy, Equality, and Popular Consent," in *Power, Inequality, and Democratic Politics: Essays in Honor of Robert Dahl*, ed. Ian Shapiro and Grant Reeher (Boulder: Westview, 1988), p. 279. In the face of arguments about the prima facie moral arbitrariness of their secular variants of the workmanship ideal, neoclassical theorists often shift to consequentialist justificatory grounds, arguing that treating productive capacities and what they generate as privately owned and alienable via the market maximizes productive efficiency. See Posner, *Economics of Justice*, p. 81. See also Nozick, *Anarchy, State, and Utopia*, pp. 149–82, 232–76. For extended criticism of such claims, see my "Richard Posner's Praxis," *Ohio State Law Journal* 48, no. 4 (1987), pp. 999–1047.

bility of human society to counteract their effects. Once these differences are considered by reference to secular understandings of workmanship, however, they are bound to become morally controversial.

Second, because human productive capacities are themselves partly produced by human work, it seems arbitrary to treat a given producing agent as the "final" owner of his productive capacities to begin with. Locke saw our productive capacities as God-given, so the question of why we might be said to own them never arose for him; indeed their very existence was part of what marked off the ultimate moral boundaries among persons. But in the absence of a theology that dictates this assumption, defenders of secular variants of the workmanship ideal have to confront the difficulty of how to specify the morally relevant boundaries among persons qua productive creatures. American courts have begun to recognize how complex this can be in divorce settlements. The domestic labor performed in support of a spouse attaining a professional qualification is treated as part of the relevant work in creating the capacity to generate the income that the qualification brings. For this reason, the divorcing spouse who performed the domestic labor is given a property interest in the stream of future income that the now qualified divorcing spouse is newly capable of generating.[33] As a philosophical matter, the intuition behind this sort of example has been generalized by feminist theorists to make the point, for instance, that it was morally arbitrary for Marx to try to measure the rate of exploitation by exclusive reference to the relation between the surplus produced and the money wage paid to the worker. Any such calculation ignores the contributions of the worker's spouse to his capacity to work, which he rents to the capitalist and which Marx arbitrarily takes to be the worker's "own." From this standpoint Marx's argument can be turned on the worker's relationship with his spouse, revealing *it* in certain circumstances to be exploitative.[34] It is indeed surprising that Marxists have attended so little to the significance of produced productive

[33]See *O'Brien v. O'Brien*, 66 NY 2d 576 (1985), in which the Appellate Division of the Supreme Court in the Second Judicial Department of New York upheld a decision that a husband's license to practice medicine was marital property on the grounds that "[t]he contributions of one spouse to the other's profession or career . . . represent investments in the economic partnership of the marriage and the product of the parties' joint efforts." Thus although New York is not a community property state, the divorcing wife was awarded 40 percent of the estimated value of the license, to be paid over eleven years, and the divorcing husband was ordered to maintain a life insurance policy for the unpaid balance of the award, with the divorcing wife as the beneficiary.

[34]See Nancy Folbre, "Exploitation Comes Home: A Critique of the Marxian Theory of Family Labor," *Cambridge Journal of Economics* 6, no. 4 (1982), pp. 317–29.

capacities, both for the coherence of the self-ownership thesis they generally embrace and for its distributive implications.[35]

In short, if the use of productive capacities generates entitlements, and if productive capacities are themselves partly produced by the work of others, then tracing the moral reach of a particular productive capacity exercised in the production of a particular nonhuman object becomes exceedingly complex, arguably impossible even in principle. For the feminist point can itself be generalized: the productive capacities a conventional wife "has" which she expends in her husband's attainment of a professional qualification were no doubt themselves partly produced by the work of others: parents, perhaps children, Sunday-school teachers who drummed into her a particular mixture of the work ethic and conventional family values, and so on. If one pushes the idea of productive capacity as the moral basis for entitlement to the limit, it seems to point in the direction of a tangled and indecipherable web of overdetermined entitlements and, indeed, to reveal a deep tension at the core of the workmanship ideal itself. The claim that we own what we make in virtue of our ownership of our productive capacities undermines the claim that we own our productive capacities, once it is conceded that those capacities are themselves produced partly by the work of others. Yet if we want to employ a variant of the workmanship ideal without pushing it to the limit, and in the absence of a theological limiting device such as Locke's, then the difficulty remains of how to do the pertinent line drawing without inviting charges of moral arbitrariness.

V. The Workmanship Ideal and the Socialization-of-Capacities Strategy

These formidable difficulties lend seriousness to the suggestion that we abandon the workmanship ideal altogether. This possibility has been most fully explored by Rawls and Dworkin in different ways in the course of contributing to a larger debate about whether resources, welfare, or some intermediate metric should form the basic unit of account of theories of distributive justice. The initial impetus for their turn to resource-based theories was the perceived defects of welfarist views such as utilitarianism which seem to require either too little or too much in the way of interpersonal judgments of utility to be morally

[35]As Cohen notes, in this respect liberals like Rawls and Dworkin, who reject self-ownership, must be accounted to the left of Marxists, who generally embrace it. Cohen, "Self-ownership: I," pp. 113–15.

satisfying. In classical (objective) welfarism, where cardinal scales and interpersonal comparisons of utility are permitted, welfarist theories are vulnerable to the charge that they fail to take seriously the differences among persons, since paternalistic judgments may be employed to increase one person's welfare at the expense of another's. Yet if the neoclassical move toward subjective welfarism is made and interpersonal comparisons are disallowed, welfarism either requires information about mental states on which it seems impossible to rely without generating perverse incentives for the systematic misrepresentation of preferences or it is managed through the market-based theory of revealed preference. This latter strategy runs into the disquieting fact that people have different resources to express preferences in a market system, neatly summed up in Anatole France's quip that the poor are free to sleep under the bridges of Paris.[36] These difficulties with welfarism are no less intractable than are they oft repeated, and resourcism is thought to be attractive partly because it appears to open up the possibility of avoiding them. Resourcism's motivating idea is that some set of instrumental goods—such as Rawls's "primary goods"—can be thought of as valuable for all rational individual conceptions of the good life and that it is those that should be justly distributed without reference to the mental states (or welfare otherwise construed) that they allegedly engender.[37]

Rawls and Dworkin both argue that, like other resources, human capacities should for certain purposes be regarded as social goods. This socialization-of-capacities strategy may be thought of as a mirror image of the classical Marxian one. For Marx, nonhuman resources cease to be of independent moral interest, being reducible to the capacities necessarily expended in their creation or their separation from nature. For Rawls and Dworkin, by contrast, human capacities cease to be of independent moral interest; they are treated as social resources like any other. Thus Rawls argues forcibly that differences both in natural abilities and in contingencies of upbringing are morally arbitrary factors

[36]This difficulty inevitably rears its head when a theory designed for the purpose of predicting prices becomes the normative basis of arguments about distribution; see Chapter 2 above.

[37]For useful accounts of what is at issue between resourcist and welfare egalitarians, see Amartya Sen, "Equality of What?" in *The Tanner Lectures on Human Values*, vol. 4, ed. Sterling M. McMurrin (Salt Lake City: University of Utah Press, 1980), pp. 197–220; and Ronald Dworkin, "What Is Equality? I. Equality of Welfare," *Philosophy and Public Affairs* 10, no.3 (summer 1981), pp. 185–246, and "What Is Equality? II. Equality of Resources," *Philosophy and Public Affairs* 10, no. 4 (fall 1981), pp. 283–345. For defense of "middle-ground" metrics, intermediate between resourcism and welfarism, see Amartya Sen "Well-being, Agency, and Freedom," *Journal of Philosophy* 82, no. 4 (April 1985), pp. 169–221; Richard Arneson, "Equality and Equal Opportunity for Welfare," *Philosophical Studies* 56 (1989), pp. 77–93; and Cohen, "Currency of Egalitarian Justice" and "Equality of What?"

that should not in principle determine the rewards people receive, usefully rendering the nature/nurture debate beside the point for arguments about distributive justice.[38] Similarly, Dworkin treats human capacities and external material resources as moral equivalents from the standpoint of distributive justice, arguing that although there may be good reasons for resisting the redistribution of physical and mental resources (insofar as this is technologically feasible), a case might nonetheless be made for compensating those with inferior physical and mental resources for their relative incapacities.[39]

Given the preceding discussion of luck and produced capacities, it might be suggested that there is no way genuinely to link entitlements to work other than by some variant of the socialization-of-capacities strategy, that it alone can consummate the workmanship ideal. This is true, I think, but the variant of the ideal thus saved is so thin that it dispenses with a good part of what gives it its intuitive appeal: the psychological side of workmanship, the sense of subjective satisfaction that attaches to the idea of making something that one can subsequently call one's own. We all know the feeling, and it is not easily argued that it can apply to a generalized notion that there is a sense in which I, along with everyone else, own everything that everyone appears at a given time and place to make. And for a species so critically reliant as is ours on productive activity for survival, it seems perverse to deny the legitimacy of so powerful a spur to productive activity as the psychic activity that producing something one can own brings.

This is why theorists such as Rawls and Dworkin balk at the implications of the socialization-of-capacities strategy. Rawls supplies a list of primary goods that are held to be desirable for any rational life plan, but he explicitly refuses to confront the implications of his account of the moral arbitrariness of differing capacities when he holds that the effectiveness with which people are able to use resources, or choose to use them, is not a relevant consideration in deciding how resources should be distributed. There are two issues here, both of which raise tensions internal to the Rawlsian account. One derives from Amartya Sen's point that if we really want justly to distribute what people of greatly different capacities are enabled to do, then we cannot use Rawlsian primary goods; we need a different metric that takes account of how different people employ capacities and resources.[40] Second, there is the

---

[38]See John Rawls, *A Theory of Justice* (Cambridge: Harvard University Press, 1971), pp. 12, 15, 72–73, 101–3, 507–11.

[39]Ibid., pp. 12, 18–19, 137–38, 172, 200; Dworkin, "What Is Equality? I," pp. 300–301.

[40]See Sen, "Equality of What?" pp. 212–20, and "Well-being, Agency, and Freedom," pp. 185–221.

point made by Cohen, Richard Arneson, and others, that different people have different preferences and goals, some more expensive and more difficult to satisfy than others. Rawls's attempt to sidestep this problem, by arguing that these are not afflictions but are chosen, scarcely meets the objection because, as Thomas Scanlon and others have noted, often they are not.[41]

Dworkin also balks at the implications of the socialization-of-capacities strategy. He invites us to speculate on how resources might in principle be equalized by use of a hypothetical auction in which all parties begin with the same finite number of bargaining chips.[42] As part of this speculation he argues that human capacities should be thought of as resources; yet there are two ways in which he dodges the full implications of the socialization-of-capacities strategy. First he claims that although capacities (his term is "physical and mental powers") are resources and as a consequence legitimate objects of a theory of distributive justice, they should nonetheless be treated differently from "independent material resources." With physical and mental powers, the goal should not be to strive to distribute them justly (which, for Dworkin, means equally). Instead the problem is construed as one of discovering "how far the ownership of independent external resources should be affected by differences that exist in physical and mental

[41]Rawls's most explicit statement of the view that people must be regarded as responsible for their preferences can be found in his "Social Unity and Primary Goods," in *Utilitarianism and Beyond*, ed. Amartya Sen and Bernard Williams (Cambridge: Cambridge University Press, 1982), pp. 168–69. For discussion of the tensions between this claim and the argument that differences in capacity are arbitrary, which Rawls defends most fully in *Theory of Justice*, pp. 101–4, see Thomas M. Scanlon, "Equality of Resources and Equality of Welfare: A Forced Marriage?" *Ethics* 97, no. 1 (1986), pp. 116–17, and "The Significance of Choice," *Tanner Lectures on Human Values*, vol. 8 (1988), pp. 192–201; Arneson, "Equality and Equal Opportunity for Welfare"; and Cohen, "Equality of What?" pp. 7–10.

[42]Dworkin, "What Is Equality? I and II." For reasons that I here lack the space to expound at length, I think Dworkin's hypothetical auction, described at "What Is Equality? II," pp. 283–90, fails on its own terms as a device for deciding on what could count as an equal initial allocation of resources. An example of one of the difficulties, which will be intelligible only to initiates of these debates, is that in the hypothetical auction Dworkin describes, it would be quite possible for some player or players to bid up the price of some good that she or they did not want but which she or they knew someone else had to have at all costs (such as the available stock of insulin on the island in Dworkin's example, assuming there was one diabetic). In this way, the diabetic could be forced either to spend all (or at least a disproportionate quantity) of his initial resources on insulin, thereby making other bundles of goods relatively cheaper for the other inhabitants, or he might be forced to buy it at an artificially high price from whoever had bought it in the initial auction. The more general point is that Dworkin's hypothetical story assumes that people do not have different strategic resources and powers to bargain and that they will not have reasons to misrepresent their preferences during the initial auction. But there is no good reason to suppose that either of these assumptions is true, and as a result there is no reason to believe that a hypothetical auction of the kind he describes can be a device that equalizes resources in the way that he claims.

powers, and the response of our theory should speak in that vocabulary."[43] For this reason he thinks that people should be compensated by reference to a standard arrived at by our speculations concerning whether and to what extent people would, on average, have insured against the particular handicap or disability or lack of talent ex ante, assuming that insurance rates would be set in a competitive market.[44]

Notice that Dworkin supplies no principled argument for why physical and mental powers should be treated differently than material resources from the standpoint of distributive justice. The assertion that they "cannot be manipulated or transferred, even so far as technology permits" is not further explained or justified, but because Dworkin has chosen to treat powers *as* resources, an explanation is surely in order.[45] This is so not least because compensation in any amount will sometimes be inadequate to equalize a power—or capacity—deficiency (as in the case of blindness), as Dworkin elsewhere notes; yet equality of resources is his basic criterion of distributive justice. In such circumstances compensation based on a standard set by a hypothetical insurance auction cannot be said to equalize the resources of two persons, one blind, one sighted.[46] Yet it is not always true, pace Dworkin, that their powers of sight *could not* be equalized.[47] The state might forcibly transplant one eye from a sighted person to the blind one in order to equalize their resources, or, for that matter, simply blind the sighted person. Less callously and more interestingly, it might invest billions of dollars on research on and development of artificial eyes, financed by a

[43]Ibid., pp. 300–301.

[44]As a result, insuring against the possibility of not having an extremely rare skill would be far more expensive than insuring against the possibility of not having a widely shared capacity such as sight. In this way, Dworkin hopes to come up with a theory of equality of resources that does not itself make implicit judgments about welfare and avoids the "slavery of the talented" problem, which any theory that permits compensation for differences in capacities must confront. See ibid., pp. 292–304. Again for initiates only: notice that for the hypothetical insurance market argument to work, it has to be assumed not only that each of the ex ante choosers has equal initial resources (see the preceding footnote) but also that none of them has any incapacity or absence of talent (for otherwise the question of whether or not to insure against the possibility of not having it could not arise). This latter I take to be an unthinkably incoherent speculation, given that talents and incapacities are treated as analytic equivalents from the standpoint of the hypothetical insurance market.

[45]Ibid, p. 301.

[46]See ibid., p. 300, where Dworkin notes—in opposition to the idea that there can be a view of "normal" human powers—that no amount of initial compensation could make someone born blind or mentally incompetent equal in physical or mental resources with someone taken to be "normal" in these ways.

[47]"Someone who is born with a serious handicap faces his life with what we concede to be fewer resources, just on that account, than others do. This justifies compensation, under a scheme devoted to equality of resources, and though the hypothetical insurance market does not right the balance—*nothing can*—it seeks to remedy one aspect of the resulting unfairness." Ibid., p. 302, italics added.

tax on the sighted. If Dworkin is to avoid such unpalatable results, he must supply an argument for why we may be said to be entitled to our powers and capacities (and in some sense responsible for having or lacking them) in different (and trumping) ways than we can be said to be entitled to material resources, given his equation of the two. In the absence of such an argument it is difficult to see how Dworkin can adopt the socialization-of-capacities strategy in principle, yet simply assert that people are entitled to, and responsible for, their capacities and incapacities in fact.

The second way in which Dworkin refuses to live with the socialization-of-capacities strategy that he otherwise embraces concerns his discussion of how our conception of a person should be distinguished from our conception of her circumstances. Dworkin argues that we need a view of distributive justice that is "ambition sensitive." It requires a view of equality by reference to which people "decide what sorts of lives to pursue against a background of information about the actual costs that their choices impose on other people and hence on the total stock of resources that may fairly be used by them." This he tries to achieve by assigning "tastes and ambitions" to the person, and "physical and mental powers" to her "circumstances," arguing that the former are not relevant considerations in deciding how resources should be distributed.[48] In this way he hopes to rescue an island of creative autonomy for the individual agent. Dworkin wants to rescue the kernel of what is intuitively attractive in the workmanship ideal, the idea that when people conceive of and put into practice productive plans, the benefits from the resulting actions should flow back to them. Yet he wants to do this without being swamped by the difficulties of overdetermination that flow from the Rawlsian claim that the distribution of physical and mental powers is morally arbitrary.[49]

Dworkin's strategy fails. The volitions we are able to form, the ambitions it occurs to us to develop; these are greatly influenced, perhaps even determined, by our powers and capacities. To "think big," to "resolve to go for broke," to steel oneself through self-control to perform demanding acts, do these reflect ambition or capacity? When we describe someone as ambitious, are we not describing something more basic to her psychology and constitution than her tastes? There are certainly circumstances in which we would say that lack of confidence is an incapacity that prevents the formation (not just the attainment) of particular ambitions. Different people have different capacities to form

[48]Ibid., pp. 311, 288, 302.
[49]Ibid., pp. 311–14.

different ambitions, and those different capacities must be as morally tainted from Dworkin's point of view as any other capacities. Donald Trump is able to develop more far-reaching ambitions than Archie Bunker owing at least partly to luck in the genetic pool and in the circumstances of his upbringing.[50]

Similar arguments can be made about the different abilities to form (or refrain from forming) different kinds of tastes, whether expensive, compulsive, or both, as Dworkin is aware. The case Dworkin considers is one in which a person might have an incapacitating obsession that he wishes he did not have, and Dworkin deals with this by arguing that such cravings may be thought of as handicaps and thus handled with his hypothetical insurance scheme.[51] But this is to sidestep my point, which is that the obsession may itself incapacitate a person from forming the relevant second-order desire to make Dworkin's hypothetical insurance solution work. Are we to say of an alcoholic whose affliction is so severe that he cannot even form the desire not to be an alcoholic that his preference for alcohol results from his *taste* rather than his *incapacity*? I think not.[52]

With all acquired tastes (not just the expensive), experiencing the taste is by definition conditional on the exercise of pertinent capacities. A taste for good beer, or even just for beer, a taste for a particular kind of music, perhaps even for any music—these can be developed only through the exercise of relevant capacities. We would not say of a deaf person that she could have a taste for music of a particular sort, or even a taste for music of any sort (although of course we could intelligibly say that such a person might perhaps wish that she was able to have such a taste). Likewise with beer and someone who had no functioning

---

[50]I should not be understood here to be saying that people always have the capacities to achieve their ambitions, or even that we cannot develop ambitions we know we cannot achieve, although I suspect that sustained analysis would reveal part of the difference between an ambition and a fantasy to reside in the fact that the former is generally a spur to action in a way that the latter need not be. Here I want only to establish that it is not credible to believe that our ambitions are developed independently of our capacities, which Dworkin's categorial distinction requires.

[51]Ibid., pp. 302–5.

[52]Cohen has tried to minimize the extent of such difficulties by suggesting that we should not confuse the true claim that our capacities for effort are "influenced" by factors beyond our control with the false claim that people like Nozick mistakenly attribute to egalitarians like Rawls: that those capacities are "determined" by factors beyond our control. Preserving this distinction enables Cohen to say that although not all effort deserves reward, it is not the case that no effort deserves reward—that effort "is partly praiseworthy, partly not"—although he concedes that in practice "we cannot separate the parts." Cohen, "Equality of What?" pp. 8–10. As I note below, however, once it is conceded that the very decision to choose to expend effort is influenced by factors that are conceded to be morally arbitrary, one suspects that the difficulty becomes one of principle rather than practicality; certainly Cohen offers no account of how that component of effort meriting reward might in principle be singled out.

tastebuds or sense of smell. The idea that we form our tastes and ambitions independently of our resources and capacities is too whiggish, as would be revealed to anyone who tried to perform a thought experiment in which she was required to decide on her future tastes and ambitions while kept in ignorance of her powers and capacities. What drives Dworkin's intuition here is the notion that people should be held responsible only for the choices they make in life, not for things over which they have no control. A variant of this thesis might be defensible, but Dworkin's treatment of it is unpersuasive. His replacement of the resources versus capacities distinction with the ambitions and tastes versus physical and mental powers distinction fails to rescue the Lockean notion of an autonomous agent, of whom rights and responsibilities may legitimately be predicated.

It might be objected that the line of reasoning I have been developing leads too quickly to pure determinism. Surely we should be open to the possibility that *some* aspects of human action are subject to autonomous choice and that people might reasonably be held to account for the aspects that fall into that category.[53] This possibility is implicit in Cohen's argument that "we should compensate for disadvantage beyond a person's control."[54] Granting that the category autonomous choice might not be empty, at least for many people, it is difficult to see how it can supply the basis for a serviceable account of distributive justice. How is the state to determine which part of a person's decisions are genuinely volitional, as opposed to determined, and how is it to measure differences in capacities for volitional behavior across persons? Beyond this difficulty, the focus on free will suggests that exotic compulsions—such as an addiction to the best available malt liquor—should trump important needs for food and shelter which people might be able to secure for themselves through voluntary action, but only at significant cost. This is to say nothing of the acute moral hazards that should be expected to arise in a regime governed by Cohen's principle. Parents would be given incentives, for instance, to avoid developing capacities for individual responsibility and autonomous choice in their children, lest they be deprived of compensation to which they would otherwise be entitled.[55]

To sum up: like Rawls, Dworkin is unable to live with the deterministic implications of the socialization-of-capacities strategy. This, I have suggested, is partly because when taken to its logical conclusion this

---

[53]John Roemer has made the argument to me in correspondence.

[54]Cohen, "Currency of Egalitarian Justice," p. 922.

[55]As noted in footnote 20 above, Cohen does not claim to have resolved these difficulties. I remain skeptical that they can be resolved.

strategy undermines what is attractive in the workmanship ideal. Yet reluctant as Rawls and Dworkin both are to abandon their intuitive commitments to the idea of moral agency that informs the ideal, neither has supplied an account of how this idea can be rendered consistent with the socialization-of-capacities strategy both feel compelled to endorse. This inability reflects deep tensions within the secular variant of the workmanship ideal itself: it presses relentlessly toward a determinism that its very terms suggest we ought to be able to deny.

VI. PRODUCTIVE FICTIONS? CONSEQUENTIALIST AND DEMOCRATIC CONSIDERATIONS

Historical linking strategies fail to tie regimes of entitlements to the work of productive agents in morally satisfying ways, yet theorists who have explored the full implications of junking them find the consequences too threatening to the idea of personal responsibility, even of personal identity, to stomach. This predicament arises partly because once the labor theories of value have been rejected, there is no evident method of assessing which work performed by whom ought to be compensated in what amount when a given object or service is produced. Liberal theorists have often argued or assumed that the market generates the appropriate system of rewards, but we saw in section III that this is not so; neoclassical variants of the workmanship ideal take for granted prevailing distributions of resources and capacities as matters of "sheer natural fact" without justificatory argument. The failure of the traditional contending theories to generate a metric by reference to which we might plausibly assess productive contributions does not, however, undermine the intuition that there are productive contributions and that these should play some role in just distribution; this fact at least partly accounts for the inability of people such as Rawls and Dworkin to stick consistently to the socialization-of-capacities strategy.

The difficulty runs deeper than a problem of measurement, however. The tensions internal to the workmanship ideal are partly reminiscent of the paradox of free will: a person may find it both rationally undeniable and psychologically impossible to accept that all his actions are determined. In a similar spirit it might be argued that, for both individual and species, some fictions about workmanship may be required for reproduction and well-being even if we know them to be fictions. The belief that autonomous productive action is possible may be indispensable to the basic integrity of the human psyche and necessary for generating and sustaining the incentive to work on which human beings are, after all, critically reliant. As a result, although facts about moral luck and produced productive capacities conspire—when confronted—to enfeeble the workmanship ideal, people may nonetheless be powerless to abandon it.

These considerations might reasonably be thought to counsel embracing a variant of the workmanship ideal on consequentialist grounds while conceding that it incorporates causal and moral fictions. There is much to be said in support of such a view, but rather than explore it at length here I will take brief note of three difficulties it is bound to confront. These should be evident from my repeated use of "may" and its cognates in the preceding paragraph. First, although a wide consensus might be possible on the principle of a consequentialist defense, it seems inevitable that there would be an equally wide dissensus over what it entails in practice. It is not only the labor theory of value and neoclassical price theory that fail to reward work impartially; no neutral system of rewards has ever been developed. As a consequence, whatever fiction is employed will work to the disproportionate benefit of some and be subject to endemic political controversy—as Marx noted so perspicaciously in his discussion of rights under socialism.[56]

Second, distributive questions aside, the consequentialist benefits of workmanship are not beyond legitimate controversy. If it gets out of control, the work ethic can be subversive of psychological well-being and promote morally unattractive kinds of acquisitiveness. Moreover, if we recognize that invisible hands can as often be malevolent as benign, we are bound to concede that the consequentialist effects of embracing the workmanship ideal will not always be beneficial. A legitimating ethic that encourages productive action can easily thus become too much of a good thing, and it can have external effects (on the environment, for instance), that are bound to be controversial politically.

Third, if a variant of the workmanship ideal is embraced on consequentialist grounds, questions must arise concerning its appropriate range, given the inevitability of its conflict with other justice values. Once it is conceded that the rights of human workmanship have no natural status or special trumping moral power, then there is bound to be controversy about where they fit into a governing distributive scheme that must cope with multiple demands on scarce resources—from redressing the effects of historical disadvantage, to caring for the sick and elderly, to supporting just causes in other countries. In short, it

[56]Marx and Engels, *Selected Works*, 3:15–18.

seems unlikely that a consequentialist scheme could be developed that would or should be beyond the bounds of political controversy.

Although these issues are about implementation, they are not merely about implementation. Once it is conceded, in a world of endemic scarcity, that there is neither a theological model nor a calculus of contribution from which correct distributive injunctions can be "read off," we are bound to come to grips with the primacy of politics to arguments about distributive justice. It is remarkable, in this light, that so little attention has been paid by justice theorists to how and by whom their principles should be implemented.[57] The idea that what is just in the distribution of social goods can be reasoned about independently of how such justice might practically be achieved rests, at bottom, on inappropriate expectations from philosophy. Whether and to what degree the workmanship ideal should be institutionalized is a political question, not a philosophical one, and as a consequence, rights of workmanship cannot fairly be thought of as anterior to the political process.

The research agenda opened up by this conclusion is to explore ways of developing and grappling with the implications of democratic distributive principles. To attempt such exploration now would take us too far from the scope of the present chapter. Here let me note in conclusion that Cohen and other justice theorists may be right that in democratic systems there is the permanent possibility for tyranny of the majority, but the risks of this tyranny should be evaluated not against some unspecified ideal of a just social order (which Cohen, among others, has done much to undermine) but against the alternative feasible systems of ordering social relations.[58] In this light I would venture

---

[57]For instance, in his only discussion of democratic decision making in the "Self-ownership" articles (to which he devotes a single paragraph), Cohen remarks that traditional socialist hostility to bills of rights has to be disavowed. The socialist reply to the liberal constitutionalist that "socialism is complete democracy, that it brings within the ambit of democratic decision issues about production and consumption which capitalism excludes from the public agenda" is now believed by Cohen to be inadequate. A defensible socialist constitution, he argues, "must contain a bill of individual rights, which specifies things which the community cannot do to, or demand of, any individual." The proffered reason derives from the fact that socialist democratic decisions require either a unanimous or a majority vote. If they require unanimity, then they have the potential to destroy individual freedom of action and trivialize self-ownership (for any action might require unanimous consent before legitimately being undertaken); and majority rule without a bill of rights "also legitimates unacceptable tyranny over the individual." Cohen, "Self-ownership: II," p. 87. Yet he does not address the much argued over issues of what the content of this bill should be and how the difficulties of unanimity and majority rule should be managed in the business of constitution making. See Chapter 2 above. In fairness to Cohen it must be said that he claims not to have done full justice to these issues, which he promises to take up more fully in the future.

[58]Cohen may be wise to insist that a socialist constitution should protect individual freedoms with a bill of rights (see the preceding footnote), but as the *Lochner* era in the United States demonstrated all too clearly, bills of rights can be used to facilitate what Cohen would regard as

that the question should not be whether or not democracy carries with it the threat of majority tyranny but whether or not this threat is better to live with than systems that carry with them the threat of minority tyranny.

------

exploitation as well as to prevent it—whatever the intentions of those who create them. This is not to say that bills of rights are undesirable, only that their benefits from the standpoint of achieving and maintaining social justice are not self-evident. Whether such bills are desirable, what their scope and content should be, who should be empowered to alter and implement them are all controversial questions that cannot be declared beyond politics (and, I would argue, beyond democratic politics). For an empirically based argument that democratic systems have best protected individual rights historically, see Robert A. Dahl, *Democracy and Its Critics* (New Haven: Yale University Press, 1989), pp. 135–92.

Democratic Innovation:
A South African Perspective
on Schumpeterianism

Many Westerners who have recently spent time behind what used to be the iron curtain have remarked that although *democracy* seems readily to be affirmed by all and sundry, it is hard to know just what the word means for people who have lived their entire lives in undemocratic systems. Like the other great 1990s catchword *market*, it seems in that part of the world to stand more for what people feel has been lacking in their lives than for any clearly conceived set of social or institutional arrangements. Indeed the frequency with which Russians and East Europeans use the two terms interchangeably reinforces the speculation that they function as little more than vague symbols of an inchoate good that people believe they have been denied.[1]

Does this matter? Does sustainable democracy require people to agree on what democracy means? Does it require them to understand how democracies work or to commit themselves to a particular understanding of the collective enterprise? Does it depend on deep-rooted commitments to democracy in the political culture? One influential strand of contemporary political theory answers these questions in the negative. Its proponents work, either explicitly or implicitly, with a view of democracy variously described as proceduralist, minimalist, antisubstantive, and rule oriented. The modern origins of this view can

---

[1]For my account, see Robert A. Dahl and Ian Shapiro, "Impressions from the Soviet Union," *Dissent* (summer 1991), pp. 342–45.

be traced to Joseph Schumpeter's classic *Capitalism, Socialism, and Democracy*, first published in 1942,[2] and it finds contemporary expression in much of the literature on democratization. My goal here is to evaluate this neo-Schumpeterian literature in light of the South African transition to democracy which captured the world's imagination in the early 1990s.

Samuel Huntington represents the genre well when he takes from Schumpeter the definition of democracy as "that institutional arrangement for arriving at political decisions in which individuals acquire the power to decide by means of a competitive struggle for the people's vote." By the 1970s, he contends, this view had effectively displaced more expansive definitions that invoked notions such as "the will of the people" or "the common good." Following Robert Dahl, he holds that for a country to be democratic, it is sufficient that there be contested elections based on universal franchise, as well as the civil and political freedoms of speech, press, assembly, and organization "that are necessary to political debate and the conduct of electoral campaigns."[3] In *Democracy and the Market*, Adam Przeworski also rejects attempts to identify democracy with the general will or the public good. He defines it instead as "a system of processing conflicts" in which parties that lose elections accept this outcome and wait for the next election rather than try to destroy the regime to attain their goals.[4] Likewise, Giuseppe Di Palma argues that a realistic view of democracy has to be disengaged "from the idea of social progress"; democracy exists when the idea of coexistence becomes sufficiently attractive to powerful groups that they can be brought to agree on the basic rules of the political game.[5] In *A Democratic South Africa?* Donald Horowitz also defines democracy procedurally, the essential procedures being a universal franchise and majority rule.[6]

The Schumpeterian account modified classical democratic theory not only by junking substantive conceptions of democracy but also by all but abandoning the representational aspects of classical democratic the-

[2]Joseph A. Schumpeter, *Capitalism, Socialism, and Democracy* (New York: Harper, 1942).

[3]Samuel P. Huntington, *The Third Wave: Democratization in the Late Twentieth Century* (Norman: University of Oklahoma Press, 1991), pp. 6–7; Robert A. Dahl, *Polyarchy: Participation and Opposition* (New Haven: Yale University Press, 1971).

[4]Adam Przeworski, *Democracy and the Market* (New York: Cambridge University Press, 1991), pp. 10–12.

[5]Giuseppe Di Palma, *To Craft Democracies: An Essay on Democratic Transitions* (Berkeley: University of California Press, 1990), pp. 23, 28, 109.

[6]Donald L. Horowitz, *A Democratic South Africa? Constitutional Engineering in a Divided Society* (Berkeley: University of California Press, 1991), pp. 98–100.

ory. Schumpeter modeled his democratic theory on the neoclassical account of markets: just as firms compete for business in economic markets, would-be political leaders compete for votes. Although political elites must in some minimal sense be responsive to voters according to this view (or at least less unresponsive than their competitors), democracy is not fundamentally about representation; it is about selling a product—governmental output—in exchange for votes.

Abandoning representativeness as a criterion of democracy gives the Schumpeterian model a top-down, elitist quality. Di Palma, for instance, is so exclusively preoccupied with the conditions that can bring elites to agree on the rules of the game that he never considers the significance of what the players actually do and how they respond to their own constituents. If betrayal of their constituents is the price of reaching the kind of mutually reassuring agreement that Di Palma regards as essential, then the elites will have crafted their own survival at the expense of what many would regard as democracy. Huntington confronts this possibility explicitly, remarking of the most recent wave of democratizations that whereas the collapse of authoritarian regimes was often exhilarating, the creation of democratic regimes often brought disillusionment: "Few political leaders who put together the compromises creating [democratic] regimes escaped the charge of having 'sold out' the interests of their constituents." Furthermore, he continues, this disaffection was, "in a sense, a measure of their success." This is because there is a trade-off in "the democratic bargain" between participation and moderation. Leaders moderate their demands in order to be included, and those who fail to realize that moderation "is the price of power" are marginalized.[7] Przeworski departs from the Schumpeterian model insofar as he does regard representativeness as a criterion of democracy. He also thinks it more or less inevitable, however, that elected leaders, once in power, ignore the interests of their followers during democratic transitions, so that negotiated democracy becomes increasingly authoritarian in practice.[8] Of these four authors, only Horowitz attends systematically to the relations between leaders and followers. In an argument that I examine in some detail below, he makes the case that democracy can function in severely divided societies only when elites from one group find themselves with incentives to cater to the interests of grass roots members of groups other than their own.

[7]Huntington, *Third Wave*, pp. 165, 169, 208.
[8]Przeworski, *Democracy and the Market*, pp. 182–87.

The Schumpeterian outlook has often been criticized for its limited democratic character.[9] But the South African example brings a prima facie response to mind: minimal as the Schumpeterian conception might be, it is better than nothing. If one starts with the ideals of classic democratic theory, or even the political reality in countries that have been democratic for some time, a Schumpeterian vision of democracy might reasonably seem impoverished. But if one starts with either civil war or authoritarian regimes and the complete absence of all democratic process, then a model that requires the circulation of elites through a competitive electoral process is not so quickly to be dismissed. Di Palma takes this tack explicitly, insisting that democracy's disengagement from the idea of social progress contains a silver lining: if (democratic) coexistence is given precedence over social and economic reform, then expectations are lowered and groups hostile to democracy are more likely to accommodate themselves to the nascent democratic order.[10] Huntington takes a similar view implicitly, by holding that the test for democratic consolidation is two successive turnovers of power after elections. As if to underline the significance of nondemocratic starting points when evaluating democracy he notes that his is a relatively tough test, one not clearly met in the United States until the Jacksonian Democrats surrendered power to the Whigs in 1840, nor one met by such nations as Turkey and Japan when he wrote in 1991, despite their democratic reputations.[11]

I return to the adequacy of this response to critics of Schumpeterianism below. I begin here by granting its adequacy for purposes of discussion and then considering what light its proponents can shed on the possibility that democracy might be sustained in South Africa in the medium term. Among the arguments I discuss, only Horowitz's is concerned exclusively with South Africa. Huntington deals with South Africa too, but as part of a comparative account of the "third wave" of attempted democratizations, between 1974 and 1990 (the first and second waves were from 1828 to 1926 and 1943 to 1962). Przeworski and Di Palma do not discuss South Africa at all; their accounts are based on developments since the 1970s in Southern and Eastern Europe and in Latin America. Yet these authors all advance general arguments about the nature of democracy and the conditions for creating and consolidating it. Acting on the rule of thumb that theories are best evaluated in

[9]For a useful discussion of the standard arguments, see Quentin Skinner, "The Empirical Theorists of Democracy and Their Critics: A Plague on Both Their Houses," *Political Theory* 1, no. 3 (1973), pp. 287–305.

[10]Di Palma, *To Craft Democracies*, pp. 22–23.

[11]Huntington, *Third Wave*, p. 267.

applied contexts, it seems potentially fruitful to consider these works from the South African standpoint here.

I. SCHUMPETERIAN DEMOCRACY AND SOUTH AFRICAN POLITICS

If any part of the world supplies us with prima facie reasons for taking seriously the case for Schumpeterian minimalism just stated, it is postcolonial Africa, where attempts to create Western democracy have been such dismal failures. As the British Empire was dismantled, parliamentary institutions cloned from the Westminster model were dumped on countries for which they would seem to have been ill suited. If there had ever been traditions of democratic politics in Africa, they had long since been undermined.[12] For over a century ethnic rivalries had been manipulated, sometimes by colonial administrators, sometimes by local elites, as modern "tribal" divisions were brought into existence. If these manipulations served the purposes of various elites they also revealed that there are limits to how much ethnicity is manipulable and that those limits are not easily identified. The institutional and national boundaries created by imperial fiat flew in the face of little-understood, yet deeply rooted, local and regional allegiances. Architects of democracy—both postimperial and local—wrongly thought that indigenous allegiances would either be co-opted or ploughed under by the forces of modernization and African nationalism.[13]

The results were catastrophic. Constitutions were swept away, ignored, or buried in systemic nepotism and corruption, leaving subjected populations to the mercy of self-appointed or (at most) once-elected leaders and single-party states. Within only a few decades the continent found itself awash in the blood of war and civil war, with millions living in abject suffering and poverty and little hope for improvement in the foreseeable future. Even the oil-rich Arab countries of the African north—with the possible exception of Egypt, where there

[12]On this contentious subject, see Noël Mostert, *Frontiers: The Epic of South Africa's Creation and the Tragedy of the Xhosa People* (New York: Knopf, 1992), and the penetrating review of that work by J. M. Coetzee, "A Betrayed People," *New York Review of Books*, January 14, 1993, pp. 8–10. See also Crawford Young, "The African Colonial State and Its Political Legacy," in *The Precarious Balance: State and Society in Africa*, ed. Donald Rothchild and Naomi Chazan (Boulder: Westview, 1988), pp. 25–66.

[13]See Leroy Vail, ed., *The Creation of Tribalism in South Africa* (Berkeley: University of California Press, 1989).

were some glimmerings of hope in the 1970s—showed scant evidence of evolving in democratic directions. Whether this outcome stemmed from inherent resistances to Western institutions in non-Western cultures continues to be debated. Whatever the explanation, Africa's first postimperial experience with democracy was less than encouraging.

At the southern tip of the continent stands the multiply anomalous South Africa. No less than any other modern African country a mercurial artifact of British imperialism, both its European and indigenous heritages are perhaps more complex than elsewhere on the African continent. On the European side, a century of conflict between Boers and British culminating in the Boer Wars left many unresolved tensions that persisted into the Union of South Africa, created in 1910, and the Republic of South Africa, which withdrew from the British Commonwealth in 1961. On the indigenous side, the various groups that inhabit modern South Africa have been shaped by conflicts rooted in their pre–nineteenth-century existences and in the legacies of British imperialism and apartheid. Although political relations within the white minority have long been relatively democratic the National Party was in power continuously between 1948 and the regime's end in 1994, so that even within the ranks of the white minority, South Africa did not meet Huntington's test for the existence of democracy in the period following independence. Since the founding elections of the new regime in April 1994, a universal franchise and the basic political and civil freedoms that Huntington deems necessary for democracy have been present for the first time; but the two-turnover test has yet to be met.

From a Schumpeterian standpoint, South Africa's undemocratic culture and history need not stand as insuperable obstacles to democratic consolidation. Przeworski, Di Palma, Huntington, and Horowitz all assume or argue that claims about the importance to democracy of something called a "democratic political culture" or "democratic civil society" are overrated. The first three all regard other factors as more important, and Horowitz argues that a type of constitutional engineering is feasible which can render the realities of South Africa's cultural divisions compatible with competitive elections based on majority rule in a unitary state.

Przeworski is the most resolutely uninterested in arguments about the importance of norms and culture for democracy. Writing from a realist perspective influenced by rational choice theory he maintains that the key to the survival of any democratic system lies in the incentives it generates for powerful groups that lose elections at any given time and, particularly, in the calculations those groups make about the future.[14] The moral of Przeworski's story is not generally encouraging: democracy is a highly fragile institutional order, unlikely to be brought into existence in a sustainable way through negotiated pacts and not easily compatible with disruptive and painful economic reforms. Democracy is fragile first and foremost because it must be spontaneously self-enforcing. As every possible outcome of a democratic process hurts some groups and helps others, the trick is to design or otherwise come by institutions that offer the relevant political forces "a prospect of eventually advancing their interests that is sufficient to incite them to comply with immediately unfavorable outcomes." Groups with the power to destroy the institutional order must believe that this prospect exists, though they need not believe in democracy.[15]

Przeworski thinks the conditions that incline the relevant actors to believe that they can pursue their interests through the democratic process are rare and not characteristic of the type of negotiated transition that took place in South Africa between 1990 and 1994. Negotiations leave institutional traces of the ancien régime, most importantly an autonomous military. Institutions adopted during negotiated transitions tend to be ad hoc "temporizing solutions" and as a result political losers inevitably try to politicize them. Although opponents to authoritarian regimes may appeal to democratic rhetoric, they are more likely to abandon the rhetoric than to alter their desires if they fail to get what they want through the political system.[16]

Particularly when radical economic reform has to occur for the sake of economic survival, the costs borne by disadvantaged groups can be expected to erode any commitment they have to democracy. Then, rather than accept defeat and wait for the next election, they will either try to destroy the system or threaten such destabilizing chaos that the military will feel compelled to intervene. Aware of this threat, fledgling democratic governments face two alternatives: they must seek a neo-corporatist solution (my term, not Przeworski's, in this context), designed to garner support from unions, opposition parties, and "other encompassing and centralized organizations," or they must render those organizations ineffective. In Przeworski's view, the neocorporatist strategy is not compatible with major economic reform because it is bound to breed resistance to the reform from groups harmed by it. As a

[14]The qualifier "influenced" flags the fact that although Przeworski sees interest maximization as basic to political action, he treats organized groups as the basic unit of politics and thus does not focus on the interests of individuals. Przeworski, *Democracy and the Market*, pp. 11–12.
[15]Ibid, p. 19.
[16]Ibid., pp. 94–95.

result, he expects those democratic governments that survive to ignore or undermine opposition and ram through economic reform from above. The price of survival is therefore likely to be the abandonment of democracy.[17] In short, it is economic needs, more than inhospitable cultures, that undermine democracy.

If this argument is sound, there would seem to be little solace in the knowledge that the absence of a democratic political culture in South Africa is not an obstacle to consolidating democracy there. To be reassured that one's house will not be destroyed by an earthquake but that it will be demolished by a tornado instead is scant cause for celebration. Nonetheless, aspects of Przeworski's argument are encouraging from the standpoint of South Africa. By his account, the most important determinants of whether or not the key actors will regard their interests as threatened are economic: will the fledgling democratic regime deliver a sufficient level of economic growth to reassure strategically powerful groups that they are not unduly threatened by its policies? The sixty-four-thousand–dollar question is what counts as an undue level of threat. Przeworski identifies two kinds of economic loss as particularly significant for thinking about this question: substantial reductions in economic well-being, and marginal reductions that move people into poverty.

Although it might at first seem counterintuitive, distinguishing between these kinds of reduction in well-being allows Przeworski to make the case that the prospects for survival of fledgling democracies are greater in highly inegalitarian countries, as in Latin America, than in egalitarian regimes like the ex-communist countries. In the former case there is wealth to redistribute downward. This will breed resistance from the wealthy, but they are comparatively small in number, and anyway they may be persuaded that a degree of redistribution is necessary and perhaps even beneficial if it promotes industrial stability and economic growth. In the ex-communist systems, by contrast, there was a more egalitarian ex ante distribution, but most people were already living just above the poverty line. Under those circumstances reforms that produce even a short-term decline in economic performance can be expected to impoverish large numbers of people, who will then oppose the reforms. Thus, despite the fact that a greater percentage of the population lived in poverty in Brazil than in the Soviet Union under the old systems, "the proportion of the population that finds itself living in

---

[17]Ibid., pp. 180–87.

absolute poverty as a result of reforms is still higher in the originally more egalitarian country."[18]

If this reasoning is sound, it bodes well for South Africa, where the structure of inequality before the transition was much closer to Brazil's than that of the former USSR.[19] Moreover, during the process of democratic consolidation, South Africa does not have to put itself through the same kinds of structural economic changes that the ex-communist countries must achieve. True, South African businessmen complain perpetually about government corruption, the low productivity of their work force, inflation, the lack of foreign investment, and an antiquarian tax structure from the point of view of incentives for job creation and economic growth. But these are questions of degree. There is a difference between the kind of corruption where bureaucrats skim a percentage off the top of public projects and the kind in kleptocracies, where they simply consume public revenues and scuttle the projects. There is a difference between a relatively unproductive work force in a functioning capitalist economy and a work force consisting of people who have no idea that there is a relationship between the work one does and what one gets paid, or even in many cases what work is. There is a difference between the sometimes high levels of inflation in South Africa and the hyperinflation and worthless currency in Russia, which by 1993 was approaching the levels of Weimar Germany, even if it has leveled off since. There is a difference between foreign capital that is staying away because of the remnants of sanctions and nervousness about political instability in the short term, and foreign capital that is staying away because of the lack of a system of banking and other financial infrastructure, let alone a predictable system of property rights, contract law, and labor relations. And there is a difference between a tax code in which the system of incentives and subsidies stands in need of growth-oriented reform and one where there is no institutional capacity to collect revenue from the only part of the economy that is producing wealth: the illegal economy run by the mafia.

For all its many economic difficulties, South Africa has a developed industrial economy and an operating market system, more so by any credible measure than the ex-communist countries or, indeed, than any other African country. Democracy there does not have to be accom-

---

[18]Ibid., p. 177.

[19]Indeed, it was more extreme. See Francis Wilson and Ramphele Mamphela, *Uprooting Poverty: The South African Challenge* (New York: Norton 1989), pp. 18–21, for evidence that by the late 1970s South Africa's gini coefficient was the highest of any country in the world for which data was available.

panied by structural economic transformation to create a viable market order. A Przeworskian analysis would hold that this increases the prospects for the survival of democracy in South Africa; the economic reforms that follow democratization are less likely to breed foundational resistance to the democratic regime, even though they will involve redistribution that will be resisted by strategically powerful groups. This comparative conjecture seems plausible. In the West, market economies were created long before democratic political institutions, and in the Third World they have usually been instituted by authoritarian regimes that have democratized later, if at all. In no instance before the postcommunist experiments currently being attempted have democratic political institutions and a market economy been created simultaneously.

There are two respects—both significant from a South Africa point of view—in which Przeworski's analysis is unpersuasively mechanical. First, he regards the key groups in the strategic politics of a democracy as internally monolithic; indeed he claims to follow Philippe Schmitter, Alfred Stepan, and Claus Offe in assuming that they are generally organized in "a coercive and monopolistic fashion."[20] In reality, political parties, trades unions, business organizations, churches, and the military contain various fissures that may be more or less latent.[21] As the political terrain shifts during and after a transition, these fissures come under pressures of various kinds, and different groups try to exploit them. The effects, though often impossible to predict, can be massively consequential for democracy's future. When F. W. De Klerk dismissed twenty-three army officers in December 1992, he seems to have sensed the existence of a fissure of this kind in the military and saw an opportunity to exploit it. He thus rid himself of those most likely to feed destabilizing violence or plan a coup and, as Tom Lodge noted at the time, succeeded in communicating a message to the rest: "Go quietly, and get your pensions."[22] Had De Klerk misjudged the divisions within the officer corps, however, his actions would have aborted the reform by precipitating a backlash from the military. Similar arguments could be made about the possible significance of latent fissures within the ranks of other strategically powerful groups. Arguably, the African National Congress (ANC) has more in common with the

---

[20]Przeworski, *Democracy and the Market*, p. 12.

[21]For a more elaborate critique of Przeworski and others for paying insufficient attention to such internal divisions, see Peter Swenson, "Bringing Capital Back In, or Social Democracy Reconsidered," *World Politics* 43 (July 1991), pp. 513–44, and "Labor and the Limits of the Welfare State," *Comparative Politics* (July 1991), pp. 379–99.

[22]See *New York Times*, December 21, 1992, p. A7.

Democratic Russia of 1991–92 than with an internally monopolistic organized political party. It is an umbrella alliance of ethnically and ideologically diverse forces, held together by fragile contingencies of its history and the apartheid system that gave it its raison d'être. Now those conditions are gone, and the ANC must confront the divisive demands of governing, which might well cause it to break up.[23] The form fragmentation will take, though unpredictable, is bound to have a decisive impact on the political order that emerges in South Africa in the medium term. Any analysis that, like Przeworski's, takes no account of the significance of internal divisions within strategically powerful groups must be judged misleadingly simplistic.

Second, Przeworski's account of the conditions required for democracy's survival is implausibly restrictive: he claims that every losing group with the capacity to destroy the fledgling regime must reason that the odds of advancing its interests are greater if it accepts the loss and waits for the next election than if it topples the regime now. That account plausibly describes one set of sufficient conditions for democracy's survival, but these may not be necessary conditions; there may be other paths to democratic survival, other sets of sufficient conditions. Strategically powerful players may develop normative commitments to democracy, or they may become persuaded that the ancien régime was unjust or illegitimate in ways that will cause them to accept frustration of their interests to a degree. In 1986, the Senate of the Dutch Reformed Church in South Africa publicly declared apartheid to be incompatible with Christianity, and in 1992, church leaders at a conference in Rustenburg publicly apologized for their church's previous support for apartheid (which apology Bishop Tutu accepted).[24] It is difficult to know what effect these proclamations will have on Afrikaner political behavior in the years after the transition. Anecdotal interview evidence suggests that they shook some Afrikaners to the core.[25] They brought some to accept that apartheid was unjust and to believe that they ought to pay a price for the structural advantages they enjoyed as a consequence of apartheid. (It is evidently possible for significant numbers within dominant groups to develop such beliefs; how else could affirmative action have become widespread policy in the United States?) Other white South Africans may have developed a

[23]For discussion of why the new electoral system is likely to reinforce tendencies toward fragmentation, see Chapter 7.

[24]See Donald Akenson, *God's Peoples* (Montreal: McGill-Queen's University Press, 1991), pp. 295–310, and Loun Alberts and Frank Chikane, eds., *The Road to Rustenburg* (Cape Town: Struik Christian, 1992).

[25]I conducted interviews of white elites during 1991, 1993, and 1995.

normative commitment to democracy for other reasons: a pragmatic judgment that separate development is unfeasible or a belief that democracy's collapse into communism no longer poses a real threat.[26]

It is of course possible to redescribe all these cases to make them consistent with Przeworski's argument, by collapsing the normative commitment to accepting a loss or affirming democracy into the definition of the relevant group's interests. But such a move would make the theory truistic and uninteresting. If every failure to oppose democratization by a group with the capacity to oppose it is seen as evidence that democracy is not believed by the group to threaten its interests, then the category of "maximizing interests" would have expanded to subsume every possible motivation. A theory that explains everything explains nothing, however.[27] Rather than adulterate Przeworski's argument thus, it is better to interpret it as describing one possible dynamic for democracy's survival and recognize that there might be others. Przeworski does try to distance himself from the claim that the dynamic he describes is literally inescapable, yet he insists that examples such as Spain, which appear to contradict it, are exceptional rather than typical. He never accounts for the Spanish case, however, which he dismisses as "a miracle."[28] At a minimum, this counterexample suggests that there might be more than one feasible dynamic of democratic consolidation. It remains an open question in South Africa whether recognition of apartheid's illegitimacy or normative commitments to democracy will cause strategically powerful players knowingly to accept the losses they expect to result from democracy.

Enter Di Palma and Huntington, who both discern an important place for belief and innovative agency in the creation and consolidation of democratic regimes. Both write in the style of the mirror-for-princes literature of the Italian Renaissance; theirs are "how-to" books, intended to help agents of democratic change. Reacting to Huntington's 1984 speculation that the prospects for the emergence of more democratic regimes in the world were slim,[29] Di Palma suggests that the lessons of the Italian and Spanish transitions may be more generally applicable. Unlike Przeworski, Di Palma thinks extrication—a negotiated

---

[26]In this connection there is some evidence, contra Przeworski, from the former communist world that democracy and liberalization can be most strongly supported by the groups that suffer most during transitions; see the poll from Moscow, St. Petersburg, and Samara reported in *Nezavisimaya Gazeta* (Moscow) March 12, 1992.

[27]See Donald P. Green and Ian Shapiro, *Pathologies of Rational Choice Theory: A Critique of Applications in Political Science* (New Haven: Yale University Press, 1994), Chap. 3.

[28]Przeworski, *Democracy and the Market*, p. 8.

[29]Samuel Huntington, "Will More Countries Become Democratic?" *Political Science Quarterly* 99, no. 2 (summer 1984), pp. 193–218.

transition—can be a promising path for the creation of workable democracy. In a functioning democracy, outcomes are inherently uncertain but the rules of the game are not. The trick, as Di Palma sees it, is to get the key players to embrace the rules and accept the uncertainty of outcomes—that is, to accept the realistic possibility of losing as a condition for winning at other times. Unlike the democratic transitions of the nineteenth century, most of those attempted since World War I have come from dictatorial regimes, not liberal ones. Although Di Palma resists every suggestion that democratization should be sacrificed by catering to the entrenched interests of the ancien régime, he thinks the old elite should be given an opportunity to compete in the new political order, else its acquiescence in the rules of the new game cannot be obtained. Rules must be agreed on that institutionalize "the openness and uncertainty of the political market" for all players in order "to avoid prejudging or loading the future wins or losses of anyone who abides by the market's intentionally easy rules of admission."[30] Rules that credibly achieve these goals can be attractive to all players; they decrease the costs of toleration by making all players think that their interests can prevail in the democratic order. That is why Di Palma believes it is essential decisively to divorce democracy from any redistributive economic agenda.[31]

There is no denying that minimalism of this kind has its strategic advantages. It is doubtful, for example, that De Klerk would have been able to move toward democratization without the worldwide collapse of communism. This had the effect of driving a wedge between democratic opposition to the apartheid state and commitment to the socialist or communist redistributive agenda with which that opposition had been inescapably associated, at least in the minds of its opponents. Democracy might lead to redistribution, but it need not. If they could be brought back to life, nineteenth-century opponents of expanding the franchise in Europe and North America would doubtless be stunned to learn how little has been its progressive impact on the distribution of income and wealth over more than a century in most capitalist countries and that, in some instances, such as the United

---

[30]Di Palma, *To Craft Democracies*, p. 55.

[31]Di Palma's discussion, ibid., pp. 97–102, of minimalism verges on the disingenuous insofar as he insists that "in the interests of democratization the corporate demands of business and the state may have to take precedence over those of labor, even when labor, after a long period of autocratic repression, may actually be escalating its demands." Labor, in his view, should therefore be compelled to trade off economic sacrifices for political gains. Assertions of this kind, unsupported by any systematic evidence in the book, belie the claim that Di Palma's minimalist view of democracy does not load the distributive dice in any particular way.

States since the 1970s, democracy has coexisted with steeply regressive change.[32]

As far as creating a democratic culture is concerned, Di Palma holds that the only way to "develop democratic skills is to exercise democracy," and he insists that prolonging transitions is more likely to scuttle than to facilitate them.[33] At first sight, this seems sound. A standard refrain of antidemocrats in the second and third worlds is that although democracy might work in the West, "we" are not ready for it because the people are backward and tribal, because Stalinism has destroyed civil society, because the economic preconditions do not yet exist, because there is no rule-of-law state, because, because, because. So one would like to believe that Di Palma is right about this, that learning to operate in a democratic order is like learning to swim; you cannot do it by standing next to the swimming pool, talking about swimming and insisting that you are busy getting ready. At some point you have to take the plunge and try to learn.[34] In fact, however, Di Palma adduces no evidence in support of the proposition that rapid transitions are more likely to be consummated than slower ones. After all, perhaps the swimming pool is too hot or too cold to survive in. Perhaps it is empty. In England, much of Western Europe, and North America, attainment of universal franchise was a gradual and protracted affair that took over a century to complete, whereas in Russia in 1917 the rapid transition was also rapidly aborted. Even when democracy is imposed, it arguably takes time. In West Germany and Japan after World War II, the Allied powers who implanted democratic institutions hovered over them for a generation to ensure that democracy took root. This contrasts sharply with the behavior of the British in Africa in the waning days of empire: they imposed democratic institutions as a parting gesture, institutions that did not survive. Some will regard such examples as prima facie evidence against Di Palma's contention (though doubtless they could be otherwise explained as well).

There are also theoretical reasons for suspecting that rapid transitions from authoritarian systems may be inimical to developing the cooperation between government and loyal opposition that workable democracy requires. Juan Linz argues, for instance, that unlike in democratic systems that evolved gradually out of semiconstitutional monarchies, in modern transitions from authoritarianism there is no

---

[32]See Kevin P. Phillips, *The Politics of Rich and Poor: Wealth and the American Electorate in the Reagan Aftermath* (New York: Random House, 1990).

[33]Di Palma, *To Craft Democracies*, p. 88.

[34]My simile, not Di Palma's.

opportunity for counterelites, the seeds of a loyal opposition, to emerge during the predemocratic order.[35] In short, to develop any confidence in the claim that speed is generally better, there must be some systematic grappling with the relevant evidence; to date this appears not to have been attempted.

Must democracy be imposed from above, or can it come about as a result of opposition? Di Palma is quick to dismiss the latter possibility, noting that except for situations in which democracy is externally installed after a military defeat (as in Germany and Japan after the war), indigenous elites must be induced to embrace democracy if it is to survive. This seems to me seriously to understate the role that opposition groups can play in forcing liberalization of authoritarian regimes and placing democracy inescapably on the public agenda. Think of the effects of *Solidarity* in forcing liberalization of the Polish regime in the early 1980s, Civic Forum in the Czech transition, and the evident effects of the frightening (to elites) mobs in Romania in 1989 and in Russia after the attempted coup in August 1991. More recently, the emergence of radical Muslim fundamentalists in the West Bank and Gaza forced the Israeli government to recognize its historical antagonist, the Palestine Liberation Organization (PLO), and begin to negotiate a transition with it in the mid-1990s—lest it confront the even more intractible opposition that threatened to displace the PLO. Di Palma's exclusive attention to the beliefs and behavior of elites ignores constraints and opportunities presented by politics from below, with which elites are bound to contend. This pressure from below matters less, perhaps, when the masses are comparatively docile; but in a highly politicized country such as South Africa, relations between elites and masses are likely to be decisive in determining whether democracy can survive.

Huntington's account plausibly recognizes that democratic transitions, consolidations, and collapses can all result from a variety of dynamics, and he explores several of them. He differs from Przeworski (and agrees with Di Palma) in arguing that negotiated transitions can be successful. Building on the work of Linz, Donald Share, Scott Mainwaring, and others, he distinguishes four possibilities: *transformations* (as in Spain, India, Hungary, and Brazil), when the elites in power take the lead in bringing about democracy; *replacements* (as in East Germany, Portugal, Romania, and Argentina), when opposition groups take the lead in bringing about democracy; *transplacements* (as in Poland, Czechoslovakia, Bolivia, and Nicaragua), when democratization occurs from

[35]Juan Linz, "Crisis, Breakdown, and Reequilibration," in *The Breakdown of Democratic Regimes*, ed. Juan Linz and Alfred Stepan (Baltimore: Johns Hopkins University Press, 1978), pt. 1, pp. 34–38.

joint action by government and opposition groups; and *interventions* (as in Japan, West Germany, Grenada, and Panama), when democratic institutions are imposed by an outside power. Of the thirty-five possible democratizations that appeared to be underway during the third wave, sixteen were transformations, six were replacements, eleven were transplacements, and two resulted from interventions, suggesting that in the third wave at least transplacements, or negotiated transitions, were common. South Africa evidently falls into this transplacement category, which results when dominant groups in both government and opposition recognize that they are "incapable of unilaterally determining the nature of the future."[36]

Huntington sees himself as developing a post hoc explanation of the third-wave democratizations rather than developing a covering-law model or predictive theory. Indeed, although he never says this, Huntington's recognition that fundamentally different dynamics may be at work in this wave as compared with the previous two, as well as in the different democratizations constituting the third wave, suggests reasons for skepticism that any general theory of democratization could be developed. If Huntington does not develop a theory, it would be a mistake to say that he does not theorize; he offers what might be called a structural-historical account of recent attempted democratizations, out of which he tries to identify generalizations about the underlying causal forces. On the basis of these he compiles pithy lists of recommendations for would-be democratizers in various transitional circumstances. The recommendations are practical, to the point, even amusing.[37] Here my focus is on the underlying argument.

For Huntington, the most fundamental necessary conditions for successful democratization are economic. Although third-wave democratizers differed greatly in their levels of economic development, none were poor (defined as having per capita incomes of less than $250 per year), and the great majority (twenty-seven out of thirty-one) were moderately well off (with per capita incomes of between $250 and $3,000). Sheer wealth appears not to be enough, however. Oil-rich Arab

[36]Huntington, *Third Wave*, pp. 113–14, 152.

[37]As in his advice on how to deal with the military in a fledgling democratic order: "Give them toys. That is, provide them with new and fancy tanks, planes, armored cars, artillery, and sophisticated electronic equipment (ships are less important; navies do not make coups). New equipment will make them happy and keep them busy trying to learn how to operate it. By playing your cards right and making a good impression in Washington, you will also be able to shift much of the cost to the American taxpayer. You then gain the added benefit that you can warn the military that they will only continue to get these toys if they behave themselves because nasty U.S. legislators take a dim view of military intervention in politics." Ibid., pp. 252–53.

countries did not democratize, indicating that broad-based economic development involving significant industrialization may be required. Huntington embraces some standard claims of modernization theory: that broad-based economic development promotes tolerance and education and makes more resources available for distribution; the expanding economic pie thus "facilitates accommodation and compromise." It also results in increased trade, which creates nongovernmental sources of wealth and influence and opens societies to the impact of democratic ideas prevalent in the industrialized world. Although the middle classes may initially be hostile to democracy, as modernization advances they become more sure of their capacities to survive in a democratic order—on his telling—and less dependent on authoritarian regimes. In virtually every country (with the exception of Poland at the time Huntington was writing, though other communist countries might now be added), landlords, peasants, and workers played marginal roles; the most active and effective supporters of democracy came from the urban middle class.[38] In this, his argument, like Przeworski's, is reminiscent of Barrington Moore's famous insistence that democracy does not emerge unless there is a middle class.[39]

Huntington is not an economic determinist, however. He recognizes that other factors, such as the level of communications, may exert autonomous pressures toward democratization.[40] One suspects that today he might make more of this point (which he based on research by Phillips Cutright from the early 1960s), given the decisive role of television in the snowballing effects of the East German demonstrations in 1989 and in the Russian transition in the fall of 1991. In a particularly useful discussion of religion, Huntington notes that the third wave belies one bit of conventional wisdom: that Protestantism is uniquely well disposed toward democracy. Most third-wave democratizations occurred in Catholic countries, a change that Huntington attributes to the Catholic Church's becoming more politically progressive worldwide, and organizationally more like Protestantism—with its stress on individual conscience, internal democracy, and self-reliance—during the 1970s and 1980s. He also conjectures that the Catholic Church may cease to be a force for democratization in the future, given the conservative theological evolution of the church under John Paul II.[41]

[38]Ibid., pp. 64–68.
[39]Barrington Moore, Jr., *The Social Origins of Dictatorship and Democracy* (Boston: Beacon, 1966), pp. 413–32.
[40]Huntington, *Third Wave*, p. 63.
[41]Ibid., pp. 75–78, 282.

How should we interpret the reality that national democracy continues to be overwhelmingly associated with Western Christianity? In 1988, Catholicism and/or Protestantism were the dominant religions in thirty-nine of the forty-six democratic countries, and democracy was notably rare in predominantly Muslim, Buddhist, or Confucian countries. Huntington explores various arguments about why these religions might generate cultural limitations to democracy, ranging from their internal hierarchies, to their refusals to accept the legitimacy of a secular public realm or the predominance of responsibilities over rights and groups over individuals in their ideologies. He thinks that although there may be something to these claims, there are limits to arguments about cultural limits to democracy. On the one hand, Christianity has exemplified many antidemocratic traits through much of its history and in many of its variations; on the other, bodies of thought such as Islam and Confucianism are internally complex and contain strands compatible with democracy as well as hostile to it.[42] It is also possible that religions other than Western Christianity may be compatible with democracy in domains of social life other than the secular nation-state. This Huntington does not consider. Like Przeworski and Di Palma, he concludes that arguments about the cultural prerequisites for democracy have been exaggerated. Cultures are dynamic; they adapt and evolve, he notes, and he reminds us that, empirically, poverty has been much more of a barrier to the spread of democracy than any cultural variable has been.[43]

Huntington does not think that democracy springs spontaneously out of economic development. The typical dynamic he identifies in the third wave is a more complex combination: the economic preconditions of relative wealth and broad-based industrialization must be present. But, by his account, democratic transitions are not triggered unless there is a period of protracted economic crisis which chrysalizes social discontent with the authoritarian regime and unless a significant part of the elite comes to believe in democratic values. Like the Italian civic humanists, Huntington believes that the legitimacy of regimes tends to decay over time, although this does not mean that as authoritarian regimes decay they are likely to be replaced by democratic ones. Indeed statistically they are more likely to be replaced by new nondemocratic regimes. In the contemporary world, democracy does have going for it the fact that aristocratic and now communist rationalizations of author-

---

[42]For one useful empirical discussion in the Egyptian context, see Bruce Rutherford, "Can an Islamic Group Aid Democracy?" in *NOMOS XXXV: Democratic Community*, ed. John Chapman and Ian Shapiro (New York: New York University Press, 1993), pp. 313–35.

[43]Huntington, *Third Wave*, pp. 72–85, 298–311.

itarianism have been almost universally discredited whereas democracy commands widespread acceptance as a public ideology, but Huntington wisely cautions that various brands of authoritarian nationalism, religious fundamentalism, oligarchic authoritarianism, and populist and communal dictatorships might well reemerge.[44] The point is well taken. At the end of the twentieth century, who could doubt that once-unfashionable repressive ideologies such as Nazism can reassert themselves or that there is any limit to the forms that ideologies of oppression can take?

If authoritarian decay is to be followed by a democratic transition, then, a necessary condition seems to be that political elites must develop commitments to democracy. In transplacements the process often starts with liberalizing elites, who have no intention of creating a full-fledged democracy, only of buying off discontent. But liberalized authoritarianisms turn out to be inherently unstable, dividing regimes between standpatters, who want to recreate the status quo ante, and reformers, who want to continue liberalization. For this reason Huntington thinks it is almost invariably a mistake for oppositions to boycott partial reforms or less than fully democratic elections (as in the 1983 and 1988 municipal elections and the 1984 and 1989 elections to the tricameral parliament in South Africa). Despite their defects, such elections will not have the shoring-up effects that authoritarian governments anticipate. On the contrary, their unstable results may precipitate further reform; indeed, they may be necessary conditions for precipitating it.[45]

Transplacements occur only when reformers are stronger than standpatters in the government and moderates are stronger than extremists in the opposition. In such circumstances standpatters and extremists can be marginalized from the emerging consensus on the new order. When Huntington wrote, it was unclear whether these conditions would transpire in South Africa. The country had moved in textbook fashion through the stages of liberalized authoritarianism he describes. But the essential coalition—between De Klerk's government and moderates in the ANC—had not yet emerged; nor had standpatters to the right or extremists to the left been successfully marginalized. The referendum on the constitutional negotiations among white voters in April 1992 (which De Klerk won by a two-thirds margin with majority support in every region of the country) went a considerable way to marginalizing the white right.

[44]Ibid., pp. 48, 35, 293–94.
[45]Ibid., pp. 186–88.

The essential agreement between the government and the ANC came at the end of 1992, despite the fact—-indeed perhaps partly because of it—-that the all-party CODESA constitutional negotiations were officially still on hold.[46] (These had broken down earlier in the year, when the ANC withdrew in response to a massacre for which it held the government responsible). New secret bilateral negotiations in September of 1992 led to a Record of Understanding between the government and the ANC, a clear indication that by then they conceived of themselves as the two principal players. The government began to moderate its criticism of the ANC, whose leaders responded in kind. In February 1993 the ANC subdued its radical wing, and the leadership approved a plan to let minorities share in governing the country for five years after the end of white monopoly rule. This was a major concession for the ANC, which had rejected power-sharing throughout its history. Both the government and the ANC leadership fixed the main terms of their agreement before multilateral talks were allowed to begin again. Inkatha and the white right believed for a time that they might be able to derail the process, but, for reasons that are discussed at length in Chapter 7, they were by now marginal to the transition. They were forced to accept constitutional and electoral arrangements that brought the ANC to power as the dominant partner in a government of national unity in April 1994. A Huntingtonian transplacement had occurred, though the prospects for democratic consolidation remained unclear.

Many factors that Huntington identifies as favorable to successful transplacements are present in South Africa: the economy, the democratically committed elites, and the history of political competition within the ruling elite under the old regime all suggest that a degree of confidence in the possibility of a successful transition is warranted.[47] In addition, there are other encouraging features that he does not mention, the most important perhaps being the existence of a tradition in which government is seen as bound by the rule of law. Even though this tradition was often honored in the breach rather than the observance during the heyday of apartheid, it left institutional traces helpful in holding the National Party government to account for violence, through such devices as the Goldstone Commission during the transition and the Truth and Reconciliation Commission afterward. There are other factors too, notably, among many groups, including

---

[46]The acronym stands for "Conference on a Democratic South Africa," a set of round-table negotiations set up in 1991 to plan for the transition and the new constitution. Most major players, except for some separatist conservative Afrikaners and the revolutionary Pan-Africanist Congress, participated in CODESA until its suspension in mid-1992.

[47]Huntington, *Third Wave*, pp. 111–12.

whites, a repository of goodwill toward the prospect of a multiracial democracy. This goodwill may be impossible to measure reliably and no doubt can easily evaporate; yet many people talked about it throughout the transition, and it seems unwise to dismiss it.

On the potentially negative side, Huntington points out that racial oligarchies have proved especially resistant to democratization historically and that high levels of violence generally undermine transitions. Even before the influx of weapons and the escalations of violence in 1992, Huntington noted that South Africa was one of the most violent countries in the world, ranking only behind Nicaragua (we should now add the former Yugoslavia, Georgia, Armenia, Azerbaijan, Tajikistan, Chechnya, and Moldova) in the numbers killed in third-wave countries in the struggle to democratize. Violence increased from the hundreds or fewer per annum in the 1970s to the thousands in the 1980s.[48] In 1992 and 1993 countless thousands were killed, although reliable figures are difficult to come by.[49] Violence can scuttle democratic consolidations even if successful transition occurs. It can abort the dynamic of governments giving up power when they become unpopular, which Huntington regards as both the essential defining characteristic and the unique advantage of democracy: when governments lose legitimacy they are replaced by other governments rather than by a collapsed democratic regime.[50] It is difficult to know what levels of violence are critically destabilizing. Certainly the experiences in Angola, Rwanda, and Bosnia reveal that, high as the level of South African violence may have been in abosolute terms during the transition, it was low when compared with the potential for violence.

In thinking about the possibilities for democratic consolidation in South Africa, it is wise not to ignore the imponderables of religion and culture. They are imponderable both because their influence is so little understood and because so little is known about them in the South African context, but this does not mean that they will be inconsequential. Huntington identifies South Africa as a predominantly Protestant country, which, on his telling, would place it in the most-receptive-to-democracy category to the extent that these considerations matter.[51] That conclusion is too simple, however. The majority of the population adheres to a variety of indigenous religions and cultural ideologies. Although these have been influenced by Christianity, it would be foolish to think that older affiliations and beliefs have been obliterated.

[48]Ibid., pp. 193–94.
[49]*Southern Africa Report,* May 14, 1993, p. 3.
[50]Huntington, *Third Wave.,* pp. 46–48.
[51]Ibid., p. 76

True, Islam and Confucianism, which Huntington identifies as particularly hostile to democracy (at least in their dominant contemporary manifestations), are not strong in South Africa, with its small and mainly Hindu Indian population of about one million and its tiny Chinese community. But little is known about the compatibility of black South African religions and cultural practices with democracy.[52]

II. The Limits of Schumpeterianism

A valid criticism of Przeworski, Di Palma, and Huntington is that their preoccupation with leaders and elites leads them to ignore constitutional factors and the dynamics of electoral politics almost entirely. This lacuna is partly filled by Horowitz, who examines South Africa's political prospects from the standpoint of the literature on constitutional engineering in divided societies. The central question in this literature is whether questions concerning electoral systems and constitutional design should be approached differently in countries where there are enduring ethnic cleavages that dominate other divisions than in the multiply-cleavaged societies of the developed West.

Consociationalism and "Divided" Societies

The literature on divided societies is contentious, partly because of its benchmark assumptions about the "pluralist" developed West. These are traceable to the so-called group theorists of American politics in the early twentieth century, of whom Arthur Bentley is perhaps the best known. As their name suggests, they believed that all politics is reducible to group dynamics and that interests that do not express themselves through organized groups are of no political consequence.[53] The group theorists were followed, in the 1950s and 1960s, by the pluralist theorists, who sought to confirm the old group theorists' claim on the basis of a series of empirical studies of American cities.[54] But it was Louis Hartz who, in the mid-1950s, first explored the implications of

[52]In this connection we await the results of important research on Ubuntu by Ziba Jiyane, "Securing Democracy and the Rule of Law in South Africa" (Ph.D. thesis in progress, Yale University).

[53]"The great task in the study of any form of social life is the analysis of these [organized] groups," he argued. "When the groups are adequately stated, everything is stated. When I say everything, I mean *everything*." A. F. Bentley, *The Process of Government* (Chicago: University of Chicago Press, 1908), pp. 208–9, Bentley's italics. See also D. B. Truman, *The Governmental Process* (New York: Knopf, 1951).

[54]Robert A. Dahl, *Who Governs?* (New Haven: Yale University Press, 1961), was the classic of this genre.

pluralism systematically. Initially, he wanted to explain why there has never been a powerful socialist tradition in American politics. His answer to this question turned on the claim that in contrast to European societies, which had exhibited a *single cleavage* between the propertied classes and the rest, America was a *multiply-cleavaged* society, with no basic or dominant division of the socioeconomic landscape.[55]

Hartz's distinction between single- and multiply-cleavaged societies has become one of the conceptual building blocks of pluralist democratic theory. The more a society approaches the multiply-cleavaged model, the less likely destabilizing revolutionary change is thought to become. Put otherwise: if I am opposed to you on one issue but also know that I may be allied with you against others on some future issue, I have an incentive to moderate my opposition to you and search for common ground. No minority ever reaches that proverbial state of affairs where its members have nothing to lose but their chains. Generalizing from this conclusion, pluralist theorists argued that building and sustaining a social landscape made up of crosscutting cleavages reinforces pluralist-democratic stability.[56] The influence of this argument has been considerable; in the present context, for instance, it implicitly informs Huntington's claim that economic development must be widespread. To insist on this is to insist in effect that economic class relations will crosscut with other bases of affiliation.

The Hartzian assumptions about both European and American politics have been subjected to trenchant criticism on the grounds that the former has never been as bipolar, nor the latter as multipolar, as the theory assumes.[57] Furthermore, cleavages are not fixed features of social orders but evolve historically—a fact that lies at the core of the Hartzian theory's contentiousness when applied to debates about divided societies in the third world. On the one side, advocates of consociational democracy contend that in societies deeply divided along ethnic lines, democracy can be realized only if the effects of majority rule are mitigated by institutional devices that require the concurrence of all groups in all major decisions and the delegation of decisions involving only the interests of particular groups to the groups

[55]Louis Hartz, *The Liberal Tradition in America* (New York: Harcourt, Brace, 1955). See also Robert A. Dahl, *A Preface to Democratic Theory* (Chicago: University of Chicago Press, 1956).

[56]For a good account of the history of the functional argument and an elaboration of its logic, see Nicholas R. Miller, "Pluralism and Social Choice," *American Political Science Review* 77, no. 3 (1983), pp. 734–47.

[57]See Eric Foner, "Why Is There No Socialism in America?" *History Workshop Journal* 17 (spring 1984), pp. 57–80; Sean Wilentz, "Against Exceptionalism: Class Consciousness and the American Labor Movement," *International Labor and Working Class History* 26 (fall 1984), pp. 1–24; and G. W. Domhoff, *Who Really Rules?* (New Brunswick, N.J.: Transaction Books, 1978).

in question.[58] On the other side, critics of consociationalism note that ethnic affiliations are not primordial givens. Rather, they are manufactured out of social and political conflicts and exploited by elites for their own purposes. They are also affected by the nature of institutional political arrangements; in Horowitz's view, this is the decisive reason for rejecting consociationalist arrangements in South Africa.

Consociationalism has been described by its best-known proponent as a system of government based on "a cartel of elites."[59] This term reflects the fact that the groups whose rights consociationalism is designed to protect are defined by leaders, who are then forced by such devices as concurrent majorities or minority veto powers to rule by agreement with one another. This model contrasts with that of the "circulating elites" of classic pluralist theory, according to which different coalitions of elites compete for power and control various parts of the political process at various times.[60]

The top-down character of consociationalism makes it vulnerable to the charge that groups whose rights are to be protected are not themselves formed or even identified in democratic ways and that in some circumstances consociational solutions reinforce and perhaps even create politicized ethnic divisions. Consociationalism solidifies the many-faceted forms that cultural affiliation can take into reified ethnic divisions; in that sense consociationalism can cause the malady it is allegedly designed to treat. Horowitz notes that successful consociational arrangements are historically rare, and he points to some difficulties that would be peculiar to a consociational solution in South Africa. These derive from the sizes and locations of the relevant minority groups; they would not necessarily balance one another by being mutually indispensable as is the case in countries such as the Netherlands.[61] But his real objection to consociationalism is more fundamental; it turns on a distinction between what he describes as "internal incentives" and "external constraints." His point is to distinguish between rules that affect the behavior of elites vis-à-vis grass roots political constituencies and the constraints on elites' strategic manipulations when dealing with one another. The central argument informing Horowitz's critique of consociationalism as well as his own proposals is that adjusting external constraints is unlikely to advance the cause of

[58]See Arend Lijphart, *Democracy in Plural Societies* (New Haven: Yale University Press, 1977).
[59]Arend Lijphart, "Consociational Democracy," *World Politics*, 4, no. 2 (January 1969), pp. 213–15, 222.
[60]See Dahl, *Who Governs?*
[61]Horowitz, *Democratic South Africa?* pp. 138–45.

democracy in severely divided societies; instead the focus should be on the structure of internal incentives.[62]

Consociationalism relies on the goodwill of leaders—on statesmanship—to foster intergroup compromise and avoid destructive intergroup conflict. But as Horowitz notes, the perceived need for consociational solutions suggests that the relevant goodwill is likely to be lacking when it is most needed. More important, however, nothing in the structure of consociationalism supplies leaders with any incentive rooted in the dynamics of electoral politics either to avoid exclusionary politics or even to support the consociational system in the long run. That is why we should expect it to be ignored or swept aside in democratic political competition. The real choice, he suggests, "is between zero-sum, high conflict contests along ethnic and racial lines— with a considerable potential for one or more actors to step in and end the democratic competition before it gets overheated or after it produces exclusionary results—and open-textured, fluid, low-conflict contests, mainly along racial and ethnic lines but with an admixture of intergroup cooperation."[63]

Essential to achieving this latter outcome, in Horowitz's view, is a system that affects the behavior of elites from one group toward the grass roots members of other groups, thereby "harnessing self-interest to the cause of peace."[64] Self-interest can be harnessed in a variety of ways, all of which require politicians to compete for votes among ethnic groups other than their own. The most obvious is a combination of coalition politics and heterogeneous constituencies. Horowitz describes a successful example of this kind from Malaysia, in which Malay and Chinese politicians were forced to rely in part on votes delivered by politicians belonging to the other ethnic group. The votes would not have been forthcoming "unless leaders could portray the candidates as moderate on issues of concern to the group that was delivering its votes across ethnic lines." In this type of situation, which Horowitz identifies as having operated for considerable periods (and then failed) in countries as different as Lebanon, Sri Lanka, and Nigeria, compromises at the top of a coalition are reinforced by electoral incentives at the bottom.[65]

Another possible device is geographic distribution requirements, such as the Nigerian formula for presidential elections employed in 1979 and 1983, in which the winning candidate had to get both the

[62]Ibid., pp. 154, 176.
[63]Ibid., p. 203.
[64]Ibid., p. 155.
[65]Ibid., pp. 154–55.

largest number of votes and at least 25 percent of the vote in two-thirds of the then-nineteen states of the Nigerian Federation. This type of system seems unlikely to work in South Africa, however, given the territorial racial dispersion. The two most promising devices there are (1) proportional representation utilizing the single transferable vote system and (2) an alternative-vote rule that also lists more than one ordered preference but declares elected only candidates who receive a majority, rather than a plurality, of votes. Both systems require politicians to cater to voters' choices other than their first preferences, assuming heterogeneous constituencies, so that the internal incentives work in the appropriate moderating directions. Horowitz thinks this moderation will be accentuated further by the alternative-vote system, assuming that parties proliferate.[66]

Horowitz makes a convincing case that such vote-pooling systems are more likely to achieve interethnic political moderation than systems, whether first past the post or proportional, that merely require seat pooling by politicians in coalition governments. He also usefully points out that debates about presidential versus parliamentary systems have generally been conducted in innocence of his distinction between incentives and constraints and that a presidential system (which he thinks might well be desirable in South Africa for some purposes) need not exhibit the defects Linz, Arend Lijphart, and others have attributed to it if it is based on a vote-pooling system of the kind he advocates.[67]

Horowitz believes it is wise to avoid specifying in advance what the groups appropriate to his system are, yet he assumes that they will be ethnically based parties that will in fact pool votes across divisive ethnic lines. The only way to ensure this result, however, would be to write it into the electoral law. If this is not done, Horowitz's system seems to "lack a mechanism," as he says of consociationalism. If it is done, on the other hand, Horowitz's system seems to be vulnerable to the criticism of consociationalism that it reifies ethnic differences. At a minimum there would have to be some constraints on the type and/or size of parties that could be represented. These constraints would inevitably be seen as proxies for race-based group rights. There is no way around this difficulty, because if there is substantial proliferation of parties, as in Poland or Russia (and which Horowitz anticipates), then Horowitz's device would not ensure that vote pooling across the relevant ethnic divides actually occurs. In the limiting case, various parties of one

[66]Ibid., pp. 184, 166, 187–96.
[67]Ibid., pp. 175–6, 206–9.

ethnic or racial group might redistribute votes among themselves until one or some coalition of them had a majority, such that other ethnic parties were excluded from power completely. This brings us back to the question of the extent to which South Africa is really ethnically divided "underneath it all" and what the quality of those divisions is. Horowitz summarizes the rather scant research conducted to date on black ethnicity, but he does not add to it.[68] Given that the immense and often overlapping complexities of racial, tribal, ethnic, linguistic, religious, and other cultural bases of affiliation are so little understood, the prudent generalization is that no one knows what the most salient groups in South African politics will be two or three elections hence. Horowitz is surely sensitive to this, but he does not explain how an electoral law that requires that the relevant groups be identified in advance can in that case be instituted.[69]

The Preoccupation with National Institutional Performance

Horowitz's discussion takes us beyond the Schumpeterian model in one important respect: in place of an exclusive focus on the jockeying of political elites, he gestures toward civil society by attending to the relations between elites and grass roots constituencies. Yet his interest in these relations is driven exclusively by an instrumental concern for the performance of national political institutions. Indeed he even acknowledges that there may be standpoints from which the forms of ethnic accommodation may militate against democracy. He notes that "there is frequently an inverse relationship between intragroup democracy and intergroup democracy. Intergroup accommodation may be easier where ethnically based parties do not need constantly to be looking over their shoulders to see which of their competitors might make political gains as a result of compromises made across group lines."[70] This possibility raises large questions about the internal structure of political parties and of civil institutions generally.

A central difficulty with Schumpeterian democratic theory is that the premium it places on stability is so high that it is often difficult, in the end, to see what is democratic about it. If it is compared to a war of all against all, in which life is inevitably nasty, brutish, and short, a prima facie case can be made for Schumpeterian minimalism, as we have seen. But is that the relevant counterfactual? Hobbes employed it to load the

---

[68]Ibid., pp. 48–61.

[69]In the event, Horowitz's proposals were not adopted; for discussion of what was and why, see Chapter 7.

[70]Horowitz, *Democratic South Africa?* p. 120.

dice in favor of unbridled absolutism; anything else, he theorized, must inevitably result in chaos, civil war, and death. Just as Hobbes's delineation of the possibilities turned out to be misleadingly narrow and malevolent, the same might be the case with the Schumpeterian approaches discussed here.

To begin with the comparatively minor point raised in the previous quotation from Horowitz, one could imagine his vote-pooling proposal being supplemented by laws about the internal structure and governance of political parties. These could require elected party leaders, open memberships, public accounting rules and regular audits, term limits, and other devices designed to diminish corruption and force a degree of democratic accountability on parties, ethnic or otherwise. Such devices might seem humdrum in light of the large and dramatic subjects I have been discussing, but think of the role they play in forcing a substantial degree of openness and elite vulnerability in American politics. The damage, possibly decisive, done to George Bush's reelection prospects by Patrick Buchanan's grass roots campaign in the 1991 Republican primaries is a case in point. As the example illustrates, the process is often not pretty but it facilitates relative openness, internal malleability, and diversity within political parties.

Promoting democracy within parties is intrinsically attractive on democratic grounds, and there might also be instrumental advantages to doing it as transitions approach. In this connection, the following hypothesis merits serious attention: the likelihood that an opposition movement will achieve sustainable democracy once it comes to power varies with the degree to which its own organization in opposition is internally democratic. There is plenty of impressionistic evidence in support of the negative, from the French to the Russian, to the Algerian revolutions. Vanguardist parties and elites acting "on behalf of" mass movements seem quick to forget or pervert their mandates once they achieve power. Evidence of the positive is by its nature harder to come by, but one notable feature of the perpetrators of the American Revolution which distinguished them from their French counterparts was their practice of internal democracy in so much of what they did.[71]

It would be a mistake to think of the practice of democracy in opposition as sufficient to ensure its survival later; the evidence belies any such claim. David Apter has shown, for example, that the Convention People's Party in Ghana was comparatively democratic in structure, modeled after the British Labour Party.[72] Yet this did not stop Nkrumah

[71]See Gordon Wood, *Creation of the American Republic, 1776–1787* (New York: Norton, 1969), pp. 3–124. See also his *The Radicalism of the American Revolution* (New York: Knopf, 1992).
[72]David Apter, *Ghana in Transition* (New York: Atheneum, 1963), pp. 203–6.

from becoming a dictator. Similar observations could be made about autocrats-to-be in Francophone West Africa (notably Senghor and Houphouet-Boigny), who served in the parliament of the Fourth Republic and were presumably well-versed in democratic practices as a result.[73] Yet if democratic practice in opposition is not sufficient for democracy's subsequent survival, it seems reasonable to conjecture that it is necessary. How will political leaders learn to practice democratic behavior in the face of the temptations of power if they have not practiced it before being subjected to those temptations? It is a source of some surprise that this issue seems completely to have been ignored in the literature on democratic transitions.

It seems reasonable to conjecture that what goes for political parties goes for civil institutions more generally. It is true that one venerable tradition of social theory affirms the contrary view, usually by appeal to the notion that once values are not authoritatively allocated by the state, as they are not in a democracy, they must emanate from civil institutions that are shielded from democracy's requirements. Thus Michael Walzer argues that although a democratic civil society "is one controlled by its members," this does not require that institutions of civil society themselves be internally democratic. Ever since this claim was first put forward by Tocqueville its democratic credentials have been suspect, however, not least because the mechanisms by which an internally undemocratic civil society will produce democratic agents and public institutions have not been spelled out by its proponents.[74] It seems to me not to be a plausible view, because democratic habits of interaction must be learned through everyday practice, and there is no convincing reason to think this will occur in an authoritarian political culture.

Given the aggressive realism with which Schumpeterianism has often been sold, it is perhaps ironic to conclude, as I do, that one of its principal demerits is its lack of realism. There are at least two reasons why this is the case. The first, suggested by the differences between the Japanese and Indian experiences, on the one hand, and much of the postcolonial African experience, on the other, is that whereas political cultures are malleable in democratic directions they are neither instantly nor infinitely so. As with the market institutions on which

---

[73]I am grateful to an anonymous referee for this point.

[74]Michael Walzer, "The Idea of Civil Society," *Dissent* (spring 1991), pp. 302–3. Tocqueville makes this claim most explicitly while discussing the relative merits of Catholicism over Protestantism in democratic systems; see Alexis de Tocqueville, *Democracy in America* (New York: Doubleday, Anchor, 1969), pp. 449, 450–51.

Schumpeter's account of democracy was modeled, they depend on habits of thought and action that have to be learned and incorporated into existing cultures and aspirations. Democrats must beware of reifying democracy in the same way that economists reify market behavior. Otherwise, like the Western economists who have been so free with advice for ex-communist countries, they run the risk of underestimating both the difficulty of creating democracy and the fragility of democratic institutions once created.

Second, if democratic institutions are to sustain themselves as legitimate, they cannot be detached from expectations that they operate to diminish injustice. This is particularly obvious in countries like South Africa, where the fight against injustice and the battle for democracy have been so intimately linked that any attempt at such separation is bound to be judged cynical and corrupt. But it is true elsewhere as well. If democracy does not function to improve the circumstances of those who appeal to it, its legitimacy as a political system will atrophy. It may well be that democratization must intrude into civil institutions, at least to a degree. The power that matters to people most is the power that most affects their lives. Much of it is manifested in the domains of employment, family life, and "traditional" cultural practices. Unless democracy operates to limit the degree to which those who have power in such settings can use it to dominate and exploit others, its impact for the better on most peoples' lives will be negligible. The normative danger is that democracy will then cease to merit their allegiance. The practical danger is that people will realize that this is so.

5

Three Ways to Be a Democrat

What is the appropriate place for democratic commitments in our convictions about social justice? My sense that this is the question to ask stems from two observations about our circumstances. First, the triumph of democratic oppositions over state socialism in the East has been sweeping, comprehensive, and rapid; yet little attention has been paid by insurgent democratic movements and governments to democracy's appropriate place in a just social order, or even to what democracy is and what it requires. Perhaps this is inevitable to a degree. Revolutionary change is by its nature reactive; sure as its proponents are about the fine details of what they are against, they are usually less clear about the texture of what they want to create. Although every anticommunist opposition since 1989 has identified itself as democratic, what they really had in common was anticommunism—just as the revolutionary European movements of 1848 had been united principally by opposition to monarchy. It is not surprising therefore that much of the public rhetoric spawned by the recent revolutions has identified democracy with communism's historical arch-antagonist, unregulated capitalism.

As the tendency to equate democracy and freedom with markets and capitalism gathers momentum in the East, many who are fully persuaded of the defects of centrally planned systems but worried by the ecological and human costs of unregulated capitalism are troubled by the implications: the possibility that failed socialist systems turning to regimes of private accumulation might end up with the worst of both worlds, and the fear that the reduced legitimacy of socialism in the East will weaken the hands of those in the West concerned to diminish defects in their own institutions. Yet a sense of unease is not an argument, and those who resist the uncritical identification of democracy with either socialism or capitalism are bound to take up the burden of rethinking democracy's nature and its place in a just social order.

The second observation motivating my question is that there is a disjunction between most of the writing on democratic theory since the war and the voluminous literature on distributive justice spawned by John Rawls's *A Theory of Justice*, published in 1971. It would be going too far to say that theorists of democracy and justice speak past one another, but there has been little systematic attention to how considerations about democracy and justice are or should be mutually related.[1] This relative inattention seems partly to have sprung from optimism among many justice theorists about what armchair reflection should be expected to deliver, a driving conviction that what is just in the distribution of social goods can be settled as a matter of speculative theory. Many of their arguments seem to take it for granted that there is a correct answer to the question *what* principles of justice ought we to affirm; that Rawls, Ronald Dworkin, Robert Nozick, Amartya Sen, or someone else will eventually get it right. On this understanding, tensions between proffered accounts of justice and the requirements of democratic politics can comfortably be thought of as problems of implementation, to be worried about later or by others.

The tendency to speculate about the nature of a just social order without attention to democratic considerations has been reinforced by democratic theory's apparently moribund condition. Joseph Schumpeter and the empirical theorists of democracy offered formidable arguments in the 1940s and 1950s that democracy's traditional aspirations could not be realized in the modern world of continental nation states and market economies, yet their attempts to redefine the democracy by reference to then prevailing American practices prompted understandable criticism that they had stripped democracy of much of what makes it morally attractive.[2] In 1979, John Dunn underlined the impasse thus created by noting that democratic theory oscillates between two vari-

---

[1]Rawls is less responsible for the existence of this disjunction than many of his successors. In his argument, rights of democratic participation are protected by his first principle of justice and thus shielded from many of the subsequent recommendations that flow from his theory, although these rights may be limited by the other (not inconsiderable) requirements of the first principle; see John Rawls, *A Theory of Justice* (Cambridge: Harvard University Press, 1971), pp. 42–43, 221–34.

[2]Joseph A. Schumpeter, *Capitalism, Socialism, and Democracy* (New York: Harper, 1942). Generally see Quentin Skinner, "The Empirical Theorists of Democracy and Their Critics: A Plaque on Both Their Houses," *Political Theory* 1, no. 3 (1973), pp. 287–305.

ants, "one dismally ideological and the other blatantly utopian."[3] Compounding democratic theory's troubles was a plethora of analytical work on the logic of decision rules, much of which purported to establish that democracy generates such perverse results as arbitrary and manipulated outcomes, logrolling politics, and continuous unplanned increases in the size of the public sector. Such findings reinforced traditional fears that democracy courts the possibility of majority tyranny and contains an ever-present potential to ride roughshod over whatever justice might be thought to require.[4]

Yet the hiatus between academic commentary on democracy and justice is surprising. Despite the rationalist temper of much recent writing on distributive justice, there are few Platonists today. Democratic intuitions play a role in most everyday conceptions of social justice, and theories of justice often appeal at some level to those intuitions. Most people would balk at the suggestion that there is a right answer to the question *what is just?* in the same way that there is an answer to the question *what is the sum of the interior angles of a triangle?* Likewise, most people—including those who fear unbridled democratic politics—are unnerved by the idea of philosopher kings. Even if one theory of justice is better than the others, there is something disconcerting about the suggestion that it ought for that reason to be imposed on the world. One naïve undergraduate reading Rawls learned this from the cynical titter of his peers when he asked why, "now that Rawls's theory has been established," the Constitution had not been changed to incorporate it? Yet a titter is not an argument, and the question what should be the relations between the demands of justice and the practices of a democratic polity remains remarkably unexplored.

What follows is an attempt to explore that question and to sketch one answer to it. My aim is to make the case that democratic commitments should play three related roles in our convictions about social justice, which I identify with the terms *metric, principle,* and *method.* The first concerns the underlying theory of value by reference to which principles of social justice are applied, the second relates to the principles themselves, and the third deals with strategies for implementing them. Collectively, they invite us to conceive of democracy as a *subordinate foundational good.* This view of democracy is elaborated in section IV, once each of my three ways to be a democrat has been explored. For

[3]John Dunn, *Western Political Theory in the Face of the Future* (Cambridge: Cambridge University Press, 1979), p. 26.

[4]William H. Riker, *Liberalism against Populism: A Confrontation between the Theory of Democracy and the Theory of Social Choice* (San Francisco: W. H. Freeman, 1982). Generally see Dennis Mueller, *Public Choice: II* (New York: Cambridge University Press, 1989), pp. 43–148.

now, suffice it to say that this view turns on the idea that although democracy is essential to ordering social relations justly, we should resist every suggestion that it is the only good for human beings, that it is the highest human good, or that it should dominate the activities we engage in. Democracy operates best when it conditions our lives without thereby determining their course; they require much else as well to be satisfactory, and it is wrongheaded to expect democracy to deliver those other things.

The democratic account of justice I defend is semicontextual; it engenders certain constraints on and possibilities for human interaction, but these work themselves out differently in different domains of social life depending on peoples' beliefs and aspirations, the causal impact of activities in one domain on others, the availability of resources within domains, and other contingent factors. A full exploration of my claim would thus involve pursuing its injunctions through various domains of social life. That is the larger task to which this chapter points and serves as a prolegomenon. My task here is limited to exploring the noncontextual part of a semicontextual ideal; I hope to explain the thinking behind the central idea and cast it in an attractive light.

I. Democracy and Metrics

Every theory of justice can be divided into two parts which can be characterized with the terms *metric* and *principle*. Metrics may be thought of as denoting the conceptions of value by reference to which principles of justice are applied, whereas principles are *what* is applied. Utility is the metric of classical utilitarianism, the greatest happiness maxim its principle; primary goods are Rawls's metric, the general and special conceptions of justice his principles; plural spheres are the metric in Michael Walzer's account, the argument against dominance embodies his principles. Although there are relations between one's conception of the metric and the principles one embraces, they are partly independent of one another. We could accept Rawls's theory of primary goods while rejecting his argument for his principles and vice versa. Metrics, however, place some constraints on the substantive principles that can be considered: we could not entertain Rawls's principles without conceding that there is some identifiable class of primary goods; nor could we entertain Walzer's critique of dominance without agreeing that there is a multiplicity of goods not reducible to a single index.[5]

[5]Rawls, *Theory of Justice*, pp. 62, 90–95, 54–117, and his "Social Unity and Primary Goods," in

Broad versus Narrow Conceptions of Politics

Where do the domains of politics begin, and where do they end? This is the primary question for any theory of social justice; arguments about different metrics rest on assumptions and convictions about it. If we think of politics as limited to what usually goes on in Congress, state-house, and town hall, one class of possibilities will seem appropriate; if we regard institutions such as the family, the workplace, and the church as political, then different possibilities will seem attractive. In the Western tradition of political theory there have been two main strategies for getting at the nature of the political; one focuses on its boundaries, the other on its essence. It is useful to take brief note of the difficulties both strategies confront, thereby opening the way to characterizing the broad conception of politics which informs the present argument.

The first strategy is one of negation; its proponents try to nail down what politics is by establishing what it is not. Their central question is: which domains of human life are beyond politics, immune from arguments about social justice? Despite an impressive array of attempts by first-class theoretical minds, at least since John Stuart Mill wrote *On Liberty*, to draw a line on the basis of which an answer to this question can be constructed, no such attempt has won the philosophical high ground. The going answers turn out, on inspection, to rest on appeals to idealized pictures of private life, of traditional communities, or of communitarian utopias yet to be created. For all their differences such appeals share in common political ideals that are beyond what Michael Sandel describes as "the limits of justice."[6] Such views depict the non-political realm in ways that cannot withstand analysis. In the family— that paradigm of the private community—justice and the sense of it play indispensable roles. The child who knows herself to be loved or respected less than her siblings, or the abused wife, will often bring to bear notions of injustice because she will feel the pertinent economy of love and affection has been violated. The language of justice comes into play whenever there is scarcity of, and conflict over, goods that people value.

Appeals to apolitical communities of the past or the future run into analogous difficulties. Sociologists and historical anthropologists have

---

Utilitarianism and Beyond, ed. Amartya Sen and Bernard Williams (Cambridge: Harvard University Press, 1982), pp. 159–85; Michael Walzer, *Spheres of Justice: A Defense of Pluralism and Equality* (New York: Basic Books, 1983), pp. 3–30, and his "Liberalism and the Art of Separation," *Political Theory* 12, no. 3 (August 1984), pp. 315–30.

[6]Michael Sandel, *Liberalism and the Limits of Justice* (Cambridge: Cambridge University Press, 1984), pp. 11–14, 183.

been waging war on the idealization of "traditional society" for decades; it is now undeniable that the search for historical communities devoid of political conflict is vain.[7] No more promising are arguments about the possibility of creating such communities in the future, as in Marx's claim that under genuine communism politics will be displaced by administration. It is sometimes thought that such a view could be persuasive if a theory of needs could be developed that distinguished them from wants; wants might be infinite, as the bourgeois economists argued, but needs are not. On this view a well-developed theory of needs might generate an Archimedean point for transcending the induced wants of the market, thereby making it possible to get rid of the scarcity that seems to make distributive conflict endemic to human interaction.[8] Yet these formulations assume a static and unrealistic (not to say surprisingly un-Marxist) view of human needs. AIDS and cancer research, dialysis machines, and other forms of medical innovation satisfy needs, not wants; yet the potential for investment in them is limitless. Once innovation is taken into account, human needs are potentially infinite, scarcity inevitable, and distributive conflict inescapable.

What many think of as the limits of justice are really limits to the politicization of social life. By declaring a sphere of action to be beyond politics, part of the private sphere, we render it immune from political criticism. Yet the accepted boundaries of politics are constantly shifting as the result of political struggles. When the law changes from denying the possibility of marital rape by conclusive presumption to creating such a crime by statute, a significant movement of this kind has occurred. The public/private dichotomy in this and other prevalent formulations misses such poignant complexities.[9] Those who invoke the idea of justice in traditionally private realms such as the family are generally those on the short end of power or distributive relationships

[7]See Edward Shils, *Tradition* (Chicago: University of Chicago Press, 1981), pp. 19, 287–330; Lloyd I. Rudolph and Susanne H. Rudolph, *The Modernity of Tradition* (Chicago: University of Chicago Press, 1967); and Joseph R. Gussfield, *Community* (Oxford: Blackwell, 1975), pp. 37–39.

[8]See Karl Marx and Friedrich Engels, *Manifesto of the Communist Party* (New York: International Publishers, 1948), pp. 22–31, for elaboration of the claim that under communism "public power will lose its political character." See also Karl Marx, *The Civil War in France* (New York: International Publishers, 1968), pp. 9–87, and *Critique of the Gotha Program*, in Karl Marx and Friedrich Engels, *Selected Works* (Moscow: Progress, 1970), 3:9–30. At times Marx embraced a more dynamic view of needs, as in his argument that what counts as subsistence is socially and historically conditioned; see Karl Marx, *Capital* (London: Lawrence and Wishart, 1974), 1:167–69, 524–28. But he never came to terms with the difficulties this view of needs raised for his account of communism as a state of permanent superabundance.

[9]On the changing law of marital rape, see "To Have and to Hold: The Marital Rape Exemption and the Fourteenth Amendment," note, *Harvard Law Review* 99 (1986), pp. 1255–73.

within them. The general rule (to which there are, doubtless, exceptions) is that the dominated try to politicize to delegitimize, whereas the dominators try to depoliticize to legitimize.

In short, negationist strategies fail. No social practice can be declared to be beyond politics and therefore beyond the possibility of political regulation. Indeed the term *regulation* is often misleading because it implies that absence of visible action by government is an indicator of the absence of politics. Were it somehow possible for society to "not undertake" collective action, as libertarian writers about its alleged irrationality often assume, such a view might in principle be defended. Because the boundaries to the private sphere are themselves politically constituted and change over time, no argument for a prepolitical distinction between public and private can be sustained.

Many who sense the conceptual vulnerabilities of strategies for bounding the political are nonetheless left uncomfortable by the thought that politics are everywhere. Some aspects of life seem at most trivially political, others momentously so; the suggestion that everything is politics threatens to obscure such distinctions in the name of a conceptual clarity that verges on the self-defeating. Partly for this reason many have pursued an alternative course of trying to specify a domain of human interaction that is basic to politics, in which fundamental conflicts are fought out and social possibilities determined. Religious theorists have sometimes thought in such terms about spiritual life, Marxists about work, feminists about family relations, liberals and fascists—from different standpoints—about the state. Strategies of this kind are conceptually tempting because they appear to make arguments about social justice manageable. Once the genuinely basic domain has been adequately characterized and understood, everything else can be thought about derivatively, as epiphenomenal. Such reductive strategies are also politically tempting; they hold out the joint possibility of focusing our energies on what really matters—spiritual life, material life, family life, civic life—and of placing limits on the demands that might be made of us in a world in which everything was politicized.

Yet no decisive case has ever been made for such reductive views; the paucity of their explanatory power as well as their unpredictable programmatic consequences routinely belie their pretensions. The troubled twentieth-century history of Marxism is a vivid confirmation of this state of affairs, but in this respect Marxism is scarcely unique. Hobbesian, Freudian, socio-biological, and other reductionisms have all been consigned to similar fates; by the late twentieth century there are good grounds for skepticism toward every reductive and essentialist venture of this kind. Rather than join a vain search for the true essence or site of politics, the account developed here rests on the view that politics are both nowhere and everywhere. They are nowhere in that there is no specifiable political realm; not buildings in Washington, not modes of production, not religious practice, not gender relations, not any bounded domain of social life. Politics are everywhere, however, because no realm of social life is immune to relations of conflict and power. To be sure, the significance of this truth varies with domain, with time and circumstance, and even from person to person in the same domain. Yet the appropriate constitution of any domain is always open to dispute; people benefit and are harmed in different ways by prevailing practices, and there is the ever-present possibility that a domain might be ordered differently than presently it is.[10]

The broad view of politics just sketched is perhaps most commonly associated with the name of Michel Foucault, yet it has progenitors in the Western tradition as distant from us as Plato and as unalike as Aristotle, Hobbes, and Marx, who agreed—for all their differences—that politics permeates every facet of human interaction. That they disagreed on so many questions signals how little of normative significance flows, by itself, from embracing a broad conception of politics. It commits us to a view of the terrain and sets some of the terms of the problem, but no more. It tells us nothing about what aspects of human interaction can be understood, controlled, or shaped, or about what policies are desirable. That politics is ubiquitous to human interaction is neither good nor bad; it is part of the reality from which we are bound to begin.

Justice in Multiple Domains

Inevitably and appropriately, arguments about justice track arguments about politics. If the requirements of justice are conceived so broadly as to range over every domain of human interaction, it seems inevitable that they must be pertinent to different domains in different ways. Family life, religion, education, leisure, and work revolve around activities that differ greatly from one another; any plausible account of social justice is bound to take account of this fact.

Few political theorists have denied this.[11] Rawls treats liberties, opportunities, income and wealth, and the "social bases of self-respect" as

---

[10]I defend this antiessentialism more fully in my *Political Criticism* (Berkeley: University of California Press, 1990), pp. 238–64.

[11]The most conspicuous example is Bentham, for whom all goods and harms are reducible to a single pleasure/pain calculus; see Jeremy Bentham, *A Fragment on Government and an Introduction to the Principles of Morals and Legislation*, ed. Wilfrid Harrison (Oxford: Blackwell, 1960), p.

pertinent to different domains (at least partly) and governed by different rules.[12] Walzer and Alasdair MacIntyre push analogous reasoning further; whereas Rawls embraces a system of lexical rankings to settle conflicts among his primary goods, they relativize the process. Goods are defined internally by reference to the logic of the relevant sphere or practice; the challenge for achieving social justice is understood as preserving the integrity of spheres and practices. This is achieved, for Walzer, by the argument that no good pertinent to conduct in one sphere should "dominate" conduct in another sphere and, for MacIntyre, by the parallel claim that social practices are functioning well when participants act by reference to "internal goods," eschewing the pursuit of "external goods." Thus if political office or familial affection can be bought for money, dominance in Walzer's sense is occurring, and if I win a game of chess by cheating when my opponent is distracted I am engaging in the pursuit of external goods in MacIntyre's sense.[13]

Both strategies confront difficulties. It has long been a stock critique of Rawls that his characterizations and orderings of human goods are idiosyncratic and rely on controversial assumptions about human psychology—particularly the propensity toward risk.[14] The early Rawls dealt with this partly by denying that the argument relied on "special" attitudes toward risk and partly by insisting that his assumptions about human motivation were uncontroversial "laws" of economics and psychology. More recently—partly in response to the skepticism both these claims engendered—he has shifted his ground to the claim that his assumptions rest on beliefs that are widely shared.[15] Yet

125. Nozick also comes close to this view when he assumes that any rights violation can in principle be fully compensated with money, which fact separates him from Rawls; see Robert Nozick, *Anarchy, State, and Utopia* (Oxford: Blackwell, 1974), pp. 54–87, and Rawls, "Social Unity and Primary Goods," pp. 159–85, 171. It is arguable that any principle in welfare economics that makes use of compensation theory implicitly assumes that all goods covered by it are reducible to a single index; see I. M. D. Little, *A Critique of Welfare Economics* (London: Oxford University Press, 1950), pp. 84–116.

[12]Thus Rawls believes that questions about political liberties can in principle be settled before economic questions concerning equality of opportunity and substantive fairness; see Rawls, *Theory of Justice*, pp. 195–227, 243–50. It is arguable that the lexical ranking device implicitly reintroduces a unitary index; see Kenneth J. Arrow, "Some Ordinalist-Utilitarian Notes on Rawls's *Theory of Justice*," *Journal of Philosophy* 70, no. 9 (1973), pp. 245–63, 254. For Rawls's response, see his "Social Unity and Primary Goods," pp. 184–85.

[13]Walzer, *Spheres of Justice*, pp. 3–20; Alasdair MacIntyre, *After Virtue*, 2d ed. (Notre Dame, Ind.: University of Notre Dame Press, 1984), pp. 181–203.

[14]See John Harsanyi, "Can the Maximin Principle Serve as a Basis for Morality? A Critique of John Rawls's Theory," *American Political Science Review* 69, no. 2 (1975), pp. 594–606.

[15]For the early formulation, see Rawls, *Theory of Justice*, 154–72; for the more recent contextualization, see John Rawls, "Justice as Fairness: Political Not Metaphysical," *Philosophy and Public Affairs* 14, no. 3 (1985), pp. 223–51.

the difficulty remains that these assumptions about human motivation will convince those who share Rawls's intuitions on this matter, but to others they are bound to seem arbitrary.[16]

The relativizing strategy runs into different difficulties. The intuition informing it is that the goods governing different social practices are and should be internally defined. Part of what makes the norms internal to practices *internal* is that they are learned from other participants, and it is the judgments of those others that are often, for a given individual, decisive. An author will want to be valued by a critic whose capacities he has come to value; there will be small nuances to every activity from child rearing to cabinet building that can be fully appreciated only by others who have learned to excel at those same activities. "He's a pitcher's pitcher" is a commendation we intuitively grasp. Defining the goods pertinent to different practices, even defining the practices themselves, seems as if it should be left to the participants. Yet internal definition appears to render outsiders impotent to make judgments about the practices.

The routes that contextualists have sought out of this difficulty are less than satisfactory. MacIntyre declares by definitional fiat that certain activities are not practices, whereas Walzer's attempts to pin down the limits to his plural spheres and the nature of the goods internal to them have provoked charges that his argument rests on an illicit Rawlsian move of simply asserting that one controversial account of these matters is correct.[17] In short, although the relativizing strategies embraced by Walzer and MacIntyre rest on an attractive resistance to the idea that choice of the theory of value underlying principles of justice is a question for philosophy, making this move creates a dilemma: it seems to require us either to allow, as just, practices that many would regard as unjust, in the name of preserving the integrity of spheres or practices, or to endorse the kind of move that makes the Rawlsian strategy objectionable.

---

[16]It is sometimes said that the critique of Rawls—that he achieves the agreement of those who accept his intuitions at the price of ensuring the disagreement of those who do not—misses the point that his reflective-equilibrium device is intended to get us to look critically at our previously unexamined intuitions. This is true of our intuitions about justice but not of empirical assumptions. At no time does Rawls suggest that these can or should be revised as a result of reflective equilibrium; on the contrary, by holding them constant he tries to use them to get people to modify their intuitions about justice.

[17]For MacIntyre's account of social practices, see his *After Virtue*, pp. 187–96. In the chapter on education in *Spheres of Justice*, Walzer treats its purpose as preparing people for democratic citizenship, yet it is unclear how he would respond to someone who disagreed with this, insisting, perhaps, that the goals of education ought to be enlightenment. See Ronald Dworkin, "To Each His Own," *New York Review of Books*, April 14, 1983.

The Place for Democratic Moral Intuitions

A principled commitment to democracy offers a way out of this bind which protagonists on both sides of the debate appear not to have noticed. This assertion might provoke initial skepticism as to its novelty; after all, both the Rawlsians and the anti-Rawlsians make claims about consensus that seem intended to appeal to democratic moral intuitions. Although the early Rawls did not discuss his foundational democratic commitments at any length in *A Theory of Justice,* they might be said to enter the picture with the requirement of unanimity in his original position.[18] The Kantian claim that everyone should be respected, as an end that motivates that requirement, suggests a commitment to the basic moral equality of persons which most democrats would affirm. But to treat a requirement of unanimity as an interpretation of the democratic ethos confuses unanimity qua decision rule with unanimity qua state of affairs because of the former's propensity to privilege the status quo.[19]

Perhaps partly for this reason Rawls appeals in later work directly to consensus as a state of affairs, displacing the foundational appeal to unanimity with a contextual justification. He now claims that his argument is supported by an "overlapping consensus," which includes "all the opposing philosophical and religious doctrines likely to persist and gain adherents in a more or less just constitutional democratic society."[20] Similarly, contextualists like Walzer appeal to consensually held norms as part of a democratically inspired resistance to the imperialism of armchair speculation about just distribution.[21] The complaint against such strategies that one philosopher's speculations about prevailing norms differ from another's is a symptom of how little democratic ice is cut by this kind of appeal; certainly none of these appealers to consensus has engaged in what a social scientist would regard as empirical study of the values in question.

It is true that the contextualists do not appeal to consensus alone. For Walzer the democratic ethos requires resisting dominance: accepted meanings should reign within their appropriate spheres but may legitimately be prevented from infiltrating other spheres. MacIntyre's argu-

---

[18]By use of the term *foundational* in this context I mean to refrain from referring to those democratic institutions that Rawls claims would be agreed on in his original position, briefly discussed in *Theory of Justice,* pp. 75–80 and 274–84, and to focus attention instead on the role played by democratic moral commitments in the characterization of the original position itself.

[19]On the antidemocratic character of unanimity rule, see Douglas W. Rae, "The Limits of Consensual Decision," *American Political Science Review* 69, no. 4 (1975), pp. 1270–94.

[20]See Rawls, "Justice as Fairness," pp. 24, 25–26, and *Theory of Justice,* pp. 387–91.

[21]See Walzer's response to Dworkin in *New York Review of Books,* July 21, 1983, p. 44.

ment against the pursuit of "external goods" rests on the analogous anti-imperial view that goods germane to one domain ought not to imperialize into others.[22] Walzer and MacIntyre both argue that such domination is illicit, and these arguments appear not to be derived exclusively from conventional meanings because they are applied to conventional meanings in a critical way; they are seen as independently justified.[23]

Such anti-imperial claims are too weak to be satisfying, intellectually or morally. By appealing for justificatory force to practices prevailing within separate domains of civil society, they ignore the forms of oppression that occur in social life when domination of one sphere by another and the pursuit of external goods are not at issue. Walzer made this observation explicit in a recent essay, claiming that although a democratic civil society "is one controlled by its members," the institutions of civil society need not themselves be internally democratic; presumably they continue to be ordered by consensual norms. One wonders, however, what the mechanisms are by which an internally undemocratic civil society will produce democratic agents and public institutions. In most formulations this argument is at bottom liberal rather than democratic inasmuch as it regards the institutions of civil society as important primarily as shields between individuals, social groups, and the state.[24]

As a more thoroughly democratic alternative, I want to make the case for bringing the democratic ethos to bear on conduct within the institutions of civil society as well as on the relations among them, a case that takes full account of the ubiquitous character of human disagreement. Theorists who appeal to consent either wish disagreement away or pursue minimalist strategies of deriving principles of social justice from the lowest common denominator of what they claim we agree on or can be brought to agree on, at least in principle. For all their differences, Rawls's aspiration to ground his argument in overlapping consensus, Walzer's attempts to divine the moral imperatives that "really" flow from our prevailing norms, MacIntyre's desire to recreate the conditions under which agreement about ends allegedly would be possible, and Jürgen Habermas's project of specifying the abstract conditions under which uncoerced agreement is possible hold in common commit-

---

[22]See Walzer, *Spheres of Justice*, pp. 10–20, and McIntyre, *After Virtue*, pp. 181–203.

[23]This state of affairs creates a noteworthy methodological symmetry: as liberal consent theorists move toward contextual justification, their communitarian critics seem to be moving away from it, back in the direction of independent principled argument.

[24]Michael Walzer, "The Idea of Civil Society," *Dissent* (spring 1991), pp. 302–3. For the classic statement, see Alexis de Tocqueville, *Democracy in America* (New York: Doubleday, Anchor, 1969), pp. 449, 450–51.

ments to consensus as the ultimate court of appeal in arguments about social justice.[25] In contrast to such ventures my claim is that the reality of absence of consensus in social life should play a central role in our thinking about ordering social practices justly. Its presence is often a sign of health and vitality, not of the valueless anomie about which philosophers and political moralists often complain.

Whereas both Rawls and the contextualists who oppose him see their appeals to consensus as flowing from democratic moral intuitions, my foundational appeal to democracy rests on the contrary intuition that absence of consensus is an essential ingredient of ordering of any domain of human interaction justly. Almost every social practice exhibits disagreement among participants as to its goals and how best to achieve them, and in the rare cases when we encounter practices unencumbered by internal dissent there are usually good reasons to be skeptical of their authenticity; one person's consensus is often another's hegemony. Most people recognize this; they know that agreement can mask all kinds of things from acts of cultish following, to strategic behavior of various kinds, to plain ignorance of interests and of how to protect them. The great premium that political philosophers so often place on consensus is thus belied by much everyday life; their attempts to come up with consensual ideals speak past too many of its realities.[26]

If there generally is not, and morally there should not be, consensus on what goods to pursue and how to pursue them, it follows *a fortiori* that political theorists cannot plausibly try to read off the "correct" account of the metrics of social justice from the prevailing norms. It is

---

[25]Rawls, "Justice as Fairness," Walzer, *Spheres of Justice*, and his "Liberalism and the Art of Separation," *Political Theory* 12, no. 3 (1984), pp. 315–30; MacIntyre, *After Virtue*, chaps. 2–3; Jürgen Habermas, *Communication and the Evolution of Society* (Boston: Beacon, 1976) and *The Theory of Communicative Action* (Boston: Beacon, 1984), vol. 1, pp. 273–337.

[26]Few empirically minded social scientists place the same premium on consent and consensus that political philosophers characteristically do. When students of comparative politics confront high levels of agreement in circumstances that they have independent reasons for thinking are based on relations of hierarchy and domination (as in Mexico), they turn to a concept like hegemony to try to explain the discrepancy. When they discern relatively little of the kinds of conflict they expect in contemporary capitalist countries, they turn to concepts such as liberal corporatism to explain the ideological incorporation of the working classes. Controversial as such explanations often are, there is no general reason to think them less likely to be true than to assume that agreement is indicative of authentic consensus. On varieties of hegemony in the contemporary world, see Alfred Stepan, *The State in Society* (Princeton: Princeton University Press, 1978), pp. 3–113, and Leo Panitch, "The Development of Corporatism in Liberal Democracies," *Comparative Political Studies* (April 1977), pp. 61–90. For philosophical arguments questioning the relevance of agreement to arguments about social justice, see Thomas M. Scanlon, "The Significance of Choice," in *The Tanner Lectures on Human Values*, vol. 8, ed. Sterling McMurrin (Salt Lake City: University of Utah Press, 1988), pp. 192–201; C. E. Lindblom, *Inquiry and Change* (New Haven: Yale University Press, 1990); and my argument in *Political Criticism*, chaps. 7–9.

not that Rawls's appeals to overlapping consensus and Walzer's appeals to prevailing meanings could be improved upon; such enterprises are flawed in principle. In short, we are bound to press—further than they have done—the contextualists' resistance to the idea that choice of metric is an appropriate task for political theorists and to make more vigorous use of the idea that people should generally be free to learn, invent, discover, and argue over the values that they will pursue in different walks of life.

With this last claim it might appear that I have opened the way for a full retreat from a communitarian to a liberal politics. To see why this conclusion would be misleading, notice that the argument developed thus far rests on assumptions about political reality that differentiate it from both the liberal and the communitarian alternatives. Most liberals accept my claim that disagreement is endemic to social life, but they see this as a reason for escaping the political, for having as few collective decisions as possible "imposed" on unwilling victims. Whether defended in contextual, contractarian, or utilitarian idiom, such flights from politics are chimerical, as we have seen. They make implausible assumptions about precollective or perfectly private states of affairs. By contrast, communitarians often affirm the ubiquitous character of politics, sharing on this score my indictment of liberalism's unrealism. But they usually make implausible assumptions of another kind: about the possibility and desirability of consensus. Moral disagreement is conceived of as a beneficially alterable condition, a view that reasonably makes liberals nervous; it conjures up images of creeping mediocrity, at best, and more often of intimidating big brotherism shrouded in fraternal communitarian rhetoric.[27]

II. DEMOCRACY AND PRINCIPLE

My remarks on metrics led to the suggestion that no theory of value can defensibly be imposed on people as correct or best in the name of a theory of social justice. In light of this claim, I want now to argue for the view that people should generally be free to decide for themselves,

[27]That Sandel appeals to a nonpolitical realm and Rawls appeals to overlapping consensus should remind us that there is no necessary correspondence between liberalism and anticontextual modes of justification, on the one hand, or between communitarianism and contextual modes of justification, on the other. I have argued elsewhere that both liberal and communitarian views can be defended by reference to both contextual and anticontextual modes of justification, so that considerably less turns on the debates about justification than many proponents in both camps would have us believe. See my "Gross Concepts in Political Argument," *Political Theory* 17, no. 1 (1989), pp. 51–76.

within an evolving framework of democratic constraints, what goods to pursue and how to pursue them. "Within an evolving framework of democratic constraints" does most of the controversial work here. A first step toward explaining what I mean by it can be taken by noting that I seek to establish the desirability of occupying a middle ground between proponents of procedural and substantive democracy. "More than process, less than substance" would be an appropriate slogan, because although I affirm the desirability of some substantive constraints on all social practices, these are conditioning constraints, defined in an open-ended and context-sensitive fashion.

For present purposes the debate between proponents of procedural and substantive democracy can be characterized as a debate between rule-centered and outcome-centered conceptions of democracy. Procedural conceptions of democracy belong to that family of decision rules which Nozick identifies as *historical*. They specify some procedural condition (unanimity rule in Nozick's case, majority rule in many arguments for democracy) and define an outcome as acceptable so long as the relevant procedure generates it. Substantive conceptions of democracy belong to the class of views that Nozick identifies as *patterned*, or *end-state*; they specify a distributive outcome or state of affairs (equality, lack of certain types or degrees of inequality, or some other) by reference to which the results of decision rules are evaluated for their adequacy.[28]

Just as defenders of end-state arguments in the distributive justice literature defend their claims by reference to the inadequacies of rule-centered views, proponents of substantive conceptions of democracy rest their arguments on objections to pure procedural democracy. Some of these objections focus on the different resources different players bring to the political process, which are often translatable into differential power within it. To this "garbage in, garbage out" rationale for suspicion of pure proceduralism is often added the fate of insular minorities, who can usually be harmed by every decision rule except unanimity rule but who can hold the rest of society to ransom if this latter rule is adopted. Pure proceduralism is objected to, third, for its perverse characteristics. Arrow's general impossibility theorem has spawned a literature that reveals all decision rules to be arbitrary and manipulable in varying degrees and throws into question even the meaning of the term *majority* in most definitions of majority rule. These and related difficulties have led defenders of substantive democracy such as Charles Beitz to contend that no system of procedures can be

[28]Nozick, *Anarchy, State, and Utopia*, pp. 28–29, 155–60, 218–24.

judged genuinely democratic until we have agreement on a theory of "just legislation" and writers such as John Hart Ely to defend the place of an activist Supreme Court in a democratic constitutional order, to limit and undermine the undemocratic effects of majoritarian legislative procedures.[29]

The difficulty with arguments for substantive democracy from the present point of view should already be plain: they assume that there is some way, independent of what democratic procedures generate, to determine what outcomes are genuinely democratic. Such a theoretical task is fraught with obstacles more formidable than those already decisive ones discussed in section I. In addition to arriving at an account of the metrics appropriate to various domains, such a theory requires us to come up with an account of how goods, measured along those metrics, should be distributed. The argument developed thus far counsels avoiding this course, yet we should nonetheless take many of the criticisms of pure proceduralism advanced by the proponents of substantive democracy seriously. The social world teems with power relations and hierarchies of different kinds which operate to impose values, and modes of pursuing them, on people in varying degrees. These hierarchies are sometimes impervious to democratic procedural rules, sometimes exacerbated by them; their endemic presence in social life threatens the integrity of domains and leads to injustice within them.

The social hierarchies that prevail at a given time and place will often be an arbitrary consequence of coercion and historical accident; they will benefit some, harm others, and sometimes benefit some at the price of harming others. Hierarchies also tend to become hostage to the imperatives for their own maintenance, and these imperatives frequently involve the creation and propagation of fictions about either the nature or the arbitrariness of the hierarchy in question. Those who benefit from the existence of a hierarchy can be expected to try—more or less consciously—to obscure its hierarchical character through ideological argument or to insist that it is rational or normal. An example of the former—brilliantly exposed in Marx's passage on the fetishism of commodities—is the standard defense of market systems on the grounds that they preserve the freedom of all to engage in voluntary transactions. An example of the latter is the Moynihan report's claim

---

[29]On procedural versus substantive democracy, see Charles Beitz, "Equal Opportunity in Political Representation," in *Equal Opportunity*, ed. Norman E. Bowie (Boulder: Westview, 1988), pp. 155–74, and Robert A. Dahl, *Democracy and Its Critics* (New Haven: Yale University Press, 1989), pp. 163–92. See also John Hart Ely, *Democracy and Distrust: A Theory of Judicial Review* (Cambridge: Harvard University Press, 1980). On the technical difficulties with different democratic procedures, see Mueller, *Public Choice: II*, pp. 43–148. These issues are discussed more fully in Chapter 2.

that the "pathological" character of poor black families derives from their failure to conform to the "normal" patriarchal pattern.[30]

Although social practices are often not designed for harm or exploitation, there is an ever-present possibility that they will atrophy into systems of domination.[31] When this begins to occur, the Walzerian arguments for respecting their integrity as practices begin to weaken. The authenticity of practices is under constant threat from a variety of sources: the scarcity of goods essential to human thriving, the unpredictability of human interaction, the fact that people are simultaneously involved in many activities that make competing and often mutually incompatible demands on them, the externalities of activities in one domain on other domains and the differential benefits within them, the fact that domains are often exclusionary in controversial respects, and the fact that the ways in which people try to integrate their different activities can be zero-sum: one life sometimes becomes more rather than less integrated at the price of another life's becoming less rather than more integrated.

Complaints about the atrophy of social practices into systems of domination may emanate either from within practices, as when domestic labor is demanded without being acknowledged, or by those affected on the outside, as when economic development in the first world is argued to promote backwardness in the third. Although no complaint of either kind can ever be ruled out as a basis for intervention in the conduct of a social practice, this is not to say that all social hierarchies can or should be eliminated. Indeed because most human activity is mediated through language, which has to be learned, a degree of hierarchy infuses everything we do. Yet hierarchies vary. Some cannot be escaped, others can. Some are essential to the pursuit of particular goods, others not. Some are embraced voluntarily, others are not. Some hierarchies are temporary, others replicate themselves more or less indefinitely.

My claim, then, is not that all social hierarchies should be eliminated but rather that there are good reasons to be nervous about them. Escapable hierarchies can be alleged to be inescapable, oppression can be shrouded in the language of agreement, unnecessary hierarchies can be

---

[30]Marx, *Capital*, 1:76–88, 582–83; Daniel Patrick Moynihan, *The Negro Family: The Case for National Action* (Washington, D.C.: U.S. Department of Labor, Office of Policy Planning and Research, August 1965), pp. 5–14.

[31]This leaves aside the difficulty of how to deal with activities whose explicit purpose does involve harm or exploitation. I do not take this up here, referring the reader instead to my treatment of it in Chaps. 5, 8, and 9 of *Political Criticism*. For a helpful discussion of oppression and its role in injustice that partly parallels mine, see Iris Marion Young, *Justice and the Politics of Difference* (Princeton: Princeton University Press, 1990), chap. 2.

declared essential to the pursuit of common goals, and fixed hierarchies can be shrouded in myths about their alterability. Accordingly, although many particular hierarchies might in the end be conceded to be justified, this concession should truly *be* in the end and *after* the defender of hierarchy has shouldered a substantial burden of persuasion.

The claim that democratic constraints are desirable but that they should occupy a subordinate role in social interaction follows from the thought that although we should aspire to get on with our lives in democratic ways, we should nonetheless aspire to get on with them. Because politics infuses everything we do while seldom being simply what we do, democracy appropriately conditions our activities; but it does not appropriately supplant them. The creative political challenge is to devise mechanisms that can achieve this result by structuring human activities while remaining subordinate in character. Put in Aristotelian terms, we might say that valuable as democratically conditioned lives are, it is wrongheaded to conceive of democracy as a final good. On this view, democracy goes to war with itself when it escapes its conditioning role because its subordinate character is integral to its value as a political ideal.

My contention that we should try to devise middle-ground principles (between procedural and substantive democracy) designed to undermine and otherwise mitigate the corrosive effects of social hierarchies is rooted in the claim that presumptive, but rebuttable, suspicion of them generally is warranted. This assertion says nothing about what is to count, and in whose judgment, as sufficient to rebut the presumption, or about what conditioning constraints should be employed in various circumstances. These context-specific issues are deferred to another occasion, but some general considerations pertinent to thinking about them are taken up in section III. For now I conclude with the observation that my middle-ground principle draws on the opposition traditions of democratic politics which have been comparatively neglected since the 1950s. After four decades of exhaustive examination, in the wake of Arrow, of different putatively democratic procedures for aggregating preferences rationally, we tend to forget that historically democracy has been as much an ideology of opposition as one of republican self-government. Democratic movements such as the nineteenth-century English Chartists and socialists emerged in opposition to an existing order; their goal was to abolish or limit what they saw as unjust hierarchy as much as it was to foster participatory politics. John Dewey summed up this reality well when he noted that modern democracy came into being as a by-product of efforts to remedy particular evils experienced in undemocratic institutions. It proceeded step

by step, and each step was taken "without foreknowledge of any ultimate result, and, for the most part, under the immediate influence of a
number of differing impulses and slogans."[32] It is this spirit of democratic oppositionalism that we need to incorporate into the evolving
constraints that condition interaction in various domains of social life.

III. DEMOCRACY AND METHOD

Just as our discussion of metrics drove us to matters of democratic
principle, so the discussion of principles has brought us to issues of
democratic method. Even if we had the best imaginable theory of the
metrics and principles of social justice, we would still be left with the
questions: Should they be implemented, how, and by whom? I begin
with summary observations culled from the road already traveled.
Nothing is beyond politics. In an evolving human world of plural
values, where there cannot be an undisputed list of goods, where there
is no reason to expect harmony, and in which all ends are potentially
subject to criticism and revision, democracy is the most attractive available foundational political commitment. Yet democracy is a complex
ideal, valuing resistance to entrenched hierarchy independently of the
traditional democratic good of participation, and it can only be
achieved—where it can—by creative adaptation to the evolving demands of various activities. Democracy is best thought of as an ethos of
adaptive opposition as well as a system of republican self-government.
Its demands are partly problem driven, varying with the characteristic
ways in which social practices atrophy into systems of domination.

Although nothing is beyond politics, democratic justice does not dictate meddling; the internal character of the goods governing most social
practices makes it advisable to leave things to the participants, within
limits. But what are those limits, and how can we know when they have
been transgressed? What happens when people disagree about these
questions? When should insiders look for outside help in achieving
democratization of their activities? When should outsiders be
permitted—perhaps even obliged—to intervene? Who should decide,
and by what criteria, who the insiders and outsiders are? To these
questions there are no general answers, but some general considerations are pertinent to thinking about them.

These considerations flow out of the third of my three ways to be a
democrat: a principled commitment to antivanguardism which advises
us to seek democratic change democratically. This commitment rests

[32]John Dewey, *The Public and Its Problems* (New York: Holt, 1927), pp. 84–85.

partly on strategic considerations, as we will see, on suspicion of the suggestion that there are cadres of experts who, having written or read the correct democratic blueprint, are best placed to impose democratic solutions. It also reflects substantive democratic commitments, however. My earlier contention that we should respect the autonomy of social practices, within limits, grew out of the claim that people should generally be free to decide for themselves what goods to pursue and how to pursue them. This commitment is bound to live in tension with any proposal that a particular set of values should be imposed on people in the name of democratic, or any other, political theory. Managing this tension implies adopting a pragmatic and problem-driven attitude toward political innovation, rooted in skepticism of claims of expertise in politics.

Distrust of Political Expertise

Expertise is relevant to politics in many ways, but its appropriate place in democratic politics needs to be specified with care. Some forms of expertise are not politically troubling, and their proponents are readily deferred to. One might reasonably believe Einstein's theory of relativity to be true even if one did not fully understand it and was incapable of relating one's everyday experience to it. In certain (though not all) circumstances one can reasonably act on the advice of an airplane pilot, an auto mechanic, an architect, or a physician without understanding its rationale or even being interested in it. But the idea that there is analogous political expertise reasonably prompts suspicion.

Most minimally, the suggestion that there is political expertise is suspect because there are few reasons to believe that there is in fact much of it. What is typically billed as knowledge about the world of politics seems so meager, and is so regularly undermined by events, that people who set themselves up as political experts often give off the whiff of snake oil. On its own this suggests only that political expertise may be primitive; after all, as medical science advances, quacks and charlatans are gradually displaced from the business of healing. Commentators who argue for the introduction of scientific modes of analysis into politics have often thought in these terms: consider Dewey's lament in 1929 that the then current way of treating such social problems as crime was still "reminiscent of the way in which diseases were once thought of and dealt with," when they were believed to have moral causes. Just as the possibility of "effective treatment" began when diseases came to be seen as having "an intrinsic origin in interactions of the organism and its natural environment," so we should now be looking for comparable solutions to social ills. "We are only just beginning to think of criminality as an equally intrinsic manifestation of interactions between an individual and the social environment," he noted, complaining that with respect to many such evils, "we persist in thinking and acting in prescientific 'moral' terms."[33]

But here we must part company with Dewey, for his view takes too little account of the enduring power dimensions of social life. To pursue his own comparison: the likely side effects of a medicine for a particular ailment on other organs of the body can reasonably be thought about in cost-benefit terms in order to decide whether, on balance, it is desirable for the person to take the particular cure. But the social analogy does not hold; for the person bearing the externality of another's benefit will be unimpressed by the claim that the benefit exceeds the harm and that society is, on balance, better off as a result, even if the accuracy of the cost-benefit calculation is conceded. One reason Dewey's reference to "treatment" in the social realm seems frighteningly Orwellian is that the suggestion that any particular form of social treatment will not in fact operate in the interests of some and to the detriment of others is no longer credible. Too often the experts turn out to be on somebody's side, and not necessarily ours.

This is not to say that expertise should be denied a role in democratic governance. It would be foolish not to recognize that economists, for instance, often have esoteric knowledge (perhaps less than they think they have) about the workings of the economy that is relevant to democratic deliberation about it. But because decisions about the limits of the market sphere and the structure of its governance are linked to the controversial exercise of power, they are inescapably political; thus economic policy making should never be ceded to professional economists. They must persuade lay representatives, in nontechnical terms, if we are to be bound by their advice. The more highly specialized the field the easier it is for political decisions to masquerade as technical ones; this is why a decisive lay component is essential to policy making concerning such technologically complex matters as nuclear weapons policy.[34]

For similar reasons people in a democratic culture will never comfortably allow psychiatric experts, ballistics experts, or fingerprint experts to decide the guilt or innocence of defendants in criminal trials, insisting instead that they persuade a lay jury if their opinions are to hold

[33]John Dewey, *Individualism Old and New* (New York: Putnam's, Capricorn, 1962), p. 164.
[34]See Robert A. Dahl, *Controlling Nuclear Weapons* (Syracuse: Syracuse University Press, 1985), pp. 69–90.

sway. This is not because most people doubt that these professionals are experts, but because of the Kafkaesque possibilities conjured up by the prospect of a legal system that begins to be held hostage to their expertise. Intelligent democratic use of expertise subordinates it to lay control through institutional devices designed to limit its imperialistic tendencies without stifling its esoteric content. Otherwise expertise threatens to become part of the entrenched hierarchical landscape; we saw in section II that there are generally good reasons for resisting this outcome. Indeed, hierarchies in systems of institutional governance invite comparatively robust democratic suspicion because they are directly involved in the management of power, whereas in the institutions of civil society power is usually exercised incidentally, in the course of pursuing some other good.

Pursuing Democracy in the Absence of Blueprints

Designing democratic institutional constraints is inevitably a pragmatic business, best pursued in a context-sensitive and incremental way. At least three kinds of reasons militate against the suggestion that we should aspire to design a democratic system *tabula rasa*. First, the sheer complexity of social life makes attention to context essential to thinking about democratic management. If democratic constraints are to range over many different and evolving domains of social life, these constraints will have to be adaptively flexible. New activities come into being; technological change, experience, and the evolution of other causally linked activities all present fresh problems and generate novel possibilities for democratic governance. Any attempt to legislate a democratic map of a just social terrain in advance is bound to run afoul of such evolving complexities.

There are good reasons, second, for trying to structure social relations so that, ceteris paribus, people will discover ways to democratize things for themselves. This can never amount to an unconditional right to be left alone, as we have seen; yet acknowledging the internal character of the goods governing various domains supplies us with grounds for a presumption in favor of internal democratization wherever possible. This presumption has force for insiders as well as for outsiders: when external help is sought to undermine domination, there is the ever-present danger that it will undermine the democratic integrity within the domain that democrats are seeking to create or sustain. One only has to think of the diminished democratic legitimacy of the Aquino government in the Philippines after the use of American air support to put down a military coup, or of the Endara government installed in

Panama by American forces, to be made aware of the costs to democrats of relying on external help. We cannot say that such help should never be sought; both these examples might perhaps be defended as cases in which the likely alternatives would, from the standpoint of achieving or sustaining democracy, have been worse. But just because seeking external help is so fraught with counterproductive danger it should be thought of as a democratizing strategy of last resort.

Although no action to advance democracy can be ruled out a priori, democrats always have more than prudential reasons to be concerned about the forms such attempts take. Certainly they cannot reasonably assume, with Roberto Unger, that every form of context smashing will undermine entrenched hierarchy and fuel greater democratic freedom.[35] Consider the three-hour, secret summary trial and execution of Nicolai and Elena Ceaucescu by a self-appointed Romanian military tribunal in December 1989. No democrat would doubt that they deserved their fates and none will likely mourn them, but the method of their disposal is bound to make democrats nervous; the absence of democratic self-restraint it evidenced seems ominous for the future. More heartening were the actions of the Czech Civic Forum in November 1989, recounted by Timothy Garton Ash. As the revolutionary tide accelerated, there were anticommunists who wanted to use a legal provision, created to purge parliament after the Soviet invasion, whereby members could be removed on a parliamentary vote and replaced by new (unelected) members. But others successfully resisted, insisting there should be free elections for the vacated seats, as in Hungary, even though it would take longer; the dangers of attempting an "undemocratic shortcut to democracy" were too great.[36]

Third, we need to get away from a way of thinking which the blueprint approach engenders, the idea that there is a "political system" the basic rules of which have to be set right, and adopt a much less state-centric view of politics. The civil-society–centric view pressed here differs from conventional liberal accounts of politics and from those of communitarian democrats, both of which reify politics by conceiving of it as a distinctive activity. Liberals often denigrate what they take to be the political realm; communitarian democrats bemoan either its passing or its recalcitrance in coming into being. My view shares something with each of these while resisting their joint preoccupation with the costs and benefits of participation. With the communitarian democrats I agree that politics ranges into all walks of life and cannot be walled into

[35]See Roberto Unger, *Politics* (Cambridge: Cambridge University Press, 1987).
[36]Timothy Garton Ash, "The Revolution of the Magic Lantern," *New York Review of Books*, January 18, 1990, p. 49.

a thing or place called a public realm, but with the liberals I resist the idea that communitarians routinely take for granted: that the highest human good is participation. Participation, as Oscar Wilde's quip about socialism taking up too many evenings underlines, can be tedious. Even communitarian democrats have now begun to concede that too much participation can be counterproductive and that the inescapable scarcity of time entails at a minimum that we are bound to confront decisions about which kinds of participation most matter in our lives.[37]

It would be going too far to say that we need democracy in the same way we need garbage cans; this would suggest a purely instrumental view that I do not mean to embrace. Instead my claim is that essential as democracy is to a tolerable existence, expecting much in the way of spiritual enrichment or edification from it is wrongheaded. This is not intended as a denial of the value of democratic participation or even that such participation will often have morally beneficial effects on participants, although the evidence on this question is mixed.[38] It is intended to emphasize that democracy should be our servant not our master; to the extent that the reverse becomes true, democracy will impoverish our lives, not enrich them.

Attending to Impediments to Democracy

Instead of trying to design institutional blueprints, we do better to work against particular undemocratic practices. The ways in which different domains can best be democratized will be conditioned partly by the nature of the domain in question, partly by the demands of activities in causally linked domains, and partly by the ways in which activities atrophy into systems of domination. Proposals to reform a given domain are bound to be controversial and to meet resistance, not least if there is much chance of their being effective. But it is wise not to think about conflicts over reform proposals too reductively, as reflecting strategic placings in the power struggle. Domination is not always by design, and the particular forms it takes are almost never by design. When atrophy occurs in the form of externalities, even its beneficiaries

[37]See Carmen Sirianni's discussion of the "paradox of participatory pluralism" in "Learning Pluralism: Democracy and Diversity in Feminist Organization," in *NOMOS XXXV: Democratic Community*, ed. John Chapman and Ian Shapiro (New York: New York University Press, 1993), pp. 283–312. This paradox derives from the fact that once politics is defined over many social domains, increasing participation in one domain may well diminish it in others.
[38]See Robert A. Dahl, *After the Revolution* (New Haven: Yale University Press, 1970), pp. 140–66; Arnold Kaufman, "Human Nature and Participatory Democracy," in *The Bias of Pluralism*, ed. William Connolly (Chicago: Aldine-Atherton, 1969), pp. 201–12; Jane Mansbridge, *Beyond Adversary Democracy* (New York: Basic Books, 1980); and Michael Walzer, "A Day in the Life of a Socialist Citizen," in *Radical Principles* (New York: Basic Books, 1989), pp. 112–38.

may be persuaded to do things differently. This may be partly because as practices begin to atrophy into systems of domination they often corrupt their ostensible goals and become susceptible to immanent criticism for Walzerian reasons. But it may also be because the fortuitous beneficiaries of such atrophy may, as a result of their own principled commitments to democracy, have no desire to dominate. Appeals to these commitments will involve immanent debate of a sort, but not over the "meaning of the good" in Walzer's sense. Rather it will be over how best to govern a practice geared to the pursuit of a particular good democratically.[39]

Disagreements over democratization may not mirror strategic interests in the power struggle for a different reason: people may be unsure about what their interests are or about how best to democratize particular domains of social life. Indeed, often nobody will know the answers to these questions. For instance, changes in the structure of American family law, making the family more of a contract and less of a status, have been motivated by a desire to undermine the patriarchal family. But it appears that one of the net effects of these changes is to render women increasingly vulnerable to the greater economic power of men in marriage.[40] As this becomes apparent, other ways of democratizing family life will be sought and new experiments tried and modified, as and when the obstacles they generate come into view. Democratizing family life will likely require changes in the organization of the economy, perhaps in other domains as well. Debates about it thus inevitably become embroiled, in unanticipated ways, in debates about other activities.

Now there will be instances in which disagreements over the allocation of a good or the governance of a domain do reflect raw differences of interest in the power struggle, but how these disagreements are related to the cooperative concerns with which they are intertwined will vary with time and circumstance, as will the possibilities for their democratic management. To get at these differences in the abstract is impossible; we have to start with complaints voiced by participants in practices, would-be participants, or others affected by them—which politics in any case obliges us to do. This leads to argument and debate about the feasibility of various courses of action, the potential costs, who should bear them, the likelihood of success, and whether attempted reform is worthwhile once these considerations are taken into account. Such issues will have to be argued and perhaps fought out in

[39]For Walzer's account, see his *Interpretation and Social Criticism* (Cambridge: Harvard University Press, 1987), pp. 3–27.
[40]See Susan Okin, *Justice, Gender, and the Family* (New York: Basic Books, 1989), pp. 134–69.

the political arena; there is no philosophical answer to them. To assume the contrary is both to expect too much from political theory and to misunderstand the nature of a foundational commitment to democracy.[41]

IV. Democracy as a Subordinate Foundational Good

At the outset I characterized democracy as a subordinate foundational good. I have since explained what I mean by "subordinate" in this context; now it is time to attend to the meaning of *foundational*. I should say immediately that by my use of this term I do not mean to take up a position here in debates about the nature of knowledge and existence. By describing a democracy as a foundational good I mean only to suggest that no prior or more basic political commitment rightly commands our allegiance.

This is not to say that my argument is philosophically neutral. Like Rawls in his "political not metaphysical" mode, my account is developed independently of claims about the metaphysical validity of contending political views.[42] Yet it is true that my account rests on skepticism toward the absolutist epistemologies and ontologies that a classical Marxist or a Platonist might embrace. This skepticism is political not metaphysical in that I take no position on whether or not they are valid (perhaps one such view is), only on whether or not it is wise to let them run the world. Evidently, partisans of such absolutist views will find their political aspirations frustrated by the politics I am advocating in ways that many philosophic fallibilists, pragmatists, empiricists, realists, and some (but not all) philosophical antifoundationalists will not.[43] My claim, then, is not that philosophical neutrality is desirable; indeed I do not think such neutrality is possible. My claim is no more and no less than this: as compared with the going alternatives, the

[41]In this connection I must confess to never having been able to see what the fuss about Richard Wollheim's paradox amounted to. That a democrat can both prefer one policy on the merits or be certain that it is the best, yet still prefer that a different policy be adopted because the majority prefers it, seems not in the least paradoxical to me; see Richard Wollheim, "A Paradox in the Theory of Democracy," in *Philosophy, Politics, and Society*, 2d ser., ed. Peter Laslett and W. G. Runciman (Oxford: Blackwell, 1962), pp. 71–87. See also Donald Weiss, "Wollheim's Paradox: Survey and Solution," *Political Theory* 1, no. 2 (May 1973); and Ross Harrison, "No Paradox in Democracy," *Political Studies* 18 (1970), pp. 514–17.

[42]John Rawls, "Fairness to Goodness," *Philosophical Review* 82 (1973), p. 228, and "Justice as Fairness," pp. 223–26.

[43]Nietzsche is an example of an antifoundationalist who would not find the politics defended here congenial. It would take us too far afield for me to explain here why I think that, by itself, a philosophic commitment to antifoundationalism entails no particular politics.

view of democracy elaborated here is the most attractive foundational political commitment.

I have tried to sketch the main contours of this foundational political view by elaborating a threefold answer to my initial question about the appropriate place for democratic commitments in our convictions about social justice, the first having to do with underlying metrics of value, the second with principles of democratic governance, and the third with methods for advancing those principles in everyday life. The middle ground they stake out in debates among procedural and substantive democrats is summed up by characterizing democracy as a subordinate foundational good, a conditioning good that is more than procedural yet less than substantive, more than instrumental yet never the point of the exercise.

My three ways to be a democrat are linked. Since there is no extrapolitical way to arrive at the appropriate metrics of social justice, discussion of the values informing them inevitably raises questions of political principle. Once a well-founded suspicion of hierarchy has been shown generally to militate in support of constraints geared to undermine the unnecessary and corrosive effects of social hierarchies, the discussion cannot advance further without attending to questions about democratic method. And because behaving democratically seems the surest path toward fostering democracy, questions of method flow back into those about metrics. That my three ways to be a democrat turn out to be mutually related should not in the end surprise us; democracy is a human artifact, as are the activities whose governance and interaction require it. The goals people pursue live in evolving tension with the democratic ideal at best; that is why there is always room and need for creative democratic agency.

My goal here has been to make the case for a foundational commitment to democracy, not to work through its implications for any particular social practice or to analyze its internal complexities. Central among these complexities, given my resistance to reducing democracy to any single imperative, are the potential conflicts among its constituent parts. Ever-present is the possibility that what people decide to do in a domain might conflict with the injunction for suspicion toward hierarchy, thereby dividing the democratic ideal against itself. This has not been the occasion to explore the possibilities for rules to settle such conflicts, but my instinct is that there is little that is general to be said about the democratic management of tensions internal to the democratic ideal. Most of the interesting argument is likely to be in the details.

Many will find my refusal to affirm any foundational political value other than democracy disquieting. Liberals will have waited in vain for the familiar list of trumping countermajoritarian rights eventually to be wheeled out. Marxists will have noticed my failure to discern democracy's entailment of socialism. Although neither a liberal constitutionalism nor a socialist political economy is ruled out on this account, these can be legitimate only if they triumph and can be sustained within democracy's constraints. Conservative communitarians may be threatened by democracy's permanent license to interfere, but I have tried to explain why the democratic ideal need be destructive only of what is genuinely illegitimate. Participatory democrats will balk at the realization that my account is more analytically than is it politically radical. To them I reiterate that there is no plausible way to think of democracy as other than a subordinate good once politics is conceived as broadly as they would rightly have us conceive of it. That statists and antistatists of the Left and the Right will all find something recognizably theirs in this view as well as something with which to quarrel should perhaps dismay me, but I prefer to think of it as indicating that in the search for a democratic third way I might be on the right track.

Democratic Autonomy
and Religious Freedom:
A Critique of *Wisconsin v. Yoder*

Richard Arneson and Ian Shapiro

Democratic politics is constitutionally at odds with paternalism and political hierarchy. For centuries democratic theorists have studied how to structure public institutions so as to diminish inegalitarian power relations and how to equalize voting power among diverse citizenries in the selection of public officials. Relatively little attention has been paid, however, to what democracy requires of the institutions that make up civil society. This is most notably true of religious and familial institutions, which are often—and perhaps in some respects inescapably—hierarchical and inegalitarian in character. This lack of democratic theoretical attention to the structure of civil institutions derives from several sources, prominent among them the prevalence of the liberal view that civil institutions form the private sphere that is, or at any rate ought to be, "beyond politics."

In recent years the feminist and communitarian critiques of liberalism have rendered its public/private dichotomy problematic (if not obsolete). The way is now open for normative reflection by political theorists on the structure of civil institutions.[1] In this chapter we take up a small piece of the newly uncovered terrain: we explore the limits of

[1]See Michael Walzer, *Spheres of Justice: A Defense of Pluralism and Equality* (New York: Basic Books, 1983); Michael Sandel, *Liberalism and the Limits of Justice* (Cambridge: Cambridge University Press, 1984); and Susan Okin, *Justice, Gender, and the Family* (New York: Basic Books, 1989).

parents' authority in the education of children who have been committed to their charge. Our use of this formulation, rather than parents'
authority over "their children," prefigures one of the central claims we
seek to defend and employ: that the relationship between parents and
children is best thought of as one of trusteeship; children are in no sense
the property of their parents. Although most people will find the claim
thus stated unexceptionable, and few would go so far as to describe
their children as their property, many of the convictions to which people find themselves drawn in thinking about the authority of parents
over children nevertheless reflect the archaic idea that the child is the
chattel of the parent (which once went hand in hand with the patriarchal idea that the wife is the chattel of the husband).

It is beyond the scope of our discussion to develop and defend a
general theory of parent-child relations. We restrict ourselves, rather, to
the specific issue of what the theory of constitutional democracy requires when parents and public officials find themselves in conflict over
the compulsory education of children for whom they have overlapping
responsibilities. This was the issue presented in *Wisconsin v. Yoder*,
decided in 1972 by the U.S. Supreme Court in favor of Old Order Amish
parents, who wanted to remove Amish children from the Wisconsin
schools after eighth grade (at age fourteen) in violation of a statutory
requirement of compulsory education to age 16.[2] The court's decision
was something of an outlier in American constitutional jurisprudence:
the result was unexpected and, although it has never been overruled, it
has not become a precedent for a general expansion of the domain of
parental authority at the expense of the public law of child rearing.
Courts (including the Supreme Court) have tended to limit *Yoder* to its
idiosyncratic facts, seeming to avoid opportunities to entrench it or to
expand its reach.

Yet the *Yoder* case is a useful vehicle for reasoning about the implications of democratic theory for adult-child relations because of the stark
and specific manner in which parental and public authority over children clashed and because the conflict involved religious freedom as
well as the education of children. Whatever our differing moral intuitions about compulsory education taken on its own, few would seriously deny that a substantial degree of religious autonomy of citizens
from the state is an important value in a modern democracy. As a
consequence, parents' claims that state authority in the education of
children should be limited are likely to be especially weighty when
their free exercise of religion is implicated in, and supplies the basis for,

[2]*Wisconsin v. Yoder*, 406 US 205 (1972).

their arguments. If one is going to argue on democratic grounds, as we do here (in sections III–IV), that the parents' claims should not displace a democratic state's requirement of compulsory education to an age when critical reason is developed and can be fully deployed, then the religiously based arguments of the kind put forward by the Amish parents are perhaps the most difficult to answer. Answering them is the burden we take on here in arguing that *Yoder* was wrongly decided. In discharging it we hope to render plausible and attractive a fiduciary model of adult-child relations in a democracy which may prove useful in other contexts. After a discussion of the context of the *Yoder* litigation, what was at issue, and why the result might initially seem attractive from the standpoint of democratic constitutional theory we turn, in section II, to an examination of democratic citizenship and the logic of its requirement of compulsory education to an age where critical reason is developed and can be fully deployed. In section III, drawing on Locke's discussion in the *Two Treatises,* we sketch and defend a fiduciary model of parent-child relations. In sections IV and V, we make the case that this model requires a rejection of the Amish parents' free-exercise claims and the acceptance by them of a responsibility to develop the critical reason of their charges, even if this threatens the existence of the Amish community from whence they come. In a final section we draw out some of the implications of our analysis of the *Yoder* problem for a democratic theory of civil institutions.

I. *Wisconsin v. Yoder:* The Dispute and Its Implications

Context of the Yoder Litigation

The Amish in North America live in self-contained and relatively self-sufficient communities, mainly in Pennsylvania, the Midwest, and Ontario. Their ancestors were the Anabaptists of sixteenth-century Europe, specifically, those who, following Jacob Amman, split from the mainstream of the Swiss Anabaptists in the 1690s. They do not seek to proselytize, and they have no desire to bring an Amish state into existence. Indeed because they conceive of themselves as a voluntary community that members are always free to leave (and from which they can be expelled and "shunned"), they are dependent on the existence of a non-Amish outside world. They reject the modern world in all its essentials, preferring a simple agricultural or semi-agricultural life geared to a subsistence existence. Their *Ordnung,* or blueprint for expected behavior, governs all public, private, and ceremonial life. It prescribes the distinctive but unostentatious Amish dress and diet. It specifies their religious rituals, patriarchal family structure, and austere work habits, and among other things it proscribes the use of mechanized farming equipment, ownership of cars, conveniencies in the home, participation in worldly public organizations, filing lawsuits, military service, divorce, all jewelry, air transportation, and high school education.[3]

More than a fifth of the children leave the community before adulthood, and very few non-Amish adults ever join. Yet, unlike the Amish communities of Europe, which have long been extinct, the North American communities have thrived and expanded, growing from about 3,700 living in 22 church districts in 1890 to more than 85,000, living in 526 districts, in 1979. This rapid expansion of between 30 and 48 percent per decade is accounted for by their high birth rate; the average Amish family has seven children.[4]

The Amish people's conception of their community as voluntary extends to their treatment of children. Like other sects of Anabaptist origin, they reject the doctrine of infant baptism.[5] In the Amish view, sin enters the world with a knowledge of good and evil, which is unavailable to a young infant; not having sinned, children do not need baptism for the removal of sin. Thus although Amish children are governed by the *Ordnung*, they do not become members of the church until they choose to be baptized—usually in late adolescence. According to John Hoestetler, the vow of baptism "embodies the spiritual meaning of becoming an Amish person, an acceptance of absolute values, and a conscious belief in religious and ethical values entirely for their own sake, quite independent of any external rewards." It includes total submission to the authority of the Amish Church and an implied promise to abide by all Amish rules, and it cannot be reversed. Whereas those who leave the community without taking the vow are not "shunned," those who take it and fail to live up to it are excommunicated from the church, and members of the community will have nothing more to do with them.[6]

Although the Amish believe that the vow of baptism must be taken

[3]John A. Hoestetler, *Amish Society*, 3d ed. (Baltimore: Johns Hopkins University Press, 1980), pp. 25–92; Donald B. Kraybill, *The Riddle of Amish Culture* (Baltimore: Johns Hopkins University Press, 1989), pp. 94–99.

[4]Hoestetler, *Amish Society*, 98–108.

[5]The term *Anabaptist* originated as a nickname, meaning "rebaptizer," for nonconformist Calvinists who believed that nothing in the scriptures supports the practice of infant baptism. Ibid., pp. 26–27.

[6]Ibid., pp. 79, 83.

voluntarily by a mature person, they go to great lengths in designing their system of education and acculturation to ensure that Amish children will take the vow and join the church. Herein lies the source of the half century of conflict between the Amish and secular educational authorities which culminated in the *Yoder* decision. The Amish educational system is designed to prepare children for life in the Amish community, not the outside world. To this end, the Amish try to shield children from the secular world, and they actively discourage critical questioning of Amish values and beliefs. They are particularly opposed to high school education, which they see as threatening to their entire way of life. By age fourteen the Amish child knows everything necessary to live successfully in the Amish community; as a result the Amish oppose further schooling, preferring on-the-job vocational training that will ease children into the community.

Amish acculturation practices have led even so sympathetic a commentator as Donald Kraybill to observe that in many respects Amish youth do not enjoy a genuine choice as to whether or not to enter the community. He goes so far as to suggest that by allowing adolescents a few flings with worldliness before they have to confront the baptismal choice, the Amish create an appearance of choice where for many there is no such thing. By the time of the choice, Amish adolescents have been so "thoroughly immersed in a total ethnic world with its own language, symbols, and world view" that to leave would involve a traumatic severing of all their significant friendships. For the great majority who join the church, "the illusion of choice" serves an important function in adult life: "Thinking they had a choice as youth, adults are more likely to comply with the demands of the *Ordnung*."[7]

Since the 1930s, conflicts between the Amish and secular authorities have surfaced whenever compulsory education requirements have seemed to Amish leaders to jeopardize their acculturation program. In 1937 in East Lampner, Pennsylvania, legislation was passed lengthening the school year and increasing the age of compulsory schooling to fifteen—a prelude to the issues that would fuel the confrontation in *Wisconsin v. Yoder*. This law produced a flurry of opposition from the Amish, who insisted that the changes would "lead our children away from the faith." The following year, writing to the Pennsylvania attorney general, Amishman Stephen Stolzfus demanded to know, "Why can't the Board of Public Instruction show us leniency and exempt our children when they have a fair education for farm and domestic work? If we educate them for businessmen, doctors and lawyers they will

[7]Kraybill, *Riddle of Amish Culture*, p. 140.

make no farmers."[8] So strongly do the otherwise placid Amish feel on this issue that some have been prepared to go to prison rather than accede to the law's requirements. Other tactics that have been used to keep children out of public high schools include having them repeat eighth grade or holding them back from first grade so that by the time they reach high school the compulsory age requirement is moot.[9]

The 1937–38 conflict abated after the Amish received a partial exemption from the statutes in question, enabling most children to avoid compulsory high school education. The Amish also began creating, and staffing, their own schools in response to the controversy. Although these schools do not meet the criteria for state certification, state officials have tended to be skittish about withholding it. Perhaps taking the path of least resistance, they have adopted a stance of "benign neglect" toward the Amish schools.[10] The unavoidable collision that came about in Wisconsin was the result of the state's decision to enforce legislation requiring compulsory education to age sixteen at a time when the public high school system was being regionalized and consolidated. Attending the public high schools would thus have made mingling in the non-Amish world and confronting secular ideas unavoidable for the Amish teenagers; as a result the Amish leadership opposed the compulsory school requirement. This resulted in the *Yoder* litigation, which found its way to the Supreme Court in its 1971–72 term.

Logic of the Yoder Decision

The opinion of the Court in *Yoder* held that the interests served by Wisconsin's compulsory education law—preparing citizens for effective and self-reliant adult life and social participation—were sufficiently served by the proposed course of action of the Old Order Amish parents. The Amish wished to withdraw their children from the public schools and train them informally in the community (though not in private community schools) for rural life in accordance with Amish religious precepts. These include eschewal of participation in the wider political and legal order, rejection of modern technology and consumer society, and affirmation of a traditional and ascetic way of life that revolves around primitive but effective farming. The Court stressed that it was dealing not "with a way of life and mode of education by a group claiming to have recently discovered some 'progressive' or more enlightened process for rearing children for modern life." In his opinion

[8]Quoted in ibid., p. 123.
[9]Ibid., p. 127.
[10]Ibid., p. 137.

for the Court, Chief Justice Burger attributed great importance to the fact that the Amish parents were sincere, that they were acting on the basis of a long-established and deep religious conviction, "shared by an organized group and intimately related to daily living."[11]

The Amish parents had contended that the compulsory education statute threatened not only the free exercise of Amish religion but the very existence of the Amish community. The basis of this claim was their experience that it was after eighth grade that Amish children in the public schools were most likely to develop, and act on, the desire to leave their community. The Court regarded this contention as decisive, "that enforcement of the State's requirement of compulsory formal education after the eighth grade would gravely endanger if not destroy the free exercise of respondents' [the parents'] religious beliefs." The Amish parents indicated that they would not seek to remove their children from the public schools before the eighth grade, and some of the justices made it clear that they would find differently were that issue presented. But the Court accepted as legitimate the Amish conception of education as "preparation . . . for life in the separated agrarian community that is the keystone of the Amish faith," concluding that compulsory education of Amish children beyond the eighth grade was unnecessary and that as a result the Amish parents were henceforth immune from criminal prosecution for violating the relevant parts of the state of Wisconsin's compulsory education law.[12]

Considerations from Democratic Theory

At first sight the *Yoder* decision might seem attractive from a civil society–centered democratic perspective; the decision was expressly crafted to preserve a viable community that is part of America's pluralistic political heritage. A commonplace of democratic theory since Tocqueville at least has been that in the modern world a well-functioning democratic political order requires a rich array of civil institutions that operate with relative autonomy from the state and to some extent in competition with it as a source of values in the culture. True, the Amish community is scarcely itself a paradigm of democracy, but democratic theorists of the relations between civil society and the state have often placed greater weight on the functional importance for democracy of a rich diversity of overlapping civil institutions than on the internal character of those institutions. Tocqueville went so far as to suggest that in a democracy, where political equality is the

[11]406 US 214, 216.
[12]Ibid., p. 216.

norm, hierarchical civil institutions might offer certain advantages for the authoritative allocation of values. Among contemporary theorists Michael Walzer insists that although a democratic civil society "is one controlled by its members," this condition does not require that institutions of civil society themselves be internally democratic. According to Walzer, that civil associations have the capacity to act as shields limiting the domination of state power is intrinsically beneficial to democracy.[13]

This pluralist-functional case for the importance of diverse civil institutions in a democracy has a venerable history that dates from the group theorists early in the twentieth century and runs through the discussion of the importance of crosscutting social cleavages by Louis Hartz and the pluralist arguments of the 1950s and 1960s.[14] Leaving to one side the much-debated question of how accurately the pluralists portrayed the distinctive features of American politics,[15] their distinction between single- and multiply-cleavaged societies has become one of the conceptual building blocks of pluralist democratic theory. The more a society approaches the multiply-cleavaged model, the less likely destabilizing revolutionary change becomes, according to the theory. If I am opposed to you on one issue, but I also know that I may be allied with you against another coalition of forces on some future issue, I have an incentive to moderate my opposition to you and search for common ground. Generalizing this reasoning, the pluralists held that a social landscape made up of crosscutting cleavages reinforces social stability in a democracy.[16]

The pluralist-functional standpoint might be thought to support broad tolerance of Amish practices, on the ground that flourishing civil society associations promote the stability of democratic institutions. Indeed there is special reason to let alone the withdrawing Amish, who do not aim to lasso state institutions in order to achieve their goals. They have interests in common with other groups who favor a heavily decentralized educational system (though they differ with them on other

[13]Tocqueville makes this claim most explicitly while discussing the relative merits of Catholicism over Protestantism in democratic systems; see Alexis de Tocqueville, *Democracy in America* (New York: Doubleday, Anchor, 1969), pp. 449, 450–51. Michael Walzer, "The Idea of Civil Society," *Dissent* (spring 1991), pp. 302–3. More generally, see Walzer, *Spheres of Justice.*

[14]See A. F. Bentley, *The Process of Government* (Chicago: University of Chicago Press, 1908); D. B. Truman, *The Governmental Process* (New York: Knopf, 1951); Louis Hartz, *The Liberal Tradition in America: An Interpretation of American Political Thought since the Revolution* (New York: Harcourt, Brace, 1955), and Robert A. Dahl, *Who Governs?* (New Haven: Yale University Press, 1961).

[15]For discussion, see Chapter 4, pp. 100–103.

[16]For a good account of the history of the functional argument and an elaboration of its logic, see Nicholas R. Miller, "Pluralism and Social Choice," *American Political Science Review* 77, no. 3 (1983), pp. 734–47.

issues); there is no danger of their pushing the nation further in the direction of a single-cleavaged society.

Even if a rich diversity of civil associations promotes democratic stability, this good hardly generates reasons for tolerating any particular questionable practice of an association. At issue here, after all, is not the mere existence of the Amish (to which we make no objection), but their child-rearing practices. It will become plain later that democratic theory reasonably requires more of civil institutions than that they not be run in such a way as to be threatening to the survival of democracy in the pluralist-functional sense.

The functional arguments aside, the *Yoder* decision can seem intrinsically attractive to democrats; it respects the autonomy of a small, self-governing group that is a source of meaning and value for its members. Culturally and economically the Amish are self-sufficient, and their mode of social organization has been revealed to be viable by centuries of testing. As Kraybill says, "Without consultants or strategic planners, the Amish, in simple and down-to-earth ways, have devised a social system that not only merits the attention of tourists and scholars but also raises profound questions about the underpinnings of happiness, freedom, and meaning. Moreover . . . despite the best efforts of the most learned planners and strategists, our modern world is strewn with fragmentation, and despair."[17]

Given the many defects of the world we live in, the Amish might reasonably be thought to exemplify the kind of face-to-face community that participatory democrats in the Rousseauist tradition (at least) would prize as something to be fostered and nurtured, rather than obliterated before the steamroller of abstract democratic principles. It is scarcely surprising, therefore, that many democratically minded communitarians took heart at the decision and have defended it vigorously.[18] Yet our claim is that these various reasons for supporting the outcome in *Yoder* are not persuasive.

II. DEMOCRATIC CITIZENSHIP

In support of its compulsory education requirements, the state of Wisconsin advanced two arguments. One is that "some degree of education is necessary to prepare citizens to participate effectively and intelligently in our open political system."[19] The second argument as-

[17]Kraybill, *Riddle of Amish Culture*, p. 259.
[18]See, e.g., Michael Sandel, "Freedom of Conscience or Freedom of Choice?" in *Articles of Faith, Articles of Peace*, ed. James Hunter and Os Guinness (Washington, D.C.: Brookings, 1990), pp. 90–91.
[19]406 US 205, 221.

serts that education is needed to prepare individuals for independent adult existence in modern society. In this section we consider the first argument.

The Supreme Court majority opinion by Chief Justice Burger accepted that the state has a compelling interest in bringing it about that children are educated in a way that prepares them for the responsibilities of democratic citizenship. Burger held that this interest could be met without keeping Amish children in school beyond age fourteen. The conception of democratic citizenship that figures in the Court's reasoning is, however, sketchy and impoverished. A more adequate understanding of the prerogatives of democratic citizenship compels the conclusion that compulsory high school attendance is a reasonable state requirement for the purpose of preparing youth for the role of citizens.

Burger's argument on this point consists of several independent assertions. He states that the fact that the Amish community has survived for more than two hundred years with little change in its way of life shows that Amish socialization practices must be instilling solid citizen virtues in their youth. Quoting from a letter of Thomas Jefferson, Burger observes that this founding father, who championed education as a shield against tyranny, apparently thought that an education providing basic literacy was adequate for this purpose. In this same vein Burger adds that an eighth-grade education fully satisfies the educational requirements of six states and that some other states have flexible requirements that partially excuse older children who have completed eighth grade from school attendance requirements so that they may take paid employment. Burger asserts approvingly that the Amish community members "are productive and very law-abiding members of society; they reject public welfare in any of its usual modern forms."[20] Finally, Burger offers the conjecture that part of the initial motivation for compulsory education laws was to prevent unhealthy child labor.[21] Given that the wholesome farm labor imposed on their children by Amish parents is not the sort of unhealthy labor that progressive legislation was designed to prevent, granting the Amish an exemption to the compulsory education law would not subvert this aspect of the state's legitimate concern, according to Burger.

This discussion is noteworthy for its lack of any specification of the responsibilities of democratic citizenship. Burger's implicit theory of citizenship would seem to be that a good citizen is law abiding, stays

---

[20]Ibid., at 222.

[21]According to Kraybill the original motivation was in fact to diminish unemployment in the aftermath of the depression by removing adolescents from the labor market; *Riddle of Amish Culture*, p. 122.

out of trouble, and stays off the welfare rolls. In contrast, we suppose that a significant aspect of citizenship includes the requirement that people have the capacity to vote in an informed way in elections that determine the membership of legislative assemblies, hence the content of the laws, as well as the identity of public officials and judges who execute and apply the laws. To be able to participate competently in democratic decision making, voters should have an adequate knowledge of contemporary science in its bearing on public policy issues, an understanding of modern world history and particularly the history of democratic institutions and the culture of their own society, and critical thinking skills that include the ability to represent the situation of others in imagination, to intuit their experience, and sympathetically to analyze and assess their attitudes, principles, and policy arguments.[22] Citizens should have the capacities to keep themselves briefed on current events relevant to governmental decisions to be made. In a diverse democracy composed of disparate creeds, faiths, races, world views, and concerns, arriving at fair and reasonable decisions about public policy is a task of delicate and complex judgment.[23]

Without entering into an extended consideration of what sort of education best prepares children for the responsibilities of democratic citizenship so conceived, we submit that education beyond basic literacy is needed to increase to an adequate level the likelihood that an individual will have the skills needed for democratic deliberation and the disposition to exercise these skills on appropriate occasions. In this regard although a high school education is not a panacea, it does provide some skills and knowledge needed to be a competent democratic deliberator. One might add that the experience of attending a typical contemporary high school—public or parochial—introduces the youth to people from different backgrounds, of different creeds, beliefs, ethnicity, and social class than her own. The experience of informal negotiating with one's classmates and adjustment to differences among them is itself a helpful preparation for the responsibilities of democratic citizenship.

Citizens in a democracy have rights to vote and to influence the

[22]On the educational attainments necessary for intelligent and responsible exercise of the franchise, see John Stuart Mill, *Considerations on Representative Government*, in *Collected Works*, vol. 19, ed. J. M. Robson (Toronto: University of Toronto Press, 1977), pp. 470–471.

[23]On the nature of deliberative democracy, see Joshua Cohen, "Deliberation and Democratic Legitimacy," in *The Good Polity*, ed. Alan Hamlin and Philip Pettit (Oxford: Blackwell, 1989); and Jon Elster, "The Market and the Forum," in *Foundations of Social Choice Theory*, ed. Jon Elster and Aanund Hylland (Cambridge: Cambridge University Press, 1986), pp. 103–32; also Jürgen Habermas, *Communication and the Evolution of Society*, trans. Thomas McCarthy (Boston: Beacon, 1979).

opinions of others through practices of free expression and the democratic process. These rights give each citizen a small amount of political power over other citizens; their collective actions produce effects that others have to endure.[24] With power comes the responsibility to use it in ways that do not wrongfully harm those who are affected by one's exercise of it. In a democracy the responsibilities of guardians of children include the duty to educate youth so that they become competent to exercise the powers of citizenship in ways that do not wrongfully threaten to impose harm on others. If parents and guardians fail to discharge this duty, the state has the obligation to intervene to ensure that the obligation is met.

The objection might be raised that the discussion of citizenship and education to this point has set an unrealistically idealistic norm both for citizenship and for the education that is to prepare individuals for citizenship. Actual majority-rule decision procedures are far from functioning as an ideal deliberative democracy. At best, ignorant voters, beset by venal and ambitious politicians and by agents of the special interests who stand to profit from manipulation of the lawmaking process, cast ballots that are honestly counted and that determine who rules. High schools in the United States today too often provide unsafe and hostile environments that reinforce the tribal anxieties and prejudices of school-aged youth and impede their intellectual development. The Amish refusal to involve their children in this process cannot be plausibly presented as a failure of citizenship responsibilities.

No doubt democratic institutions and educational practices could benefit from improvement. What aspect of contemporary society could not? But the failure of citizens generally to fulfill the responsibilities of citizenship and to provide education adequate for preparing youth for future citizenship does not justify a decision by society to cease upholding and enforcing these norms. Similarly, the unfortunate fact that some parents physically abuse their children would not excuse the state's renouncing its attempts to enforce norms against child abuse. The correct inference from the observation that there is a gap between the obligatory norms we profess and the degree to which we fulfill these

[24]Interestingly, in this connection the Supreme Court did not encounter any difficulty in 1990 in setting aside a Minnesota Supreme Court decision that exempted an Amish group from complying with a highway safety law. At issue was the refusal of the Amish to obey a state law requiring reflecting triangles on the rear of slow-moving vehicles on the grounds that compliance would mean they trusted man rather than God. Following its own precedent in *Employment Division v. Smith*, 494 US 872 (1989) (which held that religious groups could not be exempted from criminal laws against drugs on the grounds that these laws violated their religious beliefs), the Court denied the Amish request for an exemption. *Minnesota v. Hershberger*, 495 US 901 (1990).

norms is that we should narrow the gap by doing more to fulfill the norms.

Suppose it is said that if the Amish, a withdrawing sect, do not exercise voting rights, they are not obligated to educate their children into voting competence, since it is reasonably anticipated that the children will also abjure the exercise of voting rights. After all, no American citizen is under any legal obligation to vote. So far as the law is concerned, voting is optional. If the Amish do not take up this option, they have no further obligation with respect to it, and they surely need not train their children for responsibilities they will never face.

Although we would not go so far as to argue that people necessarily have an obligation to vote in a democracy, there surely is a defensible obligation to vote in any tolerably functioning democracy. Voting by many is necessary if the system is to function properly, and there is no obvious, fair way to select a subset of voters to whom the obligation does not apply. No doubt there are circumstances in which refraining from voting is permissible and even obligatory. For example, it may well be the case, for all that we say in this chapter, that the Amish practice of withdrawal from society is justified. But informed judgment about these matters can only be made by people who understand how democratic systems work and what the issues at stake in democratic elections are. One needs to be educated for competent citizenship in order to determine whether it is permissible or obligatory to abstain from exercising this or that function of citizenship.

Even if it is granted that the state has a strong, legitimate interest in compelling high school attendance in order to foster intelligent and conscientious citizenship, a judgment call is required when this interest conflicts with rights to the free exercise of religion. In our judgment, even if the state's paternalistic concern for the welfare of Amish children were to be entirely set aside, the imperative of educating future citizens into habits of intelligent and well-informed tolerance suffices by itself to justify compulsory school attendance laws like the one challenged by the Amish in this case. The duty to educate for democratic citizenship trumps any religious-exercise claims that might oppose it. But to vindicate this claim, we must clarify the nature of the parental rights and free-exercise claims at stake in *Yoder*.

III. PARENTAL RIGHTS OVER CHILDREN

In the *Yoder* case, the Court held that the Wisconsin compulsory school attendance law placed a substantial burden on the free exercise by the Old Order Amish of their religion. Having stipulated that the law burdens free exercise, the Court took the view that an exemption from the law must be granted to the Amish (or the law must be struck down), unless the state could show a compelling interest that would have to go unmet if such an exemption were granted. The free-exercise interests in question were the interests of the Amish parents in practicing their religion in their traditional way. But the state's expressed interest concerned the education of Amish children. On the face of it, there was a gap between the rights claimed by the parents, having to do with their practice of religion, and the claims of the state, having to do with *the children's* education. How do the Amish parents' rights of religious freedom extend to encompass rights to set limits to the education of the Amish children?

The obvious answer is that rights of religious freedom are understood to include the right to raise one's children in one's own faith. But it is not obvious what the source of these extended parental rights is, nor what their proper limits should be.

One useful canonical text on parental rights and obligations is John Locke's *Two Treatises of Government*. Locke there writes, referring to the natural equality of persons, "*Children,* I confess are not born in this full state of *Equality,* though they are born to it. Their Parents have a sort of Rule and Jurisdiction over them when they come into the World, and for some time after, but 'tis but a temporary one . . . The *Power,* then, *that Parents have* over their Children, arises from that Duty which is incumbent on them, to take care of their Off-spring, during the imperfect state of Childhood."[25]

On Locke's view, biological parents have fiduciary obligations to care for their children. Because children are incapable of controlling their own conduct by their reason in a steady way that adequately caters to their prudential long-term interests and the interests of others affected by their conduct, parental obligations include the duty to govern their children. These obligations are oriented to the interests of children and of humanity at large, and the concomitant rights that devolve on parents so that they may fulfill their obligations are rights to act for the good of their children (subject to moral constraints), not rights to use their children as they might wish for the parents' own benefit. Children are not in any respect the property of their parents.

My obligation to raise my children for their present and future welfare is in practice tantamount to an obligation to raise my children for

---

[25]John Locke, *Second Treatise of Government,* ed. Peter Laslett (Cambridge: Cambridge University Press, 1960), p. 346, sec. 55, and p. 348, sec. 58.

their present and future welfare as conceived by me. Similarly, my obligation to train my children to respect the rights of others and to give priority to justice and fair play translates into an obligation to train my children into proper morality as I conceive it.[26] In this way the same paternalistic duty falling on each parent leads each to a different child-rearing policy. Following your lights, you teach your child sound business practices and the lore of your tribe, and following my lights, I teach my child the religion I profess.

Locke may perhaps make too much of biological parenthood, but the rest of the story he tells remains credible. Society assigns major responsibility to particular persons to be primary guardians of particular children; in our society, biological parenthood is one way, perhaps a generally acceptable way, to assign these particular bundles of rights and responsibilities conventionally identified with parenthood. Having made an initial assignment, society does better to leave well enough alone for the most part, trusting parents whose competence and motivation have not been impugned by gross and readily verifiable tests to carry out their parental obligations as they see fit.

Society intervenes in the discharge of parental obligations in two main ways. Parents found to be unfit are separated from their children by state authority. In areas such as health, hygiene, and education, the state may set standards to be met, generally leaving wide discretion to parents as to what means to choose to meet these standards.

A complication in this picture is that being a parent looms large in the life plans of many adults who are parents. As the discharge of parental obligations allows wide scope for parental discretion, choosing and pursuing a child-rearing regimen is for many parents an important mode of self-expression and personal creativity. And because the discharge of parental obligations is sometimes fun, and over the long run deeply satisfying, for many, and for everyone strongly endorsed by powerfully entrenched cultural norms, being able to see oneself as a good parent is often a source of deep satisfaction. Even those who find parenting continuously and aggravatingly frustrating try hard to discover in their experience, or in some dimly imagined transformation of it, what they believe to be the normal pattern of harmony and mutual satisfaction. Moreover, the wide discretionary authority enjoyed by par-

---

[26]Within limits, that is. Because I know that among the set of moral beliefs I now hold to be true, some are doubtless misguided, I have an obligation to teach my child methods of reasoning and inquiry that give her a fair chance of adopting a better morality than my own. The same applies to my conception of what is prudent, which I am entitled to pass on to my child, but with a similar qualification hedging against the likelihood that my conception of prudence is in some respects in error.

ents allows them to satisfy their own desires and whims in their child rearing, sometimes in the course of fulfilling their obligations to their children, sometimes in the course of masquerading at fulfilling these obligations. If I fancy putting my child in the Little League, or in the church choir, I generally may do so. Finally, and pertinently to the Amish litigation, parents may find their own fulfillment bound up with having the freedom to raise their children in ways they deem obligatory. As the Amish parents noted, they believe that their own prospects of salvation are tied to their raising their own children properly, which means assuring their salvation, which in turn means raising them so that they in due course become loyal and conforming members of traditional Amish society.

For all these reasons, parents may feel that their own personal freedom and their rights to pursue their own happiness in their own way require that society grant them wide discretionary authority to raise their children as they see fit. So the interests and freedom of Amish parents, as well as the interests and liberties of Amish children, are at stake in *Yoder*.

IV. Free Exercise of Religion

The education of children (as opposed to adult education) by its nature involves an authoritative overriding of the judgment of the recipients of the schooling: educators seek to impart beliefs, values, attitudes, and capacities to those in their care. Indeed part of the mission of the educator of children is to shape their aspirations and desires. We have no quarrel with the conventional understanding that parents have the right to play a major role in shaping the education of their children. Nor do we quarrel with the common opinion that the religious freedom rights of parents include the right to introduce their children to their own religion and to raise their children as practicing adherents of the parents' sect. But we do argue that parents' rights to the free exercise of religion give out at the point where their preferred manner of exercise comes into conflict with the basic interests, including the basic educational interests, of their children. Inasmuch as parents and guardians do not stand in anything like an ownership relation to their immature charges, the assertion of "parents' rights" to withdraw their children from school in the circumstances of *Yoder* would have to be shown to be compatible with their overriding fiduciary obligations to their children.

What if the free-exercise interests of Amish parents and the interests of Amish children are in tension with one another? If there were a conflict between the free-exercise interests of the parents and some other legitimate interests of the children which parents had an obligation to preserve (such as an interest in receiving an adequate supply of food), then, according to the fiduciary model sketched above, the parents would have an obligation to limit their own free-exercise rights. If one's own interests prevent one from carrying out one's obligations as a trustee, one must give up one's fiduciary authority to someone else who is duly authorized to take it on.

It might be argued that this reasoning simplifies things misleadingly, because part of what is at issue is the free-exercise rights of the children. In a dissenting opinion Justice William Douglas objects that the opinions of the fourteen-year-old Amish children were not solicited by the trial court, the implication being that these opinions are relevant to the proper outcome. Here we should distinguish two questions: Do children themselves have free-exercise rights that courts should respect in cases like *Yoder,* and Should courts take children's views into account when adjudicating such cases? The two are very different. In custody disputes, for example, courts will generally appoint a social worker to interview the children as to their preferences and make a recommendation, and in some states the court is required to appoint an attorney to represent their interests in litigation over custody. Sometimes the judge will interview the children in chambers to elicit their preferences. But none of these devices is based on the idea that the minor children are free to choose a custodial parent.[27] Their preferences are but one factor taken into account, and depending on their age their preferences are given more or less weight. In practice this weighting is a rough and ready calculation, no doubt infected with the judge's own values to some degree; but conceptually it is quite different from the notion that the preferences of less than fully competent adult persons should be dispositive because they *are* their preferences. After all, if children were fully competent adults they would not need fiduciaries in the first place. Because free religious exercise (as opposed to mindless cultish behavior) can only be entered into by an act of autonomous willing,

[27]It is perhaps worth noting that even in the much-discussed Gregory Kingsley case in September 1992, in which a Florida court terminated a twelve-year-old's parents' parental rights at his request, this was not a case of a child "divorcing" his parents, as reported in the press; see *New York Times,* September 26, 1992, pp. 1, 5. The court found that the boy's natural mother had so completely neglected him for so long that her maternal rights should be terminated in favor of the foster parents with whom he had been living for a year. It was novel that the child was the named plaintiff in the suit, a tactical move on the part of the (lawyer) foster father, who wanted to avoid having the child taken out of his home while the litigation was pending. But it was not a case of child-parent "divorce" in that the court would not have allowed the boy to become parentless on his own motion or, indeed, to choose new parents other than the foster parents.

someone (like a child) who by definition is in need of fiduciary supervision in religious matters, cannot engage in free religious exercise. Thus although Justice Douglas may have been right that the children should have been interviewed, he would have been wrong to have held that their preferences in the matter should have been dispositive. The question has to be, taking everything into account, did the parents abuse their fiduciary authority by removing the children from school?

Conventional opinion in the United States and other countries holds that it is part of a parent's authority qua parent that he or she speaks for the child in religious matters. But why? Because we regard the child as too immature to speak for herself. That is reasonable from the standpoint of the fiduciary model, so long as it is subject to the proviso that the parent cannot pretend to speak for the child while really regarding the child as a mere empty vessel for the parents' own religious convictions. As a fiduciary, the parent is bound to preserve the child's own future religious freedom. Few people would deny this outright. After all, most religious people (including, presumably, the Amish) distinguish between religions and cults, and they would, presumably, see it as part of their responsibility not to let their children become prey to cults. But what is the distinction if it does not turn on preserving some freedom of will, some freedom to reject? This is a fine line, of course. Often religious people think their children should have free choice so long as they make "the right" choice in the end; this appears to be the Amish view of the matter, as we have seen. In reality such people do not believe in free religious choice.

Now the parents in *Yoder* did not invoke a fiduciary obligation to their children in support of their actions. Instead they appealed to a mixture of the right of the Amish community to reproduce itself and free-exercise rights of the parents. The first of these rests on an exceedingly powerful claim for group rights, for which it is difficult to see a coherent justification. Groups and classes are groups and classes of individuals, and talk of the "right" of the Amish community to reproduce itself glosses over the reality that group members may have conflicting rights and interests. If it is in the interest of Amish children to receive an adequate education, and their receiving it will threaten the existence of the group (assuming for now that this is true), then a conflict of this kind is evidently present. Our claim is that in such an eventuality there is no defensible reason to sacrifice the interests of the children in their education to their parents' desire to reproduce the Amish community in the name of group rights.

Our argument for resisting the notion that there is a right of the

Amish community qua community that has to be weighed against other relevant interests should not be misinterpreted. In particular it does not amount to an affirmative claim that the Amish community has no right to exist, that it should be stamped out by the state. Any such claim would run headlong into freedom of association arguments that constitutional democrats would be bound to endorse. But it is a far cry from saying that adults have the right to associate as an Amish community to saying that adults have a right to violate the rights of children to an adequate education, or to violate the legitimate interests of third parties in the education of children, *in order that they may* associate freely as an Amish community. If rights violations of either sort really are necessary conditions, then the claims of the Amish adults must give way. This is not because the Amish ought to be stamped out but because there is no reason that children and third parties should have to endure rights violations so that the Amish may freely associate.[28]

This brings us to the parents' own free-exercise rights. In *Wisconsin v. Yoder* the Court held that the Wisconsin compulsory schooling law, though not discriminatory on its face, in its application to the Amish parents qualified as a burden on the free exercise of their religion. That is, the law significantly hindered a practice central to their religious way of life. So far, we agree. In such a circumstance, according to the Court's interpretation of the free-exercise clause, the Constitution requires a decision in favor of the Amish which relieves this burden by exempting them from the law. This is so unless the state could show that granting such relief would thwart a compelling state interest, an interest "of the highest order," an interest "of sufficient magnitude" to override the free-exercise interest.[29] Balancing the interests at stake, the Court ruled that the fundamental interest in free exercise should trump the state's interest in universal education. We see no convincing basis for the Court's weighing of the interests at stake.[30]

[28]Given the high rate at which the Amish population is growing (between 30 and 48 percent per decade since 1890 at least, and well in excess of the population at large), these claims about the threat of extinction seem exaggerated. Figures taken from Hoestetler, *Amish Society,* p. 99.

[29]That, at least, was the constitutional requirement as viewed by the justices who agreed with the verdict in *Yoder.* Since *Employment Division, Department of Human Resources of the State of Oregon v. Smith,* 485 US 660 (1988) and 110 US 1595 (1990), the free-exercise constitutional requirement in relation to actions of government that neither are discriminatory on their face nor manifest an intent to discriminate has changed.

[30]One point should be mentioned here although its elaboration would take us too far afield. In deciding whether an exemption from state law could be carved out to satisfy a religious interest without unduly frustrating a substantial and legitimate state aim, the extent to which the exemption that is proposed would thwart a countervailing state interest depends in part on how broad the exemption must be. In this connection note that Justice Warren Burger attempted

In section III above we urged that the Court understand the importance of the state's interest in ensuring that each child is adequately educated for the responsibilities of democratic citizenship. In section V we argue that the Burger Court opinion underestimates the moral imperative of education for autonomy. Here, we have insisted that the Amish parents' interest in free exercise should give way when that interest comes in conflict with their fiduciary obligations to provide education for their children. But even if everything at stake in this case except free-exercise of religion rights were ignored, the Amish parents' free exercise interest in withdrawing their children from school would be countered by each Amish child's nonwaivable interest in religious freedom (the freedom as an adult to choose one's own faith), which is served by education for autonomy. If the parents' free-exercise rights genuinely do clash with the children's rights as defined by the relevant legitimate statute, then the parents must either internalize their own loss of religious freedom or, in the limiting case, decline to be parents. If their religion told them to sacrifice their children on an altar we would think nothing of terminating their parental rights (even knowing that God might, after all, be on their side). When Christian Scientists go to court to try to get permission to withhold vital medical care from their children on religious grounds, they appropriately lose, and that does not trouble our intuitions either (again God might be on their side in fact). *Yoder* presents the same kind of issue.

This understanding of parents' fiduciary obligations implies a strong role for the state as the ultimate arbiter of at least some of children's interests. But just how strong should that role be? An extreme version of the argument would require us to insist that no one has a right to be a parent. Rights of parenthood are positive rights conferred by the state. They are defined by a bundle of benefits (access to certain types of companionship, public esteem, tax breaks, etc.) and responsibilities (to nurture their charges, see that they are protected, able to develop into

---

to narrow the class of claims that could take shelter under the First Amendment religion clauses by what looks to be a tautology: "to have the protection of the Religion Clauses, the claims must be rooted in religious belief." But this seeming tautology is actually false. If one objected to compulsory schooling in a case that was just like the case of the Amish except that the choice against compulsory schooling for one's children was "philosophical and personal rather than religious," it would be utter favoritism toward religion, impermissible under a reasonable construal of the religion clauses, to allow the Amish claim for exemption because it is religious and to disallow the otherwise comparable secular claim just because it is secular in its grounding. See on this point the partially dissenting opinion in *Wisconsin v. Yoder* by Justice William Brennan. To specify when a claimed exemption for secular reasons is "otherwise comparable" to an exemption claimed for religious reasons is of course an intricate and difficult undertaking.

normal adults, etc.) and can always be rescinded. Although it is true that every state reserves the right to terminate parental rights under some conditions, most democrats would reasonably find this view unacceptably strong; it supplies too little in the way of participation by the relevant parties and too few limitations on state power.

A weaker and more plausible claim for state authority would be that although no one has an unconditional right to be a parent, people are generally presumed to have that right absent a showing to the contrary. One might start from the premises that the officials in a state (democratic or not) do not possess full knowledge of the best ways to raise children and that there are inherent economies of smallness to such knowledge. This is, for many, an attractive thought. Certainly a democratic theory of education should not commit its adherents to any single developmental or psychological theory of education.

On this view of the state's role we would say that the state can rule certain things out as clearly abusive of children or subversive of the state's interests in the production of a citizenry able to participate in its operations, but that beyond those instances it must defer to parents. This approach would issue in a "basic interests" rather than a "best interests" standard for evaluating parents' fulfillment of their fiduciary obligations. By this standard, whether or not the Amish parents lose depends simply on whether or not compulsory education up to age sixteen is a basic interest. The parents were explicit in saying that they wanted their children to miss the last two years of school both because the children had the relevant skills to survive in the Amish community and because experience had taught that it was at this age that children were most likely to develop and act on the desire to leave the community. The parents in *Yoder* thus did not begin to make the case that compulsory education to age sixteen is not a basic interest. Indeed, we argue in section VI that the parents' candid admission of motives supplies prima facie evidence that a basic interest of their children was being violated in removing them from school at age fourteen.

It is perhaps worth noting explicitly that a Supreme Court decision that required the Amish to educate their children to age sixteen would not require the Amish to submit their children to secular public high schools. The Amish would be as free as any other citizens to comply with state educational requirements by sending their children to private schools or to establish their own schools, rather than use the public ones.[31]

---

[31]In other words, a decision against the Amish in *Yoder* could consistently be reconciled with *Pierce v. Society of Sisters*, 268 US 510 (1925).

V. Autonomy: The Child's Right to an Open Future

Several commentators on *Wisconsin v. Yoder* and related issues in family law have found the key to the puzzle to be a strong value of individual autonomy which finds appropriate expression in "the child's right to an open future." On this view, the aim of education is to prepare children for lives of rational autonomy once they become adults. A "rationally autonomous" life is one that is self-chosen in a reasonable way. Education for rational autonomy thus encompasses two requirements: (1) upon onset of adulthood individuals should be enabled to choose from the widest possible variety of ways of life and conceptions of the good and (2) individuals should be trained into habits and skills of critical reflection, so that they attain to the greatest feasible extent the capacity to choose rationally among these alternative ways of life. We refer to these two aspects of education for autonomy as (1) the maximization of options and (2) the development of critical reason.

The conflict between the child's right to autonomy so conceived and the claims of the Old Order Amish parents is clear and direct; for the Amish straightforwardly believe that they should educate their children so that they embrace the traditional Amish way and that skills of critical reasoning would alienate their children from wholehearted identification with the right way to live and would therefore be corrupting.

Many commentators on children's rights are attracted to the ideal of individual autonomy. Amy Gutmann writes, "One can concede that any practical standard of education will eliminate some options that might otherwise be open to children when they mature, but so long as we must choose among paternalistic standards we are required to choose those that are most neutral among competing conceptions of the good, standards that expand rather than contract a child's future ability to exercise meaningful choice."[32] Criticizing the reasoning of Chief Justice Burger's opinion of the Court in *Yoder*, Joel Feinberg comments, "An impartial decision would assume only that education should equip the child with the knowledge and skills that will help him choose whichever sort of life best fits his native endowment and matured disposition. It should send him out into the adult world with as many open opportunities as possible, thus maximizing his chances for self-

---

[32]Amy Gutmann, "Children, Paternalism, and Education," *Philosophy and Public Affairs* 9, no. 4 (summer 1980), p. 350.

fulfillment."[33] Discussing the proper basis for child custody decisions in divorce litigation, Jon Elster describes what he asserts to be a "superior way" of conceiving the child's best interests: "Instead of being guided by the substantive preferences and choices that are imputed to the child, one could be led by the more formal goal of protecting the child's opportunity and ability to make choices. On this view, a child should be allowed, as far as possible, to reach maturity with a maximum of potentialities and the autonomy needed to choose which of them to develop. Once that point is reached, what he chooses to make of his life is up to him, but one should not knowingly preempt the choice."[34]

It might seem obvious that if one accepts that children have the right to autonomy as characterized by Gutmann, Feinberg, and Elster, then one should also accept the further claim that the state ought to uphold that right against parents who would deny it, so the state of Wisconsin should have prevailed against the Amish parents—hence *Yoder* was wrongly decided. This conflict between the *Yoder* decision and the child's right to autonomy has not seemed obvious to the commentators who have asserted the child's claim to autonomy. Feinberg views the issue as a balancing problem, with the child's interest in continued education on one side of the balance and the Amish parents' free-exercise interest on the other side. In this particular case, only two years of education were at issue, because school attendance under Wisconsin law was compulsory only to age sixteen and the Amish parents accepted the state law insofar as it prescribed school attendance through eighth grade (age fourteen). The specific balancing problem presented to the Court was delicate, according to Feinberg, and resolving it in favor of the Amish parents' right of free exercise might have been correct and certainly was not clearly mistaken.

Gutmann agrees with Feinberg that the amount of education at stake in *Yoder* was too small to force the conclusion that the child's right to education should trump the parent's right to free exercise. She also raises two further considerations that might support the decision actually reached by the Court. She suggests that the worse the education the state provides, assessed according to the standard of how well the state prepares students for successfully negotiating the wide range of valu-

---

[33]Joel Feinberg, "The Child's Right to an Open Future," in *Whose Child? Children's Rights, Parental Authority, and State Power*, ed. William Aiken and Hugh LaFollette (Totowa, N.J.: Littlefield, Adams, 1980), pp. 134–35.

[34]Jon Elster, "Solomonic Judgments: Against the Best Interests of the Child," in *Solomonic Judgments: Studies in the Limitations of Rationality* (Cambridge: Cambridge University Press, 1989), p. 137.

able ways of life feasible in modern society, the weaker the paternalistic rationale for state imposition of an educational regime on recalcitrant parents. Gutmann also flirts with the suggestion that children have a right to autonomy in the strong sense of a right "to be so educated as to be capable of choosing unprejudicially among all conceivable conceptions of the good."[35] She then observes that this right would not warrant state enforcement of education "beyond the basics" because we are substantially ignorant of how education might be set so that it does not instill some prejudices even as it removes others. She writes, "Every educational system now in existence closes children's minds to some potentially desirable conceptions of the good life and the good society." Yes, but this hardly means that all educational systems are on a par with respect to the cultivation of autonomy. If the strong sense of autonomy is so exalted that all feasible educational regimes would equally fail to achieve it, that shows not that autonomy is an irrelevant standard for judging educational regimes but that Gutmann's strong conception of autonomy is not the relevant conception.[36]

In the course of growing up, children acquire values and preferences—a conception of the good. These values and preferences of course do not spring spontaneously from the child's mind but are the outcome of interaction between the child's innate dispositions and likings and socializing environmental forces. Being social, children have a disposition to adopt the standards that are salient among significant persons in their lives, such as playmates, close relatives, teachers, and other adult figures vested with authority. Even if it were somehow possible for an educational regime to abstain from inculcating values in the child, this would not be sensible; for the vacuum left by abstaining educators would be filled by other causal influences. One way or another, the child is going to be influenced by her social environment. So the idea of arriving at adulthood without having prejudged some matters of value is a chimera. At any rate, the phenomenon of choice of values by an individual, which we associate with attainment of autonomy, always presupposes a context in which some standards and values are at least provisionally fixed and guide choice. So being prejudiced or having one's mind made up on some valuation issues is necessary for autonomy, not an obstacle that precludes it.

[35]Gutmann, "Children, Paternalism, and Education," p. 351.

[36]Ibid., p. 352. In fairness it should be noted that Gutmann alters this way of conceiving autonomy in her book *Democratic Education* (Princeton: Princeton University Press, 1987); see pp. 33–47, where she criticizes theorists, such as Bruce Ackerman, who espouse the idea that children should be educated in a way that is so far as possible neutral among all conceptions of the good life.

But then having been inculcated with Amish values as a child is not per se a hindrance to the achievement of autonomy any more than having been inculcated with capitalist consumerist values or any other values. So we had better drop the supposed ideal of unprejudiced choice among all possible ways of life and conceptions of the good.

It is worth pointing out that the maximization of options aspect of the ideal is also vulnerable to powerful objections. The idea at issue here is that education should be arranged so that the child is allowed to reach maturity with a maximum of potentialities. In some simple choice problems this norm might seem to yield advice that is both determinate and plausible. Denial of high school education to a child so that he can be socialized into an ultratraditionalist religious farming community seems to open one option while foreclosing many others. The norm of maximizing options supports provision of high school education to every child who is capable of it.

But what exactly is meant by talk of "maximizing opportunities"? To begin with, it is far from clear how to individuate and count options or opportunities. One suspects that from different evaluative standpoints, options would reasonably be individuated in different ways and that there is no neutral counting of options. From the Amish standpoint, one might say there are two relevant options, turning away from the world toward the Amish community and turning toward the world away from the community. To grant the one option is to foreclose the other. The varieties of worldly options will not appear saliently different from the Amish standpoint, and anyway there are no doubt many various alternative ways of life within the Amish community, suboptions within the unworldly option. Perhaps the neutral-sounding judgment that the Amish rejection of secondary education fails to maximize children's options is just a neutral-sounding way of registering the judgment that the Amish way of life is not worthwhile by comparison to the way of life that secondary education prepares the child for.

Assume for the sake of the argument that the difficulty raised in the last paragraph has somehow been overcome and that the Supreme Court has available to it a neutral standard for counting options which discloses that denial of secondary education reduces the total number of life options available to the child. It still is far from clear that "maximization of options" is unproblematically a good that the state ought to require all parents to provide for their children. Consider that there are many attractive ways of life such as ballet performance and competitive athletics which require dedicated, single-minded concentration and commitment on the part of any individual who aspires to one of these forms of achievement. This commitment must be made at an early age and sustained through adolescence and young adulthood. Moreover, the tremendous concentration of energy and time required to have a chance at success at a field of highly competitive performance inevitably forecloses many other valuable life options. This is not a choice that can be reserved for the adult. Either a commitment is made before the child is fully in a position to appreciate the nature of this decision problem or the child loses any realistic possibility of success at any career goal that requires early commitment. To open this door even by a crack, one must simultaneously close many other doors.

No doubt the decision by parents as to whether to permit or encourage their child to make an early commitment to a career such as ballet is delicate and open to abuse. The point we wish to make in this connection is modest. Even if one countenances the idea that it is possible to count children's opportunities and options so that the idea of educating a child so as to maximize the number of options available at the onset of adulthood is coherent, "maximizing options" is at most one desideratum among many and could not plausibly be regarded as the sole or dominant standard for child-rearing policy. Sometimes the value of a single option is sufficiently high that providing that one valuable option for the child even at the cost of foreclosing many other less valued options is, on balance, desirable for the child.

But if concentration on athletic training oriented to Olympic competition can be good for a child even if it effectively rules out college attendance for one who is academically marginal but athletically gifted, then one cannot object to Amish withdrawal of children from school in order to provide a secure Amish way of life for the child simply on the ground that this policy fails to maximize the number of opportunities available to the child at maturity. The maximization of options aspect of the ideal of autonomy does not have much force in an argument against the Supreme Court's analyses in the *Yoder* decision. Like the unprejudiced choice argument, it has to be abandoned.

What marks education for autonomy is development of skills and habits of critical thinking. The autonomous person is not the person who bears allegiance only to spontaneously self-chosen values untainted by environmental influence. The autonomous person is, rather, one who is capable of standing back from her values and engaging in critical reflection about them and altering her values to align them with the results of that critical reflection. The difficulty with the Amish program of socialization is not that it instills prejudgments—for any educational program does that—but rather that it fails to train children in skills of critical thinking and to encourage them to place a positive value on engagement in critical thinking about one's fundamental values. The

Amish acculturation program is expressly designed to limit critical thinking, to get children to accept things on faith without submitting them to reasoned reflection. As Kraybill makes clear, Amish education is "an effort to manage consciousness, to set and control the agenda of ideas. Abstract and rational modes of thought are simply not entertained in the Amish school. The uniform world view propagated by Amish education funnels ideas in prescribed channels that undergird the ethnic social system."[37] The Amish reject critical reflection partly out of fear of its effects and partly because they are philosophically opposed to it. According to the Amish sages, the wisdom of the world "makes you restless, wanting to leap and jump and not knowing where you will land."[38]

But is failure to educate for autonomous critical thinking really objectionable? Interestingly, some political philosophers have advocated a reduced liberalism stripped of what they regard as sectarian commitments and thereby capable of becoming the object of a broad consensus that includes traditionalist religious advocates. William Galston writes that the "civic standpoint," which he endorses, "does not warrant the conclusion that the state must (or may) structure public education to foster in children skeptical reflection on ways of life inherited from parents or local communities."[39] In a similar spirit, John Rawls asserts that the doctrine of autonomy of Immanuel Kant and the doctrine of individuality of John Stuart Mill are accepted by few citizens of modern diverse democracies. According to Rawls, a political conception of liberalism suitable for a modern democratic society must eschew commitment to intractably controversial philosophic views such as those of either Kant or Mill. Otherwise liberalism becomes just another sectarian doctrine, a religious view no more suited than Marxism or Methodism or Buddhism for the role of consensus moral foundation for fundamental democratic practices. Rawls seems to allude to *Wisconsin v. Yoder* when he draws the line between a commitment to rational autonomy and fair play in the public sphere which is essential to democratic citizenship and a commitment to substantive conceptions of the good and partisan ties in private life which is said to be perfectly compatible with democratic citizenship.[40]

[37]Kraybill, *Riddle of Amish Culture*, p. 131.
[38]Quoted in ibid., p. 131.
[39]William A. Galston, *Liberal Purposes: Goods, Virtues, and Diversity in the Liberal State* (Cambridge: Cambridge University Press, 1991), p. 253.
[40]We assume that Rawls has *Yoder* in mind when he writes, "Justice as fairness honors, as far as it can, the claims of those who wish to withdraw from the modern world in accordance with the injunctions of their religion, provided only that they acknowledge the principles of the political conception of justice and appreciate its political ideals of person and society." He

The Galston-Rawls position is buttressed by noting that freedom of speech as commonly understood is the right of a willing speaker to engage any willing audience on matters of public concern. No law in a democratic society commands participation in free speech practices. The laws structuring freedom of expression impose on citizens only the duty to forbear from wrongful interference with the free speech activities of other citizens. Democratic tolerance including a proper respect for freedom of expression is then (by this view) fully compatible with a firm confidence in the correctness or acceptability of one's own present values and a total absence of inclination to subject one's own fundamental values to critical scrutiny. The "civic standpoint" that Galston extols includes support for the basic institutions of democracy and their underlying rationale. If the underlying rationale of the law of freedom of expression were a commitment to the ideal of rational autonomy, it would seem more appropriate that the law should compel, not merely permit, participation in some free speech activities that would help to stimulate appropriate critical reflection. The ideal of rational autonomy is a species of perfectionism, an ideal of character that might support paternalistic restriction of the liberties of adults who would fail even to try to conform their characters to the ideal in the absence of such restriction. That the law of freedom of expression is permissive rather than compulsive suggests that its underlying rationale is civic tolerance not rational autonomy.

The Galston-Rawls position seeks to detach practices of democratic toleration from the development-of-critical-reason aspect of the ideal of autonomy. Though their arguments differ somewhat, they share a concern that the appeal to a philosophic ideal of autonomy to defend freedom of expression and to determine the limits of religious liberties is sectarian. Many, perhaps most citizens of modern democracies are committed to substantive conceptions of the good and particular ways of life and would not value the freedom to subject their fundamental ends to skeptical scrutiny. Hence one cannot resolve the conflict between Amish parents and Wisconsin public officials by stipulating that both parties to the dispute accept an ideal of rational autonomous choice of ends and subjection of current ends to critical scrutiny which in effect just presupposes that the public officials are correct and the Amish have no case. This ideal of autonomy is contested in contempo-

---

proceeds to a brief discussion of the education of children from this standpoint. See John Rawls, "The Priority of Right and Ideas of the Good," *Philosophy and Public Affairs* 17, no. 4 (fall 1988), pp. 251–76; see p. 268. See also John Rawls, "Justice as Fairness: Political Not Metaphysical," *Philosophy and Public Affairs* 14, no. 3 (1985), pp. 223–51; and "The Domain of the Political and Overlapping Consensus," *New York University Law Review* 64, no. 2 (May 1989), pp. 233–55.

rary society; to argue as though it were uncontroversial is to evade, not settle, the dispute.

But, three lines of argument do converge in support of the proposition that society, through the agency of the state, should ensure that children develop the deliberative capacities required for autonomy: the parallel with autonomous citizenship, the pressure of freedom of expression, and the instrumental case for autonomy.

The Parallel with Autonomous Citizenship

Members of a democratic society are obligated to fulfill the responsibilities of democratic citizenship, which centrally involve the assessment of public policy proposals. To assess policy proposals as a citizen one must be able to exercise critical reason by imagining what can be said for and against candidate policies from the different points of view represented in the electorate.

The claim that one ought to exercise critical reason in evaluating policies and candidates is in conflict with the claim that one is entitled to eschew critical reason altogether in forming and affirming a view of one's own individual good. A plausible surmise is that any view that justifies the claim that future citizens should be trained for the autonomous exercise of critical reason in the democratic deliberations that ought to determine the content of public policy will also justify the claim that citizens should be trained for the autonomous exercise of critical reason in their personal choices of fundamental ends. And any view that denies that citizens should be autonomous in their personal choices of fundamental ends will also deny that citizens should autonomously make up their own minds on issues of collective political choice. Hence the advocate of the Galston-Rawls position will have to deny that citizens are obligated to develop and exercise their critical reason in making up their minds on public policy issues, and this implication may be difficult to swallow.

The Pressure of Freedom of Expression

A second strand of argument supporting state-mandated provision for autonomy is that in a democratic society that honors freedom of expression, state policy toward the education of children ought to be consistent with the underlying principles that support freedom of expression. Any such policy must be designed to foster autonomy. "Freedom of expression" refers to the right of a willing speaker to address a willing audience on matters of public concern.

In a 1940 First Amendment case, *Cantwell v. Connecticut,* the Supreme Court states a rationale for broad legal protection for freedom of expression:

> In the realm of religious faith, and in that of political belief, sharp differences arise. In both fields the tenets of one man may seem the rankest error to his neighbor. To persuade others to his own point of view, the pleader, we know, at times, resorts to exaggeration, to vilification of men who have been, or are, prominent in church or state, and even to false statement. But the people of this nation have ordained in the light of history, that, in spite of the probability of excesses and abuses, these liberties are, in the long view, essential to enlightened opinion and right conduct on the part of the citizens of a democracy. . .
>
> The essential characteristic of these liberties is that, under their shield many types of life, character, opinion, and belief can develop unmolested and unobstructed. Nowhere is this shield more necessary than in our own country for a people composed of many races and of many creeds.[41]

From one angle the Court's position looks puzzling. If speakers are likely to give offense and to upset the cherished views of their audiences, perhaps proselytization across sects and argument across communal groups should be restricted or forbidden in a diverse society "composed of many races and of many creeds" so that each group can follow its own preferred way unmolested by distressing speech. Yet the Court describes free speech as a shield that protects disparate ways of life. What the Court evidently has in mind is that when free speech is protected, individuals will have access to a broad array of views supporting many ways of life and that those who take advantage of the opportunities free speech provides will make better-informed and better-considered choices of a way of life for themselves than they otherwise would. The Court asserts a democratic faith that under a regime of free expression individuals will, on the average and in the long run, make better choices as a result of intelligently sifting through the welter of considerations generated for them by free dialogue— better choices than would be made under a regime that censors speech to protect group and sect sensitivities. Free speech under the conditions of modern democracy produces "enlightened opinion," in the Court's hopeful words. This is a broad and vague empirical claim of a sort for which it is difficult to provide anything that would count as compelling

[41]310 US 296, 310 (1940).

evidence; hence we have characterized the Court's view as resting on a democratic faith. But notice that if one denied this claim one would be hard pressed to defend legal guarantees of freedom of expression. If one holds that under a regime of free expression the quality of individuals' choices of ways of life and conceptions of the good would, on the average and in the long run, deteriorate compared to what that quality would be under a regime of repression, one is well on the way to endorsement of repression. One might make the blanket assertion that individuals have basic rights to free speech even if free speech leads them to ruin, but such a fundamentalist assertion of right would be quixotic.

If adult society is conceived as a regime of free expression, in which debate is open, robust, and uninhibited, then children in order to profit from that open debate must be trained for it. Guidelines for educational policy are implicit in the rationale for freedom of expression. Education in a democratic society might well be designed to achieve other goals as well, but a society that privileges freedom of expression should establish a system of education that coheres with it.

The Instrumental Case for Autonomy

The relationship between an individual's achieving autonomy and attaining a good life for herself is complex. For one thing, a person making an autonomous choice might decide to sacrifice her own good for the sake of fulfilling moral obligations or furthering nonobligatory ideals. Leave these cases aside. Though important, they do not pertain to the issues central to this chapter.

Autonomy might be viewed as a deontological requirement the individual must pursue. But once we distinguish deciding for oneself as it bears on the interests of other people and as it bears on one's own success in leading a good life and recall that here we are considering only the latter, then it is hard to see how there could be a *moral* requirement to pursue one's own interests in a certain way, namely, autonomously.

The achievement of autonomy might be deemed worthy either instrumentally or for its own sake, quite apart from further consequences of such achievement. Conceived in this latter way, autonomy would have to be judged a sectarian goal, not suitable as a consensual basis for public policy. On what basis would autonomy be imposed on those who would reasonably regard it as not intrinsically worthwhile from the standpoint of their not unreasonable fundamental values?

The instrumental view of autonomy is difficult to disown. The idea is

168   Democracy's Place

simply that what we now regard as good might not be good in fact and that to improve the quality of our beliefs we must think for ourselves.[42] Being autonomous helps one discover reasonable values and a reasonable way to live, and discovering such values helps one to attain them. Anyone who accepts that her current beliefs that underlie her fundamental personal values might be mistaken or confused must acknowledge that critical examination of the reasoning supporting her values might reveal confusion of thought and that further acquisition of factual knowledge might remove false beliefs but for which she would not maintain her commitment to her current values. But people do not merely wish to live a valuable and worthy life according to their current beliefs about what constitutes such a life. They want to lead a life that truly is valuable and worthy. Insofar as critical reflection on one's present values is a useful means of acquiring values that could withstand informed critical reflection and that would be a reliable guide to a valuable and worthy life, one's basic goal of living a good life generates the subsidiary goal of developing and exercising critical reflection. This as we have seen is the core defensible aspect of the ideal of autonomy.

The instrumental view of autonomy does not make a fetish of it. Engaging in critical reflection about one's values can improve the quality of the values one eventually affirms; but for most of us, continued engagement in reflection quickly becomes subject to diminishing returns. Given that time spent at critical reflection is time that could have been spent seeking to fulfill one's current values, the overarching goal of leading a good life does not dictate endless dithering at reflection instead of energetic pursuit if one's aims. In principle, the prudent agent will allocate her time between reflection to improve her values and action to achieve them, so as to maximize the extent to which she is successful in leading a life that is good according to standards she affirms and which could withstand further well-informed, rational critical scrutiny. Notice that for any given person the correct allocation of time between reflection on aims and pursuit of them depends crucially on native talents that contribute to critical reflection skills. At the limit, a person whose thinking is always, unavoidably, thoroughly confused would do better to avoid critical reflection altogether and simply accept her given current aims on faith, as she is incapable of improving them by the use of her own critical powers.

In general, the practical alternative to subjecting one's fundamental aims to critical scrutiny is to accept uncritically whatever aims socializa-

[42]See Ronald Dworkin, "Foundations of Liberal Equality," in *The Tanner Lectures on Human Values*, vol. 11, ed. Grethe B. Peterson (Salt Lake City: University of Utah Press, 1990), pp. 1–119.

tion during one's childhood has instilled. The utility of this strategy of trusting local authority as it happens to have impinged on one's life depends among other things on the quality of the local authorities that have acted as socializing agents—but this is not a matter on which one can have a trustworthy opinion before undertaking a broad comparative investigation of one's local ideology rated against other ideologies and other world views.

The foregoing discussion of autonomy regarded as instrumental to a good life provides a way to model the decision problem for a guardian choosing an appropriate paternalistic policy for the upbringing of Amish youth. The model suggested here does not invoke controversial premises about the nature of the good life or about the role of the ideal of autonomy within a vision of the good life which are biased against religious traditionalists such as the Amish.

The problem of a guardian choosing an education for a youth entrusted to her care is how to maximize the expected value of the life the child will lead, subject to moral constraints reflecting the legitimate interests of others whose lives will be affected. The decision is complicated by uncertainty about the future circumstances in which the child will lead his life and uncertainty about the value to the child of the options to which education can provide access. The Amish parent must choose between a program of withdrawal from worldly concerns which prepares the child only for life in the Amish community and a program of secular education that prepares the child for different ways of life in modern society. So as not to take advantage of the perhaps unwarranted polemical claim that secular education prepares the child for many valuable ways of life whereas Amish withdrawal prepares the child at most for a single way of life, let us suppose that the child's future can be represented as a choice between just two life options, a "religious traditionalist" or a "secular worldly" one. No assumption is made about the relative value of the two options, but it is assumed that individuals differ in their traits so that for some persons, the secular way of life is better, and for some, the traditionalist way is better. The differences among persons that render one way of life or another superior for them cannot be identified in advance of maturity by guardians or by the individuals themselves. To some unknown extent the withdrawing educational program renders the recipient fit for traditionalist life and unfit for worldly life, whereas a secular education to some unknown degree renders the recipient fit for worldly life and unfit for traditionalist life. The choice of an educational program also can affect the child's capability and desire to engage in well-informed critical deliberation issuing in a choice of values and a way of life. At maturity the individual will choose a way of life autonomously or non-autonomously, where choosing one way or the other does not affect the value of the option chosen. But it is assumed that choosing after well-informed critical deliberation, or autonomously, increases the probability of a choice, secular or traditionalist, that is better for the chooser. On these assumptions the better course for a guardian is to choose a secular autonomy-promoting educational program for the child.

The assumptions presented in the previous paragraph are more favorable to the Amish case than any alternative set that could be adopted by public officials monitoring guardians without violating the establishment clause of the First Amendment. No controversial assumption is made to the effect that Amish education closes off more opportunities for the child than would secular education. No assumption is made as to the comparative value of Amish and non-Amish ways of life. No autonomy-favoring assumption is made that choosing by means of well-informed critical reflection per se enhances the value of whatever way of life is chosen. In this model, autonomous choice is not itself an element of the good life; it is merely a device for discovering the good life. Still, this instrumental value of autonomy suffices to show the superiority of an education that promotes it to one that does not when educational choice must be made ex ante, before the individual's type is known. But this assumption that educational decisions affecting a child must be made in substantial ignorance of the child's endowment of traits and dispositions is surely realistic.

This way of framing the issue might be thought to load the outcome against the Amish parent, who surely believes that he knows the comparative value of an Amish versus a non-Amish existence and believes that the former is superior for his children, regardless of their particular idiosyncratic traits. But how could he attain knowledge of these matters without having undertaken a comprehensive comparative study of Amish and non-Amish ways of life of a sort that requires wide empirical knowledge and critical reasoning skills that only secular education claims to provide? Even if he had undertaken such a comparative inquiry, its results could not be extrapolated directly to determine what life is best for his child, because the child's traits and evaluative dispositions might be significantly different in ways that would alter the outcome of the comparisons, and anyway the comparative inquiry would have to be updated with current information and a current scrutiny of pertinent evaluative arguments on offer, in order to yield a decisive answer that could sensibly guide his child's choice.

Of course in modern diverse societies the law gives parents wide latitude to attempt to pass along their own values to their children in the absence of any presumptive ground for thinking that parents know that their own values are adequate, much less superior to the values affirmed by other members of society. But there are limits to the permissible indoctrination of children by parents. One such limit that is widely accepted is that parents must cooperate with other legitimate authorities in society to develop in their children critical reasoning skills that will enable their children to stand back from the values they have been taught and to subject these values to informed critical scrutiny.

No doubt this limit is contested. But to deny the moral appropriateness of requiring all guardians to promote in their charges the disposi-tion to critical reasoning and the skills needed to practice it, it would seem that one must deny that an individual of normal potential competence is likely to benefit from such exercise of critical reasoning skills. One must hold that the epistemic strategy of uncritical acceptance of the values that the individual was taught is a superior strategy for maximizing the goodness of the life the individual will have. This across-the-board denial of the efficacy of critical reasoning in human life is a possible position to maintain, but holding that view is incompatible with any plausible rationale for democratic civil liberties including broad freedom of expression. There is no conceptual room for a "civic standpoint" that affirms wide freedom of expression for adult citizens but denies that the development in children of the capacities to engage profitably from free expression practices has any value.

VI. *Yoder* and Democratic Theory Revisited

We have argued that in a democratic society all of us have a "compelling" interest in bringing it about that each member is raised with the capacities to fulfill the responsibilities of democratic citizenship. These capacities notably include skills and habits of critical thinking that enable effective participation in democratic deliberation. In a democratic society in which there is no established religion or privileged faith, and in which many doctrines and faiths compete for allegiance, it is in each person's interest to have critical thinking skills that facilitate wise choice. In a slogan: democracy and autonomy go together.

These considerations set limits to toleration. Other things being equal, it is desirable to let associations and families carry on their own way of life in their own way; but other things are decidedly not equal in a case such as *Yoder*, in which the perceived religious interests of parents conflict with their basic fiduciary responsibilities as parents. Some parents have scruples of conscience that prevent them from taking care of the basic health care, nutritional, and educational needs of their children, but in these cases conscience must yield to basic needs.[43]

But *is* education at the high school level a basic need? The opinions of the Supreme Court justices in *Yoder* seemed to reflect the view that at the margin, whether to attend or skip two years of high school was not of much importance. In contrast, the Amish defendants themselves seemed to have a lively appreciation of the fact that early adolescence is a crucial period for defining one's identity and one's relation to the values taught as authoritative in one's childhood. If the development of children's minds from ages fourteen to sixteen is not consequential, what is the fuss about? Beyond this polemical point, our account has stressed that attaining the autonomy proper to a democratic citizen involves a mastery of sophisticated skills beyond what students could be expected to learn in grade school. So high school is pivotal, and half of high school is significant.

In section I above we mentioned two sets of considerations from democratic theory which might be thought to support the outcome in *Yoder.* First, sustaining a rich civil society fabric of associations may be functional to democracy in a variety of ways. In fact there are at least two kinds of functional claim in the democratic theory literature which turn out to be pertinent to evaluating what was at issue in *Yoder.* As far as the literature on single- versus multiply-cleavaged societies is concerned, it is clear that the Amish present no threat to the existence of a democratic political order. A (somewhat tendentious) case might be made that they are functional to democracy; certainly they are not dysfunctional in the sense of posing a threat to democratic stability. If that were the decisive test, the Amish should win.

A second argument is the Tocqueville-Walzer claim that internally undemocratic civil institutions are healthy in a democracy. In the allocation of authoritative values they act as a counterweight against the potential tyranny of the democratic state and thus help preserve its democratic character in the long run. A general difficulty with this argument, already mentioned, is that it is difficult to see how citizens will develop democratic habits of thought and interaction if these form no part of their everyday lives.[44] Our discussion here reinforces that concern. Beyond this, in a world in which conventional liberal distinctions between public and private have been called into question, the Tocqueville-Walzer position becomes yet more vulnerable. If politics

[43]See George W. Dent, Jr., "Religious Children, Secular Schools," *Southern California Law Review* 61, no. 4 (May 1988), pp. 863–941. Dent analyzes various cases in which we would say that the religious interests of parents are in conflict with the educational needs of children.
[44]See Chapter 4, pp. 106–7.

permeates civil society, a democratic theory of politics designed to leave civil society untouched scarcely deserves the name.

We have not held that the Amish constitute a threat to a democratic political order. We are not against tolerating them, only against tolerating their educational practices. Our argument has been that in a democracy, where citizens are affected by the collective actions of the majority, it is necessary that citizens develop the capacities needed to understand and evaluate the policies by which their lives might be affected and through which they might affect the lives of others. Children in a democracy should be educated to an age when critical reason is developed and can be deployed, and third parties have a right to expect parents and other educators to try to provide children with such an education.

We do not go so far as to assert that citizens in a democracy are obligated to participate in political life. We do insist, however, that even if, when they become adults, those who accept the Amish way of life choose to withdraw from participation in the political order, they need critical reasoning capacities if such a choice is to be authentic. It is because the Amish acculturation program is explicitly designed to prevent the development of critical reason that the Amish should have lost in *Yoder*. To accept a person's choice of an Amish way of life, one must have some reasonable confidence in that person's choice-making competence. This competence, we have argued, is developed in education for autonomy.

The other democratic argument in support of *Yoder* which we mentioned at the outset is communitarian in spirit. The Amish association provides the good of close community ties and a shared sense of worthwhile life for its members by withdrawing from a modern life that breaks down small-scale stable community and all that goes with it.[45] So democratic communitarianism gives one reason to tilt in favor of groups like the Amish and to applaud the decision in *Yoder* which accorded "greater respect to the claims of our encumbered selves" than the contrary decision would have done.[46]

Talking about "our" encumbered selves in the context of *Yoder* glosses over the distinct perspectives of Amish parents and Amish children. No doubt the child's self will become variously encumbered by the time adulthood is reached, but the issue is, encumbered by what? We have

[45]The movie *Witness* evenhandedly describes the appeal of Amish community solidarity and the appeal of modern individual liberties incompatible with it. See also Justice Douglas's minority opinion in *Yoder*, chiding the Burger opinion for taking an overly romantic view of Amish-style religious community.

[46]Sandel, "Freedom of Conscience?" p. 90.

maintained that it is good for each of us to become encumbered by the ability and disposition to step back from those of our current values that have been rendered problematic in some way and to think critically about them. In the absence of an argument that shows that it is possible consistently to reject this view without rejecting democratic values wholesale, the exhortation to respect encumbered selves is little more than unreasoned sentimentalism.

7

South Africa's Negotiated Transition: Democracy, Opposition, and the New Constitutional Order

Courtney Jung and Ian Shapiro

Few seasoned observers of South African politics ever expected to see Nelson Mandela inaugurated as the country's president. When this happened in May of 1994, it would have been difficult not to interpret it as a major democratic achievement. The April elections caught the world's imagination. Democrats everywhere applauded as the apartheid regime began fading into history, and the African National Congress took over the reins of power. In a country and on a continent where democracy has seldom fared well historically, the achievement seemed all the more remarkable. In an astonishingly short time South Africa had been transformed from a pariah nation, vilified around the world, into a progressive multicultural democracy, identified in the Western press as a model throughout Africa and a symbol of hope for struggling democratizers elsewhere.[1]

No less noteworthy than the result was the process that led to it. Despite considerable violence there was no civil war, no military coup, and the cooperation among the players whose cooperation was needed was impressive. Starting in 1990, after the National Party (NP) government's decision to release all political prisoners, legalize all opposition parties, and begin genuine negotiations with them on the shape of the

[1]See, e.g., *New York Times*, June 21, 1994, pp. A1, A8.

new South Africa, it was clear that real change was in the offing. Multi-party negotiations for a new constitution seemed to exemplify both the letter and spirit of a democratic transition to democracy. Even when the all-party CODESA[2] negotiations failed and were replaced by more cir-cumscribed elite negotiations, the fact that the entire process com-manded agreement among the principal players was widely heralded as an encouraging portent for the future.

The widespread popular enthusiasm for South Africa's democratic transition is in line with much recent academic orthodoxy in political science. Negotiated transitions to democracy are seen as desirable, if not necessary for democratic survival. "Pacts are not always likely or possible," Guillermo O'Donnell and Philippe Schmitter tell us, "but where they are a feature of the transition they are desirable—that is they enhance the possibility that the process will lead to a viable politi-cal democracy."[3] "How were democracies made?" asks Huntington of the third wave of democratic transformations between 1974 and 1990. His answer is that they "were made by the methods of democracy, there was no other way. They were made through negotiations, compromises and agreements."[4] Przeworski reiterates the view that democracy "can-not be dictated; it emerges from bargaining."[5] From the vantage point of these opinions, South Africa is a textbook case of a well-crafted transition; despite various fits and starts, the principals made no serious mistakes and shepherded the country safely through its first democra-tic elections.

The worldwide attention to the South African transition, and to tran-sition negotiations elsewhere, has not been matched by comparable scrutiny of what the parties to the transition negotiations agreed to or why. Yet there are serious questions as to whether constitutional orders that emerge from negotiations facilitate democratic politics in the me-dium term. In particular, South Africa's transitional constitution lacks a system of opposition institutions that any healthy democracy requires. Although terms such as *group rights, consociationalism,* and *minority vetoes* are anathema in the South African political vocabulary, the politi-cal order that has been created is consociational in many critical re-spects; as such it is designed to give every powerful player a say in government. The electoral system, the rules of parliamentary control,

[2]See Chapter 4, note 46, p. 98 above.

[3]Guillermo O'Donnell and Philippe Schmitter, *Transitions from Authoritarian Rule* (Baltimore: Johns Hopkins University Press, 1986), p. 39.

[4]Samuel P. Huntington, *The Third Wave: Democratization in the Late Twentieth Century* (Norman: University of Oklahoma Press, 1991), p. 164.

[5]Adam Przeworski, *Democracy and the Market* (New York: Cambridge University Press, 1991), p. 80.

and the powers and composition of the cabinet and the executive all reinforce this reality. The result is that there are no powerful actors to play the role of "loyal" opponents to the new government and its policies. A system designed to involve every player of political consequence in government leaves no institutional space for a loyal opposition.

In this chapter we examine the disquieting possibility that the new South Africa's lack of these basic ingredients of a viable democracy is a direct result of the transition's having been negotiated between reformers in the NP government and the moderate leadership of the ANC. We explore and evaluate the conjecture that the dynamics of negotiated transitions such as South Africa's make it virtually impossible for the principal players to converge on an agreement that includes provision for effective opposition forces in the new democratic order. If our analysis is persuasive, then it leads to the conclusion that although the interim constitution may well have been the best possible device to end apartheid without a civil war, it should not be replicated in the permanent constitution.[6] This means that the advice of such analysts as Arend Lijphart, who makes the contrary recommendation, should be ignored.

The reasons for our conclusion are elaborated in section VII. In sections I and II, we discuss the nature and value of strong opposition institutions in a democracy and the types of political systems that tend to sustain them. In section III we describe what was agreed to in the South African negotiations in this regard. In section IV we conjecture about the dynamics of negotiated transitions; in section V we explain how these dynamics appear to have played out in South Africa. In section VI we elaborate on our conjecture by reference to similar negotiated transitions elsewhere in the world, though we do not attempt a systematic empirical test of it here. Whether our account of the

[6]The National Assembly and the Senate jointly form the Constitutional Assembly, which was required to adopt a final constitution with a two-thirds majority by May 1996. This constitution comes into operation only if the Constitutional Court certifies that it complies with the constitutional principles laid down in the provisional constitution. These include a democratic system of government, universal franchise, regular elections, a multiparty system, one class of citizenship for all, recognition of individual rights, antidiscrimination provisions, equality before the law, separation of powers, three levels of government (national, provincial, and local), and an entrenched constitution that—as interpreted by the Constitutional Court—is the supreme law of the land. This last feature was a notable change from the old British-style system of the supremacy of parliament. Other features of the interim arrangements, such as the boundaries of the provinces, could not be changed in the final constitution. There was no requirement, however, that the interim system of constitutionally mandated power sharing (the central focus of this chapter) be retained in the final document. See *South Africa 1995* (Johannesburg: South Africa Foundation, 1995), pp. 14–15.

dynamics of transitions can be developed into a general theory is a question for another day. Our discussion of the defects of the interim constitution and our recommendations for the final constitution are not, in any case, dependent on it.

I. POLITICAL OPPOSITION AND DEMOCRATIC POLITICS

In 1965, Robert Dahl remarked that "of the three great milestones in the development of democratic institutions—the right to participate in governmental decisions by casting a vote, the right to be represented, and the right of an organized opposition to appeal for votes against the government in elections and in parliament—the last is, in a highly developed form, so wholly modern that there are people now living who were born before it had appeared in most of Western Europe."[7] He might perhaps have added that opposition is also the milestone that has been least studied by contemporary political scientists. Since the 1950s, the subject of representation has received substantial attention from figures as different as Giovanni Sartori and Hanna Pitkin, but opposition is scarcely mentioned in the works of either.[8] The rational choice tradition since Arrow has also been centrally concerned with problems of representation, focusing on the difficulties involved in devising rules that can aggregate preferences in a meaningful way. As its name suggests, the participatory tradition sought to shift attention from representation to participation, but one can search the works of Carole Pateman and Benjamin Barber without finding any more attention to the subject of opposition than is contained in the works of Buchanan and Tullock or Riker.[9]

Considering the importance of opposition in democratic politics, this is a surprising state of affairs. One need not go as far as Barrington Moore, for whom the central defining characteristic of a democratic political order is "the existence of a legitimate and, to some extent

[7]Robert A. Dahl, *Political Opposition in Western Democracies* (New Haven: Yale University Press, 1965), p. xiii.

[8]See Giovanni Sartori, *The Theory of Democracy Revisited* (Chatham, N.J.: Chatham House, 1987), and Hanna Pitkin, *The Concept of Representation* (Berkeley: University of California Press, 1967).

[9]See Carole Pateman, *Participation and Democratic Theory* (New York: Cambridge University Press, 1970); Benjamin Barber, *Strong Democracy: Participatory Politics for a New Age* (Berkeley: University of California Press, 1984); James Buchanan and Gordon Tullock, *The Calculus of Consent: Logical Foundations of Constitutional Democracy* (Ann Arbor: University of Michigan Press, 1962); and William H. Riker, *Liberalism against Populism: A Confrontation between the Theory of Democracy and the Theory of Social Choice* (San Francisco: W. H. Freeman, 1982).

effective, opposition," to hold that a functioning political opposition is essential to democracy. Although the notion of a loyal opposition finds its origins in monarchical rather than democratic politics, democratic systems rely on institutionalized oppositions, and it is doubtful that any regime could long survive as minimally democratic without them.[10]

This is true for at least three related reasons. The first is functional, having to do with the peaceful turnover of power by governments that lose elections. Huntington identifies peaceful turnover as the sine qua non of democratic politics. Although one might not want to go all the way with him in regarding it as sufficient, he is surely right that it is necessary.[11] If democratic politics is seen as requiring at a minimum that there be turnover of power among elites, then there must be sites for counterelites to form and campaign as potential alternative governments. Such opposition requires the permissive freedoms of speech and association as well as the presence of institutions and practices that make it possible for counterelites to organize and inform themselves so as to be able to contest for power. An organized parliamentary opposition, a shadow cabinet, access to security briefings, and civil service support are all necessary for an opposition to be perceived as a realistic alternative to the government of the day. If the opposition is not thus perceived, then the possibility of turnover is diminished and crises for the government are correspondingly more likely to become crises for the democratic regime.

This suggests a second reason why opposition institutions matter: for the legitimacy of the democratic political order. Providing the institutional space for opposition is essential for ensuring that discontent and dissatisfaction can be directed at particular governments rather than at the democratic regime itself. As Przeworski has argued, if we think of a democracy as, among other things, "a system for processing conflicts," it is important that those who lose particular political battles do not forfeit the right to criticize and compete against the government, the capacity to try to influence legislation and the bureaucracy and to seek recourse through the courts.[12] Unless there are such institutional outlets for dissent within the regime's institutions, those who are discontented with the status quo may not even distinguish the government from the regime, undermining the possibility of the ebb and flow of competitive party politics that democracies require.

[10]Barrington Moore, Jr., *Liberal Prospects under Soviet Socialism: A Comparative Historical Perspective* (New York: Averell Harriman Institute, 1989), pp. 8, 25. For a more elaborate discussion of the importance of opposition to democracy, see my Chapter 8.

[11]Huntington, *Third Wave*, p. 267.

[12]Przeworski, *Democracy and the Market*, pp. 11–12.

Last, institutional arrangements that facilitate loyal opposition perform important public-interest functions in democracies. They are necessary to ensure the presence of healthy political debate. They encourage competition over ideas among elites and counterelites, and this leads to demands for reason giving and coherence in public debate. Moreover, opposition institutions empower groups and individuals who have an interest in asking awkward questions, shining light in dark places, and exposing abuses of power. Without an organized political opposition that has rights to information and other resources, governing in secret becomes all too tempting for the administration of the day. Governments always have incentives to camouflage mistakes or controversial decisions that might otherwise threaten their popularity and to misuse the perquisites of office. Unless their members know that they can be called to public account for their actions, the temptation to act on these incentives will in many cases prove irresistible.

II. The Opposition/Nonopposition Continuum

Although the principal alternative to democratic systems that institutionalize opposition may be authoritarian systems that repress it, many systems of government are designed to channel dissent and opposition away from national political institutions and otherwise to diffuse it. Such systems are usually defended on the grounds that disagreements in the society in question are so potentially explosive that anything else will result in the war of all against all. Many orthodox prescriptions for "divided" societies—those in which unbridgeable divisions among the population are thought to preclude pluralist politics—take this form. Perhaps the best known of these is Lijphart's consociational model of minority vetoes and enforced coalitions, which might be thought of as occupying a position at the far end of a continuum from the opposition model just sketched.[13]

Consociational models of democracy emphasize participation and representation to the virtual exclusion of opposition. Their organizing principles are proportionality in the electoral system, an institutional structure that forces power sharing and a system of mutual vetoes among "a cartel of elites,"[14] and a predisposition toward robust federal-

[13]See Arend Lijphart, *Democracy in Plural Societies* (New Haven: Yale University Press, 1977), and *Power-Sharing in South Africa* (Berkeley: University of California Institute of International Studies, 1985).

[14]Arend Lijphart, "Consociational Democracy," *World Politics* 4, no. 2 (January 1969), pp. 213–15, 222.

ism to insulate territorially based minorities from the power of whoever controls national political institutions. Advocates of consociational democracy contend that particularly when societies are deeply divided along ethnic lines, if democracy can be realized at all it will be only if the effects of majority rule are mitigated by institutional devices of this sort. The assumption is that ethnic divisions so completely overdetermine other conflicts, and that they are so intense and enduring (if not primordial), that the only viable institutional recipe is one that is designed to minimize political competition and keep the groups from getting at one anothers' throats.

Consociational systems undermine the functional, legitimacy-generating, and public-interest roles of opposition discussed in section I. With regard to the first, consociational systems are not designed to foster alternation of major parties in power. Instead, they permit the same combination of elites to entrench themselves at the peaks of spoils and patronage hierarchies more or less continuously. The democratic benefits that can accrue from "tossing the rascals out" are therefore unavailable. On the legitimacy front, because consociational arrangements ensure that every major political player is part of the government, there is little basis for the disaffected to differentiate the government from the regime. It is hard for an ethos of loyal opposition to develop when there is no institutional outlet.[15] Those who are not in government are removed from politics altogether, making it more likely that they will turn to extra-institutional politics if they can. With regard to the public-interest role of opposition politics, consociational systems do not give powerful parliamentary players incentives to keep government honest by shining light in dark corners. Because consociational systems require high levels of consensus among governing elites, the only way for anyone in the governing elite to get her way on issues that matter intensely to her is to give other powerful players what they want on issues that matter intensely to them. Therefore, mutual vetoes can be expected to lead to mutual logrolling, rather than to political confrontations among elites, and to promote insider clubism. By the same token, logrolling minimizes the likelihood that government elites will be called to account by members of potential alternative governments. In short, consociational systems, based on the politics of elite coalitions, maximize both representation and participation in government, but at

[15]This insight is at the core of Horowitz's critique of consociational systems: that the very circumstances in which they are most needed—when there are powerful divisions in the society—are the circumstances when they are also least likely to be effective; see Donald L. Horowitz, *A Democratic South Africa? Constitutional Engineering in a Divided Society* (Berkeley: University of California Press, 1991), pp. 142–43.

the price of almost complete abandonment of a viable opposition politics.

The position of a regime along the opposition/nonopposition continuum depends on the electoral system and on the divisions of power within the legislature and between the legislature and the executive. First-past-the-post electoral systems based on single-member districts are likely to produce two-party systems and, as a result, strong parliamentary oppositions.[16] These oppositions may or may not have the potential to become alternative governments (depending on their potential grass roots support). Nonetheless, they will have an interest in becoming magnets for antigovernment sentiment, which should give them incentives to perform at least some of the conventional functions of loyal oppositions: organizing and channeling dissent, disseminating information, and exposing government corruption. Thus although two-party–dominated plurality systems have high barriers to entry and are comparatively unrepresentative, they produce significant institutionalized opposition.

Things will be less predictable in multiparty systems dependent on coalition governments. Given the well-documented propensity of proportional representation to produce party fractionalization, particularly when constituencies are large and thresholds are low,[17] unconstrained proportional representation makes parliamentary structure unpredictable. In certain circumstances it may produce strong opposition coalitions and alternation in government, as is sometimes the case in Israel and The Netherlands. In other circumstances, such as Austria and Switzerland, the major parties will often govern in coalition. Given the unpredictability of unconstrained proportional representation versus the predictability of first-past-the-post plurality systems in generating two-party politics, one would not choose the former over the latter if the goal was to produce oppositional rather than consociational parliamentary politics.

Whether a system is presidential or parliamentary also affects the prospects for institutionalized opposition. Parliamentary systems link the fortunes of the executive to those of the majority party in parliament, so that institutionalized opposition is apt to be centered in the

---

[16]Douglas W. Rae, *The Political Consequences of Electoral Laws* (New Haven: Yale University Press, 1967).

[17]Arend Lijphart, *Electoral Systems and Party Systems* (Oxford: Oxford University Press, 1994). Rae suggests that with proportional representation, small and medium-sized constituencies and higher thresholds combine to limit fractionalization and give parties incentives to form blocs, whether in government or opposition. In effect the constraints make multiparty systems operate more like two-party systems; see Douglas W. Rae "Using District Magnitude to Regulate Political Party Competition," *Journal of Economic Perspectives* 9, no. 1 (winter 1995), pp. 65–75.

legislature. In presidential systems, significant opposition may occur between the executive and the legislature, depending on the powers of the presidency (e.g., whether they include the power to appoint a cabinet or to conduct some affairs unilaterally) and the interactions between the electoral rules for parliament and presidency. An electoral system that produces a government consisting of all the powerful players in the legislature is likely to weaken the presidency, reducing the president, in the limiting case, to a figurehead. If the president's party is a minority in the legislature, as is often the case in Brazil for instance, he has to seek support from the majority (opposition) party to avoid governmental paralysis. This type of system tends closely to approximate a power-sharing type of arrangement. If, however, the constitution confers substantial autonomous power on the president, as it does in the United States, the president may be an institutional figure to be reckoned with even if his party is a minority in the legislature. For presidential systems to be relatively close to the opposition end of the continuum in virtue of their presidentialism, then, either presidents must be institutionally powerful or there must be significant minority parties in the legislature with which they can ally themselves. As the latter is less predictably so in proportional representation systems, it is less predictably the case in presidential proportional representation systems. Perhaps for this reason, observers have noticed a coincidence of presidential proportional representation systems and power-sharing governments.[18]

Those who negotiate transitions to democracy all bring to the bargaining table interests that will lead them to see the costs and benefits of various institutional outcomes differently. Negotiators representing a party that expects to be in the minority in the new democratic order should be expected to prefer a power-sharing arrangement in which they are guaranteed some of the spoils of office and veto powers on measures that affect their critical interests. Leaders of parties that expect to alternate in government and opposition in the new regime might reasonably take a more mixed view of things: when they are in government, they will want the power to govern but when they are in opposition they will want to be able to frustrate as much of the government's agenda as possible. Parties that anticipate being able to win a majority can be expected to prefer an oppositional model that will give them the power and authority to govern and to enact as much of their agenda as

[18]Scott Mainwaring, "Presidentialism, Multiparty Systems, and Democracy: The Difficult Equation," *Comparative Political Studies* 26, no. 2 (1993), pp. 198–230; Arend Lijphart, "Democratization and Constitutional Choices in Czechoslovakia, Hungary, and Poland, 1989–1991," *Journal of Theoretical Politics* 4, no. 2 (1993), p. 209.

they can. Consequently, they should be expected to push for a majority system during the transition negotiations and to be more resistant than any of the other players to power sharing and other consociational arrangements.

The story of the South African transition partly belies these expectations. As anticipated, the National Party insisted on a consociational outcome throughout the negotiations and eventually prevailed, making few concessions. But the ANC, with its overwhelming grass roots support and its well-founded expectation that it would hold an absolute majority in the new parliament, made concession after concession, eventually accepting constitutionally mandated power sharing, for the rest of the century at least, almost without a whimper. As power sharing had been anathema to the ANC as late as mid-1992 and as most observers inside and outside South Africa seemed to think that the ANC held most of the cards, this outcome needs an explanation.

III. Democratic Opposition in the New South Africa

The 1993 constitution negotiated between the NP and the ANC, and adopted by the all-white South African parliament as its final act in December 1993, appears close to the nonopposition extreme on our continuum. By acts of both omission and commission its authors created an electoral system and institutional structure that contains no provision for an official opposition, let alone a shadow cabinet or access to information and resources for those who are not part of the new government. Instead they mandated a government of national unity in which every player of consequence is expected to participate, have seats in the cabinet, and be bound by the doctrine of collective responsibility. This system is entrenched in the interim constitution.

The electoral law is a cornerstone of the new system. The constitutional negotiators replaced the old (British-inspired) system of single-member first-past-the-post constituencies with a lower house based on list-system proportional representation with half the four hundred members elected at large and the other half from party lists in each of the nine regions that replace the old four provinces. The ninety-member senate has ten members from each region nominated by the parties represented in its provincial legislature, which is also elected on the basis of list-system proportional representation.[19]

[19]Secs. 40, 48.

If Rae is correct that in order to make proportional representation systems function more like two-party systems, a combination of small and medium-sized constituencies and high thresholds are needed, the South African system—which has neither—does not fit the bill.[20] The particular brand of proportional representation adopted in South Africa is especially inimical to the formation of parliamentary opposition because of the way in which power is allocated in parliament. Not only are seats in the National Assembly proportionately distributed, but so are cabinet portfolios. Any party that holds at least 20 seats in the National Assembly is entitled to cabinet portfolios in proportion to the number of seats it holds in the National Assembly.[21] Thus the April 1994 elections, which gave the ANC 62.6 percent of the popular vote, the NP 20.4 percent, and the Inkatha Freedom Party (IFP) 10.5 percent, resulted in a parliamentary distribution of 252 ANC seats, 82 NP seats, and 43 IFP seats. The vote translated into a 27-member cabinet in which 18 were ANC, 6 were NP, and 3 were IFP, and deputy ministers distributed among the same parties 8, 3, and 1.[22] Any party that wins at least 80 seats in Parliament—and if none does, then each of the two largest parties—is also entitled to designate an Executive Deputy President. This rule, which resulted in F. W. De Klerk's appointment to the post for the NP in 1994 along with Thabo Mbeki for the ANC, extends the principle of incorporating the powerful players throughout the executive branch. Thus, although the system overrepresents larger parties in the cabinet and the executive, it also ensures that all parties with substantial bases of electoral support are part of the government.

This system makes effective opposition to the government in Parliament virtually impossible. Powerful parliamentary players will be reluctant to give up the influence, perquisites, and patronage that accompany their positions as part of the government. No potentially effective parliamentary group exists outside the cabinet but inside Parliament to oppose government policy. Small wonder that as early as May 1994, Derek Keys, the NP minister of finance held over from the previous government, was publicly wondering how the doctrine of collective cabinet responsibility could be compatible with running against the ANC-led government's record in future elections.[23]

If effective political opposition cannot come from party competition, another place to look for it is on the back benches. Here, too, the rules

[20]Rae, "Using District Magnitude."

[21]Sec. 88 (2).

[22]Election results taken from *Foreign Broadcasting Information Service Daily Report,* May 6, 1994, p. 5. Cabinet portfolios from Associated Press wire, May 9, 1994.

[23]*New York Times,* May 9, 1994, p. A6.

seem to have been designed to preclude meaningful opposition. Chapter 4 of the constitution provides that any MP who ceases to be a member of his political party will also lose his seat and be replaced by someone else from the party list.[24] Depending on how the rules concerning the internal governance of parliamentary parties develop, this feature of the constitution could give governing party elites the most powerful whip system in the parliamentary world. If they can cause members to be threatened with expulsion from their parties, backbenchers will have no leverage of any kind in dealing with their own party leaderships. Even if legislation is passed to curb leadership power, at a minimum the constitutional provision rules out the possibility of disgruntled backbenchers crossing the floor to join an opposition party in protest against government action. Poignantly, the 1993 constitution rules out the sort of defiant act undertaken by Helen Suzman and eleven other MPs in 1959, when they crossed the floor to form the Progressive Party after their United Party decided to play along with apartheid.[25]

We noted in section II that in certain circumstances a presidential system might promote institutionalized opposition. This is not so of the new South African presidency, which is institutionally weak by comparative standards and by comparison with the old South African presidency. The president is not elected independently, and he or she must select the cabinet proportionately from the major parliamentary parties. The president has few powers of appointment—as compared with U.S. presidents, for example—and is explicitly required to exercise his major powers "in consultation with" the cabinet and the executive deputy presidents.[26] In short, the president must govern by consensus and with the support of most of the powerful parliamentary players.

Facilitating and institutionalizing loyal opposition was not a goal of those who wrote the 1993 constitution. They mandated a government of national unity. They designed a parliamentary and electoral structure that limits effective opposition politics, gives substantial amounts of political power to elites who represent salient minorities, minimizes party competition and conflict between the executive and legislature, and renders backbenchers impotent.[27] That this is not a recipe for a

[24]Sec. 43, art. 200.
[25]Helen Suzman, *In No Uncertain Terms: A South African Memoir* (New York: Knopf, 1993), pp. 46–51.
[26]Sec. 82 (2) and (3).
[27]In this light, it is not surprising that Lijphart describes the new constitution as "fundamentally a consociational document" and characterizes it as "close to the optimal power-sharing

viable democratic order should be clear from our discussion in section I. But why was it chosen?[28]

IV. THE DYNAMICS OF TRANSITION NEGOTIATIONS

Transplacements, as Huntington describes negotiated transitions,[29] should be expected to occur only when two conditions are present. First, dominant groups in both government and opposition must bargain with one another while recognizing that neither party is capable of determining the future unilaterally. Second, at critical junctures reformers must appear to be stronger than standpatters in the government while moderates seem stronger than extremists in the opposition.[30] Elites who negotiate transitions are thus subject to constraints that arise both out of the negotiations and out of their relations with their own grass roots constituencies. The negotiating partners are concerned to maximize power along two dimensions. First, each tries to maximize power in relation to the other in the negotiations. Because both sides expect to lead parties that will compete in the new democratic regime, each has an interest in trying to get the upper hand in the negotiations to secure the result most favorable to its future political fortunes. Second, the negotiating partners (the reformers in the government and the moderates in the opposition) have incentives to maximize grass roots support for themselves (thereby continuing to marginalize standpatters and extremists) while causing their negotiating partner merely to satisfice with respect to its grass roots supporters. Each wants the other to retain enough constituent support—but no more—to be able to deliver an agreement, and each seeks to achieve this result in an evolving context. Thus negotiators are bound by three constraints as they move toward an agreement: time, their respective constituencies, and the changing demands of the other party.

---

system that could have been devised"; see Arend Lijphart, "Prospects for Power-Sharing in the new South Africa," in *Election 1994 South Africa* ed. Andrew Reynolds (Cape Town: Philip, 1994), pp. 222–24. Lijphart's celebration of the new order is taken up in section VII below.

[28]By focusing on the importance of parliamentary opposition here, we do not mean to imply that opposition to government outside parliament is unimportant in a democracy. In this respect the constitutional guarantees of free speech, assembly, habeas corpus, and defendant's rights are not without significance (see secs. 7–35). Unless, however, there are forces within Parliament which can translate dissent into effective politics, the political impact of these freedoms is bound to be limited, at best, and, more likely perhaps, institutionally destabilizing.

[29]Huntington, *Third Wave*, pp. 113–14; and see above, Chapter 4, pp. 93–94.

[30]Huntington, *Third Wave*, pp. 124, 152.

Government Reformers

Reformers willing to begin the process of liberalizing an authoritarian regime might come to the fore in the government for a variety of reasons. A list would include sanctions and other forms of external pressure; fissures within their own ranks (perhaps as a result of the collapse of their legitimating ideology); the growth of a normative commitment to democracy among strategically placed members of the government; intractable economic problems; and civil unrest that threatens to spiral out of control. Reformist elites will be divided about what course of change to follow and how far they intend to go. No doubt some will intend to liberalize the regime while retaining its basic authoritarian character. The evidence suggests, however, that this option is not feasible. Liberalized authoritarianisms appear to be inherently unstable, perhaps because, as Huntington suggests, liberalizing reforms provoke demands for greater reform rather than the stability that their proponents anticipate.[31] Others in the government may intend to go further, but they are likely to be unsure or divided as to whether to pursue negotiations with opposition moderates or opt for a transformation. They may begin a transition to test the waters, using the threat of unilateral transformation as a weapon in the negotiations and believing that they can revert to it if the negotiations do not yield what they want.

Although they may not initially perceive it, reformers have a strategic interest in an early settlement because of the unequal but evolving distribution of power among the negotiating principals. In transition negotiations, the principals are defined by their capacity to veto a proposed settlement, either alone or in combination with other players. (Those who lack the power to veto—because they lack sufficient control of coercive force, grass roots support, or both—will be marginal players.) Those who do have the power to veto proposals are not equally powerful in the negotiations, however, because the consequences of a collapse in negotiations will affect them differently. This fact creates an asymmetry in the government's favor and strengthens the hand of reformers in negotiations, vis-à-vis their moderate opponents, from the outset: so long as the governing party retains control of the state's coercive institutions, a collapse in the negotiations means a return to authoritarian rule.

Negotiations are, at the same time, risky for reformers. Although the threat of a return to authoritarianism gives the regime an advantage in the negotiations, even making this threat is dangerous for the political

[31]See ibid., pp. 136–37.

prospects of the reformers, who would surely be discredited by an actual reversal. As a result, the value of the authoritarian threat as a negotiating instrument should be expected to diminish as the negotiations proceed, inasmuch as the opposition moderates can be expected to know that the costs to the reformers of playing that card are increasing. In the limiting case, reformers will be reduced to the role of a bee who fatally stings an enemy to save the queen but then dies.

Reformers face a threat from standpatters who, perhaps in conjunction with hard-liners in the military, stand poised to scuttle the whole process. These standpatters may or may not be bolstered by a constituency that opposes negotiations. So long as constituent support for the transition is uncertain, every move the reformers make toward their negotiating opponents will bring attacks from the right which threaten to pull the rug out from under them. Unless and until they can marginalize these standpatters, the reformers cannot embark on a negotiated transition. They may be able to continue liberalizing the authoritarian regime, and they may flirt with the possibility of a unilateral transformation if they think they have the power to achieve it. But they will be able to make the concessions required of a bargaining process only after neutralizing the hard-liners and their constituents. To do so, they must gather popular support for the transition, perhaps by demonstrating the danger of a return to authoritarianism. Once the reformers decide to face the standpatters down in public confrontation, they become committed to achieving a successful transition. If opposition moderates remain intransigent, government reformers will likely threaten to play the transformation card at this point and perhaps even play it if they can.

If reformers cannot achieve a unilateral transformation, it will now be in their interest to conclude an agreement as quickly as possible. As negotiations continue, the cost to reformers of a collapse in the process should be expected to increase. Once their credibility and legitimacy become tied to the transition, so too does the likelihood that failure or stalemate will fracture their base of support and lead them to lose the initiative to standpatters to their right. The reformers' strength vis-à-vis opposition moderates will also diminish, as the latter can be expected to foment unrest and raise expectations among their own grass roots constituencies to force the government to make concessions (discussed below). As the costs to reformers of backing away from the transition begin to increase, their leeway will diminish and they can be expected to start negotiating seriously.

The government reformers' interest in reaching a settlement does not, however, eclipse all other considerations. Although the prospect of losing the initiative to the right wing will be frightening to them, it will not be as frightening as losing the initiative to the opposition. The latter outcome means either a replacement, or, if the opposition lacks the resources to achieve that, civil war. Losing initiative to the opposition should thus seem more dangerous to government reformers because it precludes the possibility of a second attempt at transplacement or transformation and because it is more likely to cause them and their families to face catastrophic consequences than would a reversion to authoritarianism.

Opposition Moderates

Opposition leaders may become moderate and develop an interest in negotiating with the authoritarian government for a number of reasons. If the government is able to withstand military or popular pressure against it for a considerable time without apparent signs of breakdown, then elements in the opposition leadership may eventually be forced to abandon more radical tactics. Opposition leaders may also have allies, either externally or internally based, who begin to advocate negotiations for reasons of their own. If these allies are persuasive or exercise some power over the democratic opposition—ideologically, economically, or militarily—they may sway the opposition leadership's perception of its options. The leadership may also respond to events in neighboring countries where negotiations appear successful, using other transitions as a model. Finally, a change in the government itself may alter the opposition's perception of the equation, convincing it that previously unacceptable negotiations are now possible.

As with government reformers, opposition moderates face incentives that are likely to change as the negotiations evolve. Initially, time seems to be on their side. For a period, the opposition derives legitimacy and strength among its grass roots constituencies simply by the recognition that the negotiating process affords. As social demands and attendant violence escalate, opposition moderates' relative strength in the negotiating process will also grow as the costs, for government reformers, of failing to reach a settlement start to increase. Perceiving this shift, opposition moderates can be expected to believe that their own power is growing during this initial period and they will be relatively intractable in the negotiations. They may well actively encourage social discontent in this period, raising the stakes by making the country increasingly difficult to govern.

The bargaining power of opposition moderates continues to increase, however, only to the point at which their grass roots constituencies begin to fragment. If violence grows and their supporters become increasingly politicized, opposition moderates should start to sense a Hobson's choice on the horizon. If they begin to move toward a settlement in the negotiations they will be attacked by radicals on their left flank, who will accuse them of selling out and begin vying for their grass roots support. The increasingly politicized masses, who until this point have been a useful weapon for moderates in the negotiations, now begin to be seen as a potential threat that might get out of control and even engulf the moderate leadership. The more that moderate opposition leaders really begin to think of themselves as a "government-in-waiting," the more worried they will become about escalating expectations and radicalizing a population that they are going to have to deal with after the transition.

If, however, the moderate leadership does not move toward a settlement, its grass roots support can be expected to erode anyway. The mere fact of participating in negotiations cannot sustain legitimacy if there is no perception of progress. If negotiations appear to be stalled or moving too slowly, then other opposition leaders can be expected to emerge and to siphon off support from the moderates. Furthermore, the moderate leadership will begin to perceive that the further leftward they are pulled by the grass roots mobilization, the harder it will become for them to propose anything that their negotiating partners, the government moderates, can accept, making a collapse back into authoritarianism correspondingly more likely. Once opposition moderates find themselves confronting the Hobson's choice, they know that their grass roots support is likely to erode whatever they do, perhaps precipitously, unless an enforceable settlement is quickly reached. This diminishes their capacity to force concessions from the government.

The Point of No Return

Negotiations begin in earnest once negotiating elites on both sides realize that they are approaching the point of no return: when retreat from the negotiations would be followed by a collapse of support from which political recovery is unlikely. Both leaderships, and perhaps their political parties as well, will by then have become so identified with the negotiated transition that, if the negotiations collapse, they will lose their leadership positions, presumably to standpatters and radicals. From this point on, political survival for reformers and moderates depends on concluding a successful agreement. This is most likely to occur if negotiators on both sides come to believe that their leverage to force concessions from the other side has reached its maximum or begun to diminish and that replacement and transformation continue not to be viable options. These beliefs will give both sides strong incentives to make the compromises necessary to reach an agreement, once they face what appears to them to be secular erosion of their own grass roots support.

A transplacement, or negotiated transition, differs from a Huntingtonian replacement in that in the former the authoritarian regime does not cede control of the armed forces until after the agreement has been concluded. Both government reformers and opposition moderates know, therefore, that there are hard-liners in the military who will insist on security guarantees and also that grass roots support for government reformers is likely to be critically reliant on their being able credibly to claim that they can guarantee their constituents' physical security. Thus the government reformers have a structural advantage over the opposition moderates throughout the negotiations, as we have noted. It also suggests that, if an agreement is reached, in the end it will involve more substantial concessions from the opposition than from the government because the government retains control of the means of coercion. Once the opposition moderates realize that they have passed their point of no return, so that their political survival is contingent on reaching an agreement, they can be expected to accept demands rejected earlier. Even if the government reformers have passed their own point of no return, both sides are likely to assume that, in the event of a terminal collapse of negotiations, government reformers will turn control over to (or be pushed aside by) standpatters rather than accept the complete loss of control suggested by replacement or civil war.

The government will have an incentive not to force too many concessions out of the opposition moderates, however. It needs them to satisfice, to retain enough support among their grass roots to be able to sell the agreement and continue to marginalize the radical opposition elites waiting in the wings. The government must, therefore, simultaneously reassure its own constituent base, give the opposition just enough to crow about to its supporters, and claim as credibly as possible to undecided potential voters to have made the deal that is in their best interest. Opposition moderates confront the no less delicate task of convincing their core supporters that they have made the best possible bargain and concurrently presenting their concessions to others as evidence of their moderation and lack of partisanship.

In short, in negotiated transitions government reformers have more valuable cards going in than do the opposition moderates, deriving from their monopoly control of the state's coercive institutions. They may lack the power to impose what Huntington describes as a transformation, but by the same token the opposition lacks the power to impose a replacement. (Were this not so, negotiations would, presumably, not begin; and should it not remain so, they would not continue to an agreement.) The test of the government reformers' negotiating skill is how successfully they manage to use their structural advantage to get the opposition moderates to concede the maximum possible while forcing them to satisfice with respect to their grass roots constituency. They must do this in a way that alienates as few of the government's own potential supporters as possible. The test for the opposition moderates is how successfully they can undermine the government's structural advantage, reach an agreement with which their core supporters can live, and make themselves attractive to as many other potential voters as possible. How these interacting imperatives were played out in the South African transition between 1990 and 1994 is the subject to which we now turn.

V. SOUTH AFRICA'S NEGOTIATED TRANSITION

The National Party's grand design for apartheid ran into trouble almost as soon as its leaders began to implement it when they came to power in 1948. When basic tenets of separate racial and ethnic development proved unworkable, parts of the strategy were abandoned and others were redesigned.[32] With various liberalizing fits and starts, South Africa was thus an unstable authoritarian regime for some forty-two years before the NP government of F. W. De Klerk decided, in 1990, to dismantle the apartheid regime and create a new multiracial political order.

The Failure of Liberalized Apartheid

Economic necessity led to the first tangible wave of liberalization in the late 1970s, when the government relaxed certain labor laws and legalized black trade unions. The pinnacle of then-president P. W. Botha's strategy to mollify the opposition and undermine its uncooperative stance was the creation of the Tricameral Parliament in 1984. Pretoria hoped to draw in the "Coloured" and Indian communities and separate them from the rest of the disenfranchised black majority by creating separate parliaments (still subordinate to the white parliament) in which they would be represented.

[32]See Hermann Giliomee, *The Parting of the Ways: South African Politics, 1976–1982* (Cape Town: Philip, 1982), and Heribert Adam and Hermann Giliomee, *The Rise and Crisis of Afrikaner Power* (Cape Town: Philip, 1979).

This strategy backfired. The Tricameral Parliament provided the impetus for the organization of the United Democratic Front, an umbrella group of antiapartheid forces. By allowing elections for the Tricameral Parliament and easing strict apartheid bans on freedom of movement and gathering, the government unwittingly opened the space for a mass politicized boycott that changed the terms of political debate. As Nigel Gibson puts it, the "overwhelming rejection [of the Tricameral Parliament] and struggles against the reforms were the starting point for a new stage of experiments with democratic forms of rule."[33] The 1980s were marked by nationwide boycotts, strikes, stay-aways, and demonstrations, seemingly in line with Huntington's conjecture about the instability of liberalized authoritarianisms.[34] This widespread refusal to cooperate, together with the refusal of any country outside South Africa to recognize the tricameral solution as legitimate, weakened the government's position and was followed by increasingly militant grass roots mobilization, notably among the urban black youth.

The government responded to the popular upsurge with repression. In mid-1986, President Botha declared a nationwide state of emergency that gave the government wide-ranging powers to implement detention without trial, break up gatherings of two or more people, and generally to suppress political activity. Thousands of activists were detained. Nonetheless, the militancy of the townships and the momentum of "people's power" were not seriously affected. By the late 1980s it was clear to most observers that what remained of the government's legitimacy was fast eroding, and that a combination of growing internal opposition, international pressure and sanctions, and a spiraling economic crisis meant that major change of some kind was all but inevitable.

Prenegotiations

The National Party reformers. Yet many observers were caught off guard by the speed and decisiveness with which change came in February 1990. President De Klerk, a conservative Afrikaner by history and reputation who had been one of the mainstays of apartheid in previous cabinets, surprised both the South African opposition and the world by unbanning the ANC, the Pan-Africanist Congress (PAC), and the South African Communist Party (which had been illegal since 1960). He simultaneously announced plans to release all political prisoners, includ-

---

[33]Nigel Gibson, "Why Is Participation a Dirty Word in South African Politics?" *Africa Today* (second quarter 1990), p. 27.

[34]Huntington, *Third Wave*, pp. 136–37.

ing Nelson Mandela, and to begin negotiations toward democracy. Given the NP's history of relentlessly demonizing these groups while sustaining the apartheid order behind a veil of cosmetic adjustments, these decisions left little room for doubt that fundamental change was at hand.

The government's decision to act suddenly and release Mandela before his role within the ANC had been agreed upon seemed calculated to promote and capitalize on the ANC's disorganization and to enable the NP to structure the terms of future negotiations as much as possible. De Klerk's relentless forward pressure, in stark contrast to the NP history of stonewalling and temporizing, suggests an awareness on his part of the advantages to the government of an early settlement.[35] He seems to have realized that although the government had the upper hand—it controlled the means of coercion and unilaterally directed the transition process—its strength was bound to decline as negotiations legitimated the opposition groups and reduced the government to lame duck status.

De Klerk's NP reformers also faced significant opposition from political hard-liners and a right-wing movement that had garnered substantial support from whites who feared the end of minority rule. De Klerk could and did use the threat from the Right as a negotiating tool, to demonstrate to the ANC the government's limited room to make concessions. But in the early stages the right wing really was an unknown quantity, widely perceived to be a credible threat to the transition and to the political strength of the reformers. De Klerk's early attempts at unilateral democratization seem to have grown partly out of his tenuous position vis-à-vis his own constituency and with respect to his right flank. He had no mandate actually to negotiate with the ANC and he could not ensure that he could bind his party or constituency to an agreement that represented a compromise.

The ANC moderates. In much of 1990 and 1991, the ANC showed little interest in starting serious negotiations. For the first few months of the apparent negotiating period, there was no agreement within the ANC about who could legitimately represent it or what its policies should be on a host of issues from the handling of the economy (given the ANC's now obviously anachronistic links with orthodox communism) to land reform, education, housing, regional power, international relations, and

---

[35]Press reports from the first ten months of 1990 show that De Klerk moved quickly to establish an NP negotiating position, draft a proposed constitution, remove some remnants of apartheid, and generally pave the way for an early settlement. In the absence of negotiations, the ANC complained that De Klerk was negotiating with the media rather than with the opposition; see *Star* (Johannesburg), July 1, 1990.

the constitutional future of the country. Mandela toured southern Africa and Europe soon after he was released from prison, strengthening the ANC's negotiating position by exploiting his fame as a political prisoner of conscience and an international symbol of black oppression. While scrambling to formulate a negotiating position and assemble a credible negotiating team, the ANC enjoyed and capitalized on the legitimation that unbanning and planned negotiations afforded it.

For the first two years, talks moved slowly, with a good deal of grandstanding at CODESA from all sides. During this period, the ANC was faced with the dual task of transforming itself from a liberation movement into a political party and trying not to alienate its traditional supporters, who in many cases preferred revolution to negotiation. The leadership faced the danger of appearing too conciliatory at the same time as it needed to make concessions to keep the process alive. For instance, the ANC announced the suspension of the armed struggle in August 1990 but refused to disband Umkhonto we Sizwe (its military wing), hand over weapons, or disclose the location of weapons caches inside the country. The storm of controversy the suspension precipitated among ANC supporters, as well as mid-level leaders who resented exclusion from decision making, forced the leadership to back away from the suspension, brushing aside government assertions that if they were serious about negotiations they would disband.[36]

Partly in an effort to rebuild and consolidate its constituent base, and partly to demonstrate its strength to the NP, the ANC dubbed 1991 "the year of mass action." Clearly still in the demand-escalating mode, the ANC leadership organized nationwide strikes, stay-aways, protest marches, and rallies while imploring people to remain peaceful and to trust in the negotiation process as the primary vehicle of change. The ANC leadership was locked within very narrow parameters as it tried to maximize its own base of support without derailing the negotiating process or alienating the NP and its core constituency.

The ANC was reluctant to let the negotiations move rapidly. Whereas the NP pressed for a substantive agreement on a postapartheid government, the ANC focused on reaching agreement on a procedure by which a democratic government could be formed.[37] To this end, it sought partly to remain a liberation movement, demanding an interim government and an elected constituent assembly to write the first constitution. ANC leaders sought to undermine the legitimacy and strate-

[36]Hermann Giliomee and Johannes Rantete, "Transition to Democracy through Transaction? Bilateral Negotiations between the ANC and the NP in South Africa," *African Affairs* no. 91 (1992), p. 529.
[37]Ibid., p. 526.

gic advantage of the NP by challenging its role as legitimate government and primary negotiator. An interim government would assume
(some undefined degree of) responsibility for governing while the two
sides negotiated on what the ANC termed "a more level playing field."
Additionally, ANC leaders argued that only an elected constituent assembly would lead to a democratic process in which the constitution
would be drafted by democratically elected delegates. Confident that
they would win a majority in elections for a constituent assembly, they
expected that they would then have a free rein to draft the new constitution and control the new government.[38]

The Central Issue: Majority Rule

The debate over majority rule plagued discussions even in the pre-
negotiating phase. Despite extravagant claims by Mangosuthu
Buthelezi to be a coequal player with large support for his ethnically
based IFP throughout the negotiations, the polls systematically belied
his assertions. All parties to the negotiations assumed throughout—
accurately, as it turned out—that the ANC would easily win an absolute majority in any election based on universal franchise. As a result,
negotiations for democracy centered on the issue of majority rule
versus some sort of power-sharing arrangement.

Initially, the government seems to have thought that it could dictate
the terms of a settlement. De Klerk said, in 1990, "We did not wait until
the position of power dominance turned against us before we decided
to negotiate a peaceful settlement. The initiative is in our hands. We
have the means to ensure that the process develops peacefully and in an
orderly way."[39] His intention was formally to entrench power sharing
in the new constitution. The NP proposed that minority parties with
significant support be assured of cabinet representation, that the presidency rotate among three to five members, and that decisions be based
on consensus in both bodies.[40]

Power sharing had been anathema to the ANC for its entire history. It
seemed too obviously to be a euphemism for "group rights," in turn
little more than a smoke screen for apartheid by another name. Given
this history and the ANC's knowledge of the extent of its own grass
roots support, it is not surprising that initially the ANC regarded all talk
of power sharing as taboo. In his early campaigning and international

[38]Ibid., p. 527.
[39]*Die Burger,* March 31, 1990. See also Giliomee and Rantete, "Transition to Democracy," p.
518.
[40]Giliomee and Rantete, "Transition to Democracy," p. 523.

travels, Mandela heaped scorn on assertions by the government that South Africa was unique in its ethnic and racial composition and that as a result it needed a political system tailored to its idiosyncrasies. The ANC rejected all such claims, insisting that they wanted no more—but also no less—than an "ordinary democracy."[41]

Negotiations Begin

Early in 1992, a series of Conservative Party wins in local by-elections in former NP strongholds served to warn reformers in the NP that substantial numbers of whites might not support a transition. De Klerk responded by calling a referendum, held in March 1992, in which white voters were asked whether they supported negotiations. In so doing, he took a substantial political risk. Had the referendum results been negative, he would certainly have had to reverse policy, and he would likely have been deposed as leader of the NP and head of the government. But he won a resounding two-thirds majority, revealing the white-right electoral threat to be chimerical. The "no" voters in the referendum failed to win a majority even in the Afrikaner heartlands in the Orange Free State and the Northern Transvaal. Rumblings about a military coup continued until December 1992, when De Klerk called the bluff of the hard-liners in the military by firing twenty-three senior officers with a message, as Tom Lodge put it, to "go quietly, and take your pensions."[42] These events effectively marginalized the white right and substantially expanded De Klerk's room for maneuver in the negotiations.

De Klerk was quick to declare that the referendum result was a mandate to negotiate a settlement, and he insisted throughout the remainder of the negotiating process and the 1994 election campaign that everything he agreed to had been outlined in the referendum and thus previously endorsed by an overwhelming majority of the whites.[43] His freedom in this regard was not unlimited, however. Although the referendum gave De Klerk the political leverage he needed to negotiate a settlement on behalf of the white population, it committed him to some version of power sharing. This had been explicit in the referendum

---

[41]In 1990, Mandela wrote in his best-selling autobiography that there would be no peace until majority rule was fully implemented; see Nelson Mandela, *The Struggle Is My Life* (London: IDAF Publications, 1990), p. 206. As late as April 1992 he was still insisting at press conferences that the ANC could never accept the various "fancy proposals" for power sharing that were on offer from the government: "We want an ordinary democracy as practiced elsewhere in the world." ANC press conference, *BBC Summary of World Broadcasts*, April 9, 1992.

[42]Quoted in *New York Times*, December 21, 1992, p. A7.

[43]*SAPA* (Johannesburg), June 8, 1993.

campaign, in effect making the referendum a contract between De Klerk and the white minority that he would not devolve all power to the black majority.[44] Had he ventured beyond the terms of this contract, his support would have fragmented and the far right would likely have re-emerged as a serious force. Within the constraints implied by the contract, however, De Klerk was now free to begin genuine negotiations with the moderate leadership of the ANC.

The ANC leadership's incentive and capacity to negotiate emerged gradually. In the June 1992 Boipatong massacre, thirty-nine unarmed ANC supporters were killed by apparent Inkatha members while South African police and vehicles stood idly by. Mandela immediately pulled out of the talks in protest against the security forces' unwillingness to stem so-called black-on-black violence as well as Inkatha attacks against the ANC, precipitating the end of the all-party round-table negotiations.[45] The ANC backed up its dramatic walkout by calling for mass action and popular protest. The leadership used this, its most valuable extra-institutional bargaining chip, to demonstrate that it retained the capacity to mobilize its following against the government. The mass-action campaign was successful in bringing tens of thousands of people into the negotiating process by using them to back up ANC demands. It became evident, however, that mass action once mobilized was no longer controllable by the ANC leadership. Although Mandela called repeatedly for peaceful demonstrations, South Africa's highest levels of transitional violence occurred in the month after Boipatong.[46]

Three months after Boipatong, the Ciskei government opened fire on a group of ANC followers marching in support of the mass-action campaign at Bisho. This event in particular made the human cost of the transition graphically evident to the ANC leadership. Although the ANC had organized the demonstration, it was powerless to protect the demonstrators or to punish those responsible for the massacre. The mass-action campaign and the Bisho incident demonstrated that it was the ANC's constituency—and not the government's—that was suffer-

---

[44]De Klerk launched the referendum campaign by saying, "We will not say yes to a suicide plan. We will once again reiterate the importance that in such a new constitution, whether it be a first phase or a fully encompassing constitution, how important we regard it that there must be effective protection against domination of minorities"; *SABC Network* (Johannesburg), February 24, 1992. After his victory, De Klerk said, "We want to share power, we want a new dispensation, want it to be fair, we want it to be equitable"; ibid., March 19, 1992.

[45]These negotiations had been stalled for some time over the percentage of votes needed for acceptance of the constitution, with the ANC advocating two-thirds, which it thought it might be able to win outright, and the government insisting on 75 percent.

[46]In that month, there were 1,535 incidents of political violence with 240 deaths, the highest number to that date; *Southern Africa Report*, May 14, 1993, p. 3. That number was to be exceeded only in the final weeks before the April 1994 elections.

ing the greatest repercussions from the breakdown of negotiations. Even nationwide mass action was not likely to destabilize the government to the point that it would cede ground to the ANC in the absence of talks.

The ANC's visible inability either to control or protect its increasingly frustrated constituency seems to have changed the leadership's appreciation of time constraints. Mandela signaled that the economic and social dislocations of the transition were threatening to spiral out of control when he said, in September 1992, "We are trying to push the country away from . . . horror . . . We haven't got much time . . . the economy is falling to pieces, and that we cannot afford."[47] If the ANC leadership lost control of the mass action, it would lose both its grass roots support and its role as a negotiating principal. At least some in the ANC leadership seemed to be realizing that even if they did manage to negotiate a settlement, waiting too long might undermine the electoral support they would need to ensure a dominant position even in a multiparty government.[48]

At the same time as social unrest was threatening to spiral out of the ANC leadership's control, De Klerk was greatly increasing the stakes for both sides by threatening to play the transformation card. Having faced down the hard right, he was now approaching his point of no return; now he needed to get a settlement. During this period he declared repeatedly that he would negotiate with anyone or no one, that he would arrange the transition by himself if need be, but that, no matter what, it would occur. Illustrating this determination, he held a series of bilateral talks with the PAC in Botswana,[49] held a conference with key advisers to outline a new strategy to jump start negotiations,[50] and broadened invitations for talks on violence to include other political parties after the ANC declined the invitation.[51]

The dual triggers of Boipatong and Bisho, and their repercussions, seem to have caused the ANC leadership to look into the abyss and realize that time for a negotiated settlement over which they could have

[47]*Star*, September 15, 1992.
[48]Support for the ANC dropped from 75 percent in May 1992 to 65 percent in March 1993; "Election Watch," *Work in Progress*, June 1993, p. 3. "Our people have experienced us negotiating for three years with no tangible advance. We need, as politicians, to be aware that they have seen no change in their lives and for that a nation that is divided, torn asunder, rent by violence, needs to see where is this country going by when," said Mac Maharaj, ANC leader, *SABC TV*, June 3, 1993.
[49]*Star*, September 17, 1992, p. 9.
[50]*SABC TV*, July 30, 1992.
[51]*SAPA*, July 30, 1992.

substantial influence was running out.[52] In any event, ANC leaders returned to bilateral talks with the government immediately after the Ciskei massacre, and the real negotiations began. Unlike the two earlier CODESA round-table negotiations, which had been public events adorned by many marginal players, the post-Boipatong talks involved the government and the ANC only, they were held in secret, and both sides appeared determined to fix the main terms of their agreement before multilateral talks would again be allowed to begin. These terms were announced in the Record of Understanding, made public in February 1993, between the ANC and the government.[53]

From "Ordinary Democracy" to Power Sharing

Once the ANC leaders became convinced that all the alternatives to a relatively quick negotiated settlement were worse, they faced the Hobson's choice described in the previous section, and the government's structural advantage in the negotiations became manifest. De Klerk's commitment to power sharing was nonnegotiable; this meant that the ANC would make the principal concessions. A successful agreement thus came to hinge on whether the moderate ANC leadership could move itself tactically and ideologically into a position where it could accept power sharing before its core constituency support was lost. The leadership had to shift its policy to accept power sharing and marginalize other elites inside and outside the ANC who might challenge its position as the principal representative of the opposition. The government, which had been ready to negotiate seriously since mid-1992 but needed a serious partner, did everything it could to help with the second matter. Once the bilateral talks began in September, government ministers began to mute public criticism of the ANC leaders (who responded in kind), and the government began trying to marginalize opposition groups that were in competition with the ANC—most notably the IFP. This marked a distinct change in government strategy. As late as May of 1992 the government had seemed bent on pumping up non-ANC opposition groups through such actions as meeting with the PAC (which was then boycotting CODESA) outside the country and disputing ANC claims about its own grass roots support (insisting, for example, that the IFP had more substantial support than the ANC

[52]It is hard to believe that the daily news of civil war and ethnic slaughter in Bosnia and the recent memories of what had happened in Angola had no impact, though it would be difficult to determine just what that impact was.

[53]*New York Times*, February 19, 1993, pp. A1, A7.

among the Zulu in Natal). The old strategy of seeking to divide the opposition as much as possible—consistent with a transformative strategy—was now shelved in favor of finding, and to some extent even creating, a negotiating partner with whom a deal could be made.

By the end of 1992, the government and the ANC leadership were being criticized from the left and the right in ways that suggested that the alliance necessary for transplacement to occur was close to being cemented in place. In December, Buthelezi was reduced to desperate talk about unilaterally calling a referendum on self-rule for Natal, and he furiously denounced the February 1993 agreement. A common assertion that could be heard emanating from all parts of the political landscape by early 1993 was that the government and the ANC were now fully dependent on one another. The government had evidently abandoned the transformation strategy, and, indeed, seemed to be welcoming the opportunity to externalize some of the responsibility for controlling urban violence onto the ANC leadership. There was even discussion of integrating Umkhonto we Sizwe into the South African Defense Force, an idea dismissed by the government as unthinkably radical only nine months earlier at CODESA. Both sides had managed to marshal sufficient support to sustain the negotiation process, and both sides seemed aware that this support would not last indefinitely. Each side had maneuvered itself into a position from which it could afford to reach an agreement *and* from which the costs of failing to reach one were growing all the time.[54]

The other essential ingredient was that the ANC leadership subdue its radical wing and get its core supporters to accept power sharing. In November 1992 the ANC National Executive adopted a document that formally conceded the basic principle. Noting that "the regime commands vast state and military resources, and continues to enjoy the support of powerful economic forces," the document recognized a need "to accept the fact that, even after the adoption of a new constitution, the balance of forces and the interests of the country may still require us to consider the establishment of a government of national unity."[55] This position stood in marked contrast to the ANC's insistence, some eight months earlier at CODESA, that it unalterably opposed all forms of "enforced coalitions/power sharing/minority vetoes." At that time the

[54]The impression that these shifts in strategy had occurred is based on interviews with people close to the principal negotiating partners, conducted during visits to South Africa in May and December 1992.

[55]African National Congress, "Negotiations: A Strategic Perspective" (adopted by the ANC National Executive Committee, November 25, 1992); quoted in Steven Friedman, "A Reluctant Transition," *Journal of Democracy* 4 no. 2 (April 1993), p. 61.

ANC had reiterated its long-held view that under majority rule the legitimate aspirations of the white minority could be expressed through the opposition in the legislature, and it had dismissed the NP argument for a constitution that would ensure minority participation in government as "a code for guaranteed power for racial groups."[56]

The fight over power sharing within the ANC lasted several months. It was not clear that the radical wing had been subdued until the end of a fractious three-day debate in February 1993. The issue was whether the Congress's one hundred–member governing committee would endorse the agreement that had been negotiated with the government. Cyril Ramaphosa, the ANC's chief negotiator and longtime leader of the Conference of South African Trade Unions (the powerful black trade union movement), denied that the agreement amounted to a power-sharing arrangement. But the reality was clearly different, as militants such as Harry Gwala and Chris Hani were quick to point out and as De Klerk and his aides were busily announcing to their supporters. The agreement called for a legally mandated five-year government of national unity regardless of the election outcome, with cabinet representation for all parties that won at least 5 percent of the vote, and a share of executive power for the strongest minority party. The government made marginal concessions on the size of supermajority thresholds and agreed for the first time to defer some questions about regional powers to the next parliament.[57] But on the central question of majority rule, the ANC reversed its decades-old policy and accepted a strong consociational arrangement, at least for the rest of the century.

However accurate the militants' portrayal of the agreement as a sellout might have been, they were unable to secure the votes on the ANC's governing committee for a nationwide membership conference to debate the issue.[58] The agreement that had been negotiated was approved, and from that point through the elections, the ANC leadership faced no serious threat from its left. Although multiparty talks began the following month, the bilateral agreement of February 1993 set the basic terms of the constitution that was adopted by the white parlia-

---

[56]The African National Congress, "The Constitution, Minorities, and the New Constitution" (undated response to the National Party paper "The Meaningful Participation of Political Minorities," submitted to CODESA Working Group 4 on February 25, 1992); quoted in Steven Friedman, *The Long Journey: South Africa's Quest for a Negotiated Settlement* (Johannesburg: Ravan, 1993), p. 68.

[57]The changes on regional powers were not really concessions because they mattered more to white separatists and the IFP, neither of whom were serious players by this time, than to the government, which never considered abandoning the concept of a unitary state once negotiations began.

[58]*New York Times*, February 19, 1993, pp. A1, A7.

ment in its final act in December of that year. In October, an act was passed creating the Transitional Executive Council (TEC), a multiparty executive body designed to oversee the government in the run-up to the elections of April 1994.[59] Although the act limited the TEC's powers to matters having to do with ensuring a level playing field for the elections, the TEC quickly became a kind of supercabinet. When the TEC successfully ordered the military to go into Bophuthatswana to put down a white separatist group that was supporting the local black leader in opposing the coming elections, two things became clear for the first time: the army was loyal to the TEC, and the transition to multiracial government in South Africa was a fait accompli before a single black vote had been cast.

The Absence of Democratic Opposition

Huntington advises the leaders of authoritarian regimes who are engaged in negotiated transitions to begin planning for politics in opposition.[60] Not only did De Klerk fail to take this advice, he could not have taken it while still negotiating a transition to a multiracial state with the ANC moderate leadership. The necessary condition for his marginalizing the standpatters to his right was that he commit to a power-sharing model that would ensure the white minority a role, if a junior one, in the next government. Once the moderate ANC leaders had passed their point of no return and needed an agreement, they had to accept this reality as well—hence the mutual convergence on power sharing. Beyond these constraints, the negotiating principals had few incentives to pay attention to opposition institutions in the new order because at no time did either of them intend not to be in the next government. Whether either would have found a different model more attractive had they considered the longer term turned out to be irrelevant; both were prisoners of the myopia that, in the last analysis, became the minimum price of a negotiated transition.

As they moved closer together, the government and the ANC leadership developed a common interest in marginalizing all opposition to their joint venture, so that there was no dissent, for example, when the TEC made the ominous decision to suspend the planned abolition of Section 29 of the Internal Security Act permitting detention without trial, which had been inherited from the apartheid regime.[61] During the

[59]"Transitional Executive Council Act," Act no. 151 (1993), *Government Gazette*, October 27, 1993.

[60]Huntington, *Third Wave*, p. 162.

[61]*Southscan*, February 11, 1994.

heady final months of the transition negotiations and the run-up to the elections, co-opting or marginalizing opposition seemed desirable to the principals and to most observers. This is understandable because the opposition being expressed was opposition to the end of the apartheid regime. But because the principals expected to be major players in the new political order, they were engaged in more than regime building. And in ensuring that there could be no serious opposition to the new order they were creating, they also ensured that there would be little scope for democratic opposition within it.

VI. COMPARATIVE CONSIDERATIONS

We hesitate to speculate that a negotiated settlement will always lead to a particular type of constitutional arrangement. The nature of the political order that prevails in a country depends on a number of factors: there may be a regional bias in favor of a particular type of government; constitution framers may perceive a need to attenuate potentially divisive ethnic, linguistic, or religious cleavages; or a nascent state may be influenced by its colonial heritage—to name three obvious candidates. Nonetheless, our discussions of the dynamics of transition negotiations in section IV and of the South African negotiations in section V suggest that the following conjecture merits serious consideration: negotiated transitions are unlikely to lead to constitutional arrangements that contain strong opposition institutions when the outgoing government expects to be a minority player in the new political order. Other things being equal, such transitions are more likely to converge on arrangements toward the non-opposition end of the continuum discussed in section II.

Since this conjecture and the model of transition negotiations that gave rise to it were developed in the course of a retrospective attempt to understand the South African developments, the next step is to consider the following questions: how does our conjecture square with data culled from other sources, and how does it compare with other plausible explanations of the South African developments we sought to explain? To address the first of these would require a systematic look at the outcomes of other transitions with respect to opposition institutions and an accounting of the ways in which democracies that do have strong institutionalized oppositions came to have them. To address the second, we would need to see how our conjecture stacks up against competing explanations for why those who designed the 1993 South African constitution agreed on a model that has notably less institutional space for political opposition than was the case during the apartheid era. An empirical test of our conjecture would thus require systematic comparison of different types of transitions with variation in the independent variable. That is too large a task to attempt here. Nonetheless, some consideration of our conjecture seems in order at this point to get a prima facie sense of whether the South African transition appears to belong to a class of negotiated transition types (and if so, just what that class is) or whether it is better thought of as a sui generis phenomenon.

Huntington's transplacements most closely resemble the transitions we are interested in understanding.[62] In *The Third Wave*, he identifies eleven instances, to which we would add Chile and Zimbabwe. Huntington classified Chile as an instance of a hybrid between a transformation and a transplacement, but, as we point out below, since he wrote it has became clear that substantial parts of the transition were negotiated. Huntington also excludes Zimbabwe as a nondemocratic country, but the Zimbabwean transition from colonial rule led to a seven-year power-sharing agreement: precisely the kind of truncated democracy that, we suspect, negotiations may often yield. It may, indeed, be a mark of the kind of negotiated transition we are examining that the ensuing regime does not meet Huntington's definitional test of a democracy: two peaceful turnovers of power following elections.

Not all of Huntington's transplacements should, however, be expected to follow the logic we have identified. A different subgroup consists of transplacements in which the power holders in the outgoing regime do not intend to be players in the new order, as in Uruguay, Bolivia, and Nepal. In such circumstances, reformers in the authoritar-

---

[62]The negotiated transitions we are considering differ from Huntingtonian transformations, such as occurred in Spain, in that they are not put into effect unilaterally by agents of the authoritarian regime. The Spanish transition was controlled by a third party, King Juan Carlos, who was eager to restore democracy after the death of Franco, had majority support to do so, and did not intend to participate in democratic elections. No doubt during transformations exiting governments can often exert substantial influence on the future institutional structure. This would scarcely be counterintuitive, given the fact that they hold all the cards from the beginning to the end of the transition. What motivates our present research is the different question Why do opposition moderates concede so much in negotiated transitions, when government reformers have less power than in transformations? For an opposite reason, we exclude replacements, such as exemplified by East Germany and Romania, and interventions, exemplified by West Germany, Japan, and Panama. In the former, the authoritarian regime collapses before negotiations about the structure of the new political order begin. In the latter, the key determinant of future institutional arrangements is likely to be the preference of the intervening power—usually a victor in war. In both these circumstances the animating force that structures negotiated transitions—the outgoing government's decisive hold on power throughout the negotiations—is absent. They should be expected to exhibit their own distinctive dynamics.

ian regime do not confront the incentives that face a power holder in the old order who is planning to be a potential electoral competitor in the new one. Accordingly, the dynamics we identify should not be present.[63] Huntington also describes Honduras and El Salvador as having undergone transplacements. In these cases, the principal negotiations were between the authoritarian regime and the U.S. government in the role of a kind of surrogate opposition.[64] They were thus hybrids between transplacements and interventions. They, too, should be expected to follow a distinctive logic. Finally, in our view, Huntington misclassifies the change in Czechoslovakia as a transplacement instead of a replacement because the Communist government there collapsed before negotiations began. A multiparty coalition headed by Vaclav Havel took over, presiding over the transition and first elections.[65] After these additions and deletions we are left with six negotiated transitions that seem similar to South Africa's: those in Zimbabwe, Poland, Chile, Mongolia, Nicaragua, and Korea.

ZIMBABWE. After a decade-long civil war between Rhodesia's white minority government and the nationalist Patriotic Front, the opposing sides entered negotiations to end the war and design a mutually agreeable political system. Although the war had seriously undercut the legitimacy of the Rhodesian government as well as its ability to protect its white constituency, the regime was by no means spent militarily; and both sides knew that it retained the capacity to return to the battlefield if its demands were not met. Government negotiators, as well as British mediators trying to safeguard white interests, insisted on guarantees that would allow the authoritarian regime to maintain political influence in a postcolonial democratic system. The Patriotic Front plan, conversely, simply offered all Zimbabweans equal rights without discrimination. It was forced to make the major concession. The 1979 Lancaster House agreement included special clauses to prevent changes to the constitution for seven years and to reserve 20 percent of the seats in Parliament for whites, who constituted 2 or 3 percent of the population.[66] In the event that the African vote should be seriously

[63]In Uruguay and Bolivia the military negotiated with an eye to extracting itself from the political process while retaining its institutional legitimacy; it had no intention of contesting future elections. Similarly in Nepal the monarchy, which controlled the government and means of coercion, did not negotiate a political role for itself in a democratic system. King Birendra retains only ceremonial status.

[64]Huntington, *Third Wave*, p. 152.

[65]Gordon Wightman, "The Collapse of Communist Rule in Czechoslovakia and the June 1990 Parliamentary Elections," *Parliamentary Affairs* 44, no.1 (1991), pp. 28–57.

[66]Jeffrey Herbst, *State Politics in Zimbabwe* (Berkeley: University of California Press, 1990), pp. 29–30.

fractured, twenty seats in a one hundred–member parliament could place the whites in a kingmaking role.[67]

POLAND. Poland's 1989 round-table negotiations were the result of popular opposition and trade union demands for liberalization and democratization going back to as early as 1979. The Communist Party government agreed to negotiate with Lech Walesa's Solidarity movement in order to stem the erosion of its legitimacy, and its continued close ties to the Soviet Union gave it leverage throughout the negotiating process. Although it thus had sufficient power significantly to determine the terms of the settlement, it was pessimistic about its chances for winning an election against the democratic opposition. It calculated that a semipresidential proportional representation system, with certain guarantees, would ensure its interests in a nascent democracy. The system finally agreed to included a strong presidency, elected by both chambers of a parliament but not subject to its confidence, as well as a prime minister and cabinet subject to parliament.[68] The agreement included a tacit understanding that General Wojciech Jaruzelski, the Communist Party leader, would be elected president and a guarantee that 65 percent of the seats in the lower chamber would be reserved for the Communist Party.[69]

CHILE. Chile's authoritarian regime undertook democratic transition after a 1988 plebiscite on Augusto Pinochet's continuation in power produced a majority "no" vote. The transition is commonly analyzed as a negotiation between a strong authoritarian regime and a strong democratic coalition,[70] although in the end, as Pamela Constable and Arturo Valenzuela point out, "all of Chile's democratic forces realized they would have to swallow the bitter pill of the regime's legal transition formula."[71] In the final settlement, Pinochet retained the right to appoint nine of forty-seven senators and established a complex electoral system that favored minority proregime candidates and overrepresented the rural areas where conservatives believed they had

[67]Jeffrey Davidow, *A Peace in Southern Africa* (Boulder: Westview, 1984) p. 59.

[68]Richard F. Staar, ed., *Transition to Democracy in Poland* (New York: St. Martin's, 1993) pp. 57–77.

[69]Arend Lijphart, "Democratization and Constitutional Choices in Czechoslovakia, Hungary, and Poland, 1989–1991," *Journal of Theoretical Politics* 4, no. 2 (1992), pp. 207–33; Wictor Osiatynski, "The Polish Constitution," *Law and Policy* 13, no. 2 (April 1991), p. 130.

[70]Helgio Trinidade, "Presidential Elections and Political Transition in Latin America," *International Social Science Journal*, no. 128 (1991), p. 304.

[71]Pamela Constable and Arturo Valenzuela, "Democracy Restored," *Journal of Democracy* 1, no. 2 (1990), p. 8.

greater appeal.[72] The combination of a favorable electoral system and designated senators gave the conservatives a majority in Congress and veto power. Mayoral posts were distributed between the government and the opposition coalition.[73] Finally, Pinochet himself was guaranteed his position as commander of the armed forces until 1997.

MONGOLIA. The ruling Mongolian People's Revolutionary Party moved toward reform in response to popular demonstrations for democratization in 1989 and 1990. The party initially tried to shore up its legitimacy by reorganizing itself and held elections for the Great People's Hural (GPH) in 1990. The election law negotiated between regime and opposition allowed the ruling party to retain dominance by favoring the rural areas and overrepresenting the majority party, which won 86 percent of the seats in the GPH with 60 percent of the vote. The GPH in turn elected party leader Punsalmaagiyn Ochirbat president of Mongolia, although in separate elections an opposition party member won the vice-presidency. Negotiations subsequently led to the creation of the Small Hural—whose fifty members were appointed in proportion to the percentage of the vote they received in the 1990 election—to assume responsibility for governing and constitutional reform. The Small Hural took the unusual step in 1991 of banning all political parties and requiring the president and vice-president to drop their party affiliations. The explicit intention was to reduce interparty conflict and facilitate power sharing among all parties.[74] Mongolia appears to be undergoing what might best be described as a rolling transition in which a series of elections have each changed the parameters of political competition, but it is still far from clear whether a formal agreement on a democratic system will be reached.

NICARAGUA. Nicaragua's Sandinista government believed that it could shore up its power and image by agreeing to hold elections in 1990. Because it thought it still had more than enough support to pass an electoral test without having to resort to fraud, the government did not negotiate the terms of the elections or of alternation in power.[75] Contrary to widespread expectations, however, Violeta Chamorro and her fourteen-party coalition won the 1990 elections in a

[72]Ibid., p. 9

[73]Alan Angell, "The Transition to Democracy in Chile: A Model or an Exceptional Case?" *Parliamentary Affairs* 46, no. 4 (1993), pp. 569–70.

[74]William Heaton, "Mongolia in 1991: The Uneasy Transition," *Asian Survey* 33, no. 1 (January 1992), p. 50, and "Mongolia in 1992," *Asian Survey* 34, no. 1 (January 1993), p. 53.

[75]Pablo Antonio Cuadra, "Reclaiming the Revolution," *Journal of Democracy* 1, no.3 (summer 1990), p. 43.

landslide. A peaceful transition still depended on Sandinista cooperation, and the two sides met over the following weeks to negotiate the
transfer of power. It was during this period, when the authoritarian
regime still controlled access to power but had already lost democratic
elections, that the Sandinistas held out for the type of power-sharing
guarantees usually agreed to in the preelectoral phase. Most important,
Chamorro agreed to "respect the integrity of the armed forces as an
institution," a de facto recognition that the military was still under
Sandinista control (she was forced to appoint Humberto Ortega, Daniel
Ortega's brother, as chief of the armed forces). Thus, although what
emerged was not an explicit power-sharing arrangement—there were
no quotas for cabinet representation, for instance—it was widely seen
in Nicaragua as a classical dynastic pact between two powerful families
and was hailed as a government of national unity.[76]

KOREA. In response to widespread demands for democratization,
Korea's ruling Democratic Justice Party (DJP) unilaterally announced
that it would hold direct presidential elections in December 1987. The
DJP won the presidency with 36 percent of the vote and entered negotiations with the two leading opposition parties to determine the arrangement of National Assembly elections. Because of its relative success in the presidential elections, DJP negotiators believed they would
win a majority in parliamentary elections. Accordingly, they created an
electoral system designed to overrepresent the majority party: a presidential system with a national assembly elected by a complex mixture
of first-past-the-post and proportional representation rules.[77] As in Nicaragua, then, in Korea the outgoing authoritarian regime did not insist
on power-sharing arrangements because its leaders believed (however
incorrectly) that these were unnecessary to protect its power in the new
democratic order.

Our brief look at these six transitions suggests that the conjecture we
developed in attempting to account for the outcome of the South Afri-

[76]Robert S. Leiken, "Old and New Politics in Managua," ibid., pp. 35–37.

[77]David Brady and Jongryn Mo, "Electoral Systems and Institutional Choice: A Case Study of
the 1988 Korean Elections," *Comparative Political Studies* 24, no. 4 (January 1992), p. 419. As it
happened, the DJP overestimated its electoral strength and won only 34 percent of the popular
vote, which translated into 39 percent of direct-constituency seats. Consequently, it had a
minority in the National Assembly and was paralyzed by the three leading opposition parties,
which cooperated to reject presidential nominations, stall budget deliberations, and control the
legislative schedule. In an effort to break the deadlock, the ruling DJP eventually joined forces
with two of the primary opposition parties. In January 1990 the three parties merged to form the
Democratic Liberal Party, with more than two-thirds of the seats in the National Assembly,
effectively, if only temporarily, hamstringing national politics. See Sung Joo Han, "The Korean
Experiment," *Journal of Democracy* 2, no. 2 (1991), p. 96.

can negotiations does merit systematic comparative examination. The outcomes are compatible with the logic behind our conjecture that negotiated transitions yield democratic systems capable of sustaining strong opposition only when leaders of the outgoing regime expect to be majority winners in the new political order, as in Nicaragua and Korea. In the more usual case, as in South Africa, they correctly calculate that they will lose the founding election, and they manage to insist on power sharing as the price of a negotiated settlement. These outcomes may, of course, be compatible with alternative logics as well, which suggests the need for systematic comparison of this sufficient account of the outcomes with other plausible alternatives. The logic we have identified might also be the result of a different causal process that would come to light only if larger numbers of negotiated and non-negotiated transitions were compared systematically with respect to the emergence of institutionalized political opposition.[78]

Although the preceding observations do not furnish us with enough variation in the independent variable to allow a decisive test, they are illuminating for two reasons. They suggest, first, that the South African outcome is not unusual. Given the propensity of academic commentators to classify South African politics as sui generis, this point is worth making. Within the subset of negotiated transitions in which the outgo-

---

[78]See Donald P. Green and Ian Shapiro, *Pathologies of Rational Choice Theory: A Critique of Applications in Political Science* (New Haven: Yale University Press, 1994), chap. 3, for discussion of these methodological issues. Initiates of the debate about that book will note that the present account of the dynamics of transition negotiations hypothesizes that the participants seek to maximize their strategic advantages, subject to the constraints imposed by the evolving situation. To avoid misunderstandings it should perhaps be reiterated that Green and Shapiro never maintained that strategic maximization plays no part in politics. Indeed they argued that it is most likely to account for outcomes where (1) the stakes are high and the players are self-conscious optimizers; (2) there is a clear range of options and little room, therefore, for strategic innovation; (3) preferences are relatively fixed and well ordered; (4) the strategic complexity of the situation is not overwhelmingly great for the actors; and (5) they have the capacity to learn from feedback in the environment and adapt; see ibid., pp. 10–11, 27–28, 192–93, and "Pathologies Revisited: Reflections on Our Critics," their contribution to a double issue of *Critical Review* devoted to discussion of *Pathologies*; see *Critical Review* 9, nos. 2–3 (Winter/Spring 1995, pp. 235–76). Inasmuch as negotiated transitions appear to meet these criteria, this is an area where one might expect rational choice explanations to be vindicated. As noted in the text, whether or not this or a similar model will be vindicated as a general explanatory account remains to be seen. Green and Shapiro differ from rational choice theorists in recommending that explanatory arguments be arrived at inductively rather than being deduced from a rational choice model. In this connection it should perhaps be said that when the present authors began work on this problem, we asked several game theorists for help in trying to model the interactions characterized verbally in section IV of this chapter. The universal response was that the number of players, variables, constraints, and interactions made the problem too difficult to model as a formal game. It is not, therefore, evident that deductive theory has much to contribute to the analysis of this problem (other than the less-than-arresting proposition that in self-consciously strategic situations, people can be expected to behave strategically). We do await with interest, however, the efforts of Leonard Houantchekon to model these dynamics.

ing government reformers expected to be a minority party, South Africa appears to have followed a common pattern. Second, if we are right, political calculations and the evolving distribution of power during transition negotiations may play a more important role in determining the electoral system of a nascent democracy than regional factors or preexisting sociocultural cleavages. As we noted earlier, consociational power-sharing arrangements are often understood and sometimes recommended as electoral systems that can attenuate otherwise polarizing ethnic, religious, or linguistic cleavages. If we are right, power sharing and consociationalism may result instead from the dynamics of negotiations.[79]

In South Africa consociational arrangements cater to political parties that are not, for the most part, ethnically based. The April 1994 election results belie the oft-repeated conventional wisdom that, politically, South Africa is deeply divided along ethnic lines.[80] Although confrontations between Inkatha and the ANC are often portrayed in the Western media as proxies for "tribal" confrontations between Zulu and Xhosa, it should be remembered that the Xhosa constitute 11.6 percent of the population but that the ANC won 62.6 percent of the vote. The IFP was the only major party that ran as an ethnic party in the election. Although Zulus are 29.2 percent of the population (38.5 percent of the black population), the IFP won only 10.5 percent of the vote, suggesting that almost two out of every three Zulus voted for another party (the majority for the ANC). Even in the IFP stronghold of Kwazulu/Natal, the IFP managed to get only 50.3 percent of the vote (and that amid widespread charges of election fraud on their part), with the ANC winning 32.2 percent and the NP 11.2 percent. Both the ANC and the NP campaigned as nonracial parties throughout, collecting substantial numbers of votes from various population groups.

Despite the fact that whites are only 13.1 percent of the population, the NP won 20.4 percent of the vote, indicating that they picked up millions of votes from other population groups. The majority of both

[79]In this connection it should be noted that negotiations (of a different sort than those examined here) have, after all, led to consociational arrangements in countries as different as Venezuela, Colombia, and East Germany, despite the fact that ethnic or other apparently primordial groupings were not politically mobilized and at any rate were not accommodated by the consociational system that negotiators agreed to. Prima facie this seems to be a strike against the "divided-society" hypothesis.

[80]For the received wisdom, see Arend Lijphart, "Constitutional Choices for New Democracies," *Journal of Democracy* 2, no. 1 (1991), p. 75. It is standard to refer to South Africa as an "ethnically divided society," even for those, like Horowitz, who are skeptical of consociational arguments; see his *Democratic South Africa?*, chap. 2, where the scant empirical research that has been done on this question is helpfully summarized.

the "Coloured" and Indian vote went to the National Party,[81] and 14 percent of the NP vote came from black South Africans. Although this translates into only 3–4 percent of the total black vote, it is more than three times the vote garnered by the ethnically exclusive PAC. Even the white vote did not split predictably along ethnic lines; indeed the vast majority of the white Afrikaner vote went to the NP, despite the presence of a well-organized Afrikaner ethnic party. White Afrikaners make up 7.5 percent of the population (57.5 percent of the white population); yet the Afrikaner separatist Freedom Front won 2.2 percent of the vote, indicating that three out of four white Afrikaners voted for another party—the great majority for the NP.[82]

VII. IMPLICATIONS FOR THE FUTURE

How troubled should democrats be that the "democratic route to democracy" fails to generate some of the institutions essential to a viable democratic order? In reflecting on this question we should begin by wondering just how democratic a negotiated transition really is. After all, in South Africa the CODESA round-table talks, although genuinely inclusive and consultative of all parties, were notable failures. They were followed by a classic elite pact, for the most part secretly negotiated, between the two most powerful players. This pact set the terms of the new constitution in all important particulars. Other political players were told to like it or lump it, and the IFP was paid attention to only to the extent that the principals thought it had the power to disrupt the negotiations. Indeed we saw that either co-opting or marginalizing potential opposition to the emerging agreement was, at several critical junctures, necessary for success.

In response it might be argued that however much negotiated transitions impose results from above, they do so less than interventions or transformations. There is truth in this argument, but it raises the possi-

[81]It is sometimes said that the "Coloured" NP vote was really an ethnic vote insofar as it was motivated by "Coloured" fear of blacks. Jung expects to publish data in the not too distant future which reveal that this claim is more easily sustained for the Western Cape than the Northern Cape, where the "Coloured" NP vote appears to have been motivated more by economic concerns. Beyond this it should be noted that Colourds and Afrikaners are linked by their common language, not an unimportant fact if crosscutting cleavages are thought to be salient to democratic consolidation.

[82]Election results taken from the Associated Press wire, May 9, 1994; *Foreign Broadcasting Information Service Daily Report*, May 6, 1994, p. 5; and Andrew Reynolds, "The Results," in *Election 1994 South Africa*, ed. Andrew Reynolds (Cape Town: Philip, 1994), pp. 183–220. Population statistics computed from *South Africa 1994* (Johannesburg: South Africa Foundation, 1994), pp. 14–15.

bility that negotiated transitions might combine the worst of both mechanisms from the standpoint of democratic institutional design. On the one hand, an elite pact agreed to by the most powerful principals is not really democratic. On the other, the institutions imposed are not chosen for their democratic durability. In transplacements, the negotiating principals are usually jockeying for position in the next government at the same time as they are designing the new institutional rules. This means that they respond to imperatives generated both by the internal logic of the negotiations and by future electoral politics rather than try to design viable democratic institutions. To be sure, nothing in the logic of transformations, replacements, or interventions requires that institutions will be better designed from the standpoint of democratic durability than with transplacements of the South African kind; but at least the principals do not confront the incentives we have identified to design them poorly.

A democratic constitutional order is a public good; it must be jointly supplied and no one can be excluded from it. That a public good is not well supplied through bilateral negotiations will not surprise economists. Not only may it be misleading, then, to think of the negotiated transition procedure as a democratic path to democracy; it may be misguided to think of it as an effective path to sustainable democracy. From the standpoint of a public goods analysis, the problem with negotiated transitions is not that the institutions are imposed from above but rather that they are not imposed in a sufficiently thoroughgoing fashion. Here we might think of transition negotiators as confronting a quasi prisoners' dilemma: the parties converge on a suboptimal outcome in response to the immediate incentives that they face. They design an order that they are likely to come to regret having designed, and perhaps they even know this in advance. But the logic of negotiated settlements holds them hostage to this outcome.

One way to get constitutional designers who are also future players to agree on a system of rules which promotes alternation in power is to ensure that they are uncertain about everyone's future electoral prospects. Each then has a reason to calculate that, despite a failure to prevail in the first election, the possibility of prevailing obtains in the next, or the next, or the next. This uncertainty gives the players incentives to create, and to continue to support, democratic opposition institutions rather than to try to topple the regime if they fail to get their way initially.[83] From this point of view, the difficulty with negotiated

[83]See Przeworski, *Democracy and the Market*, pp. 10–50, and Giuseppe di Palma, *To Craft Democracies: An Essay on Democratic Transitions* (Berkeley: University of California Press, 1990), pp. 27–75.

transitions is that they are devices for minimizing unpredictibility. Constrained by their grass roots supporters, by standpatters and radicals, and by the escalating costs of failure to agree, the negotiators settle on the system that is most likely to guarantee them a presence and as much power in the new government as possible. Other considerations are all to easily thrown to the wind.[84]

If negotiated transitions are neither notably democratic nor effective means for creating viable democratic institutions, this does not necessarily mean that they are a bad thing. They may have other virtues, such as minimizing bloodshed, and in many circumstances there may be no other way to get an authoritarian regime out of power. It is difficult to know whether this is the case in any given situation. Sometimes the authoritarian regime will be weaker than everyone believes it is; the collapse of the Soviet Union, which took the whole world by surprise, is an incontrovertible reminder of that possibility. We will never know whether the apartheid regime in South Africa would similarly have imploded had it not been for the decision by reformers in the NP and moderates in the ANC to effect a negotiated settlement—or had their efforts failed. Nor can we know whether a viable democracy would have followed a replacement in South Africa had the apartheid regime collapsed.

Acknowledging these imponderables should not lead us to misunderstand what did occur or why it happened. The 1993 South African constitution is an interim one; the new Parliament is mandated to write and approve a permanent constitution within two years of the 1994 elections. A greater appreciation of the weaknesses of the present document might lead those who write the new constitution to improve it. This is a tall order, and in early 1996 it remained unclear whether the deadline for the permanent constitution would be met. As the old saying about the most long-lived, but "provisional," 1875 constitution in the Third French Republic suggests, "C'est seul le provisoire qui dure." Supposedly interim political arrangements have a way of hanging on for decades, as at different times they have in West Germany, Ireland, Israel, France, and elsewhere. They often incorporate hard-won compromises, and the specter of revisiting their basic terms can seem too problematic—if not potentially explosive—to too many players to be

---

[84]It should be commented that the public choice literature on institutional design from Buchanan and Tullock to Rawls is not helpful in thinking about this problem. The central difficulty is not that this literature assumes that the players are ignorant of their future prospects (for as our discussion of the Korean transition indicated, at least sometimes they turn out to be wrong). The real difficulty is that this literature assumes that institutional designers have more or less equal power and resources (see Chapter 2). In fact this is seldom the case, and in the class of transplacements we have been considering, it is never the case.

worth attempting. This is not inevitable. Indeed, if the analysis presented here is correct, then the decisive feature of the transition negotiations that led to power sharing—the outgoing government's monopoly
control of the military—disappears once the transition has occurred,
creating a new reality subject to new constraints. If a coalition that has
enough power to alter the system emerges in the new parliament, as in
Poland after the 1989 elections, then power sharing may begin to evolve
in more democratic directions.

It is often understandably hard, however, to get politicians to agree to
alter the system of rules that has put them into power. Supermajority
requirements for constitutional reform usually necessitate high levels of
consensus, effectively entrenching transitional arrangements.[85] Fear of
conflict may also play a role in the durability of transitional power-
sharing arrangements. When the predemocratic history has been
characterized by violence and warfare, people may readily accept the
notions that opposition is just too dangerous to allow and that consensus will unify the country and bring peace. Alan Angell, for instance, describes the evolution of the ideology of consensus in Chile:
"What was originally a tactical agreement amongst the parties of the
then opposition. . . . soon became a strategy, but has now become a
dominant ideology."[86] In South Africa, too, the Government of National
Unity had an emotional resonance that spoke to healing the racist divisions of apartheid. Hence Lijphart's observation, in 1994, that there
was a "general expectation" among the principal players "that the
final constitution [would] bear a strong resemblance to the interim
constitution."[87]

Lijphart celebrates South Africa's new consociational institutions as
"just about the best that could have been designed," urging that they be

[85]See Vernon Bogdanor, "The Electoral System, Government, and Democracy," in *Israeli
Democracy under Stress*, ed. Ehud Sprinzak and Larry Diamond (Boulder: Rienner, 1993), pp. 83–
106. In South Africa both houses of Parliament, sitting jointly as the Constitutional Assembly,
must approve the final constitution by a two-thirds vote. If they fail to do this, the matter is
referred to a panel of experts who must come up with a unanimous recommendation within
thirty days. If the Constitutional Assembly adopts their recommended text by a two-thirds
margin, it becomes the final constitution. If this procedure fails, the Constitutional Assembly
may, at its discretion, vote a constitution by a strict majority, which would not be adopted unless
it was then approved by a 60 percent majority in a referendum. If this mechanism does not
produce a final constitution within two years, the president must dissolve Parliament for an
election, and the new Constitutional Assembly must approve a constitution with a 60 percent
majority. If this fails, the process is to be repeated. *South Africa 1995*, p. 15.
[86]Angell, "Transition to Democracy in Chile," p. 573. Comparable arguments have been made
about Venezuela and Colombia; see Michael Coppege, "Venezuela's Vulnerable Democracy,"
Journal of Democracy 3, no. 4 (October 1992), pp. 34–37; and John Peeler, *Latin American
Democracies* (Chapel Hill: University of North Carolina Press, 1985), pp. 98–99.
[87]Lijphart, "Prospects for Power-Sharing" p. 223.

replicated in the final constitution.[88] If we are right, this is wrong-headed advice. The power-sharing arrangement may have been essential to achieve a negotiated end to the apartheid order, and it may also head off open conflict in the short term. But those who care about democracy in South Africa must remember that constitutional arrangements are tested during times of crisis, not political honeymoons, and think about their operation in the future.[89] Unless institutions are put in place that can give dissatisfaction and opposition meaningful institutional expression, it seems reasonable to assume that, as the government of national unity begins to lose popularity, it will be the democratic constitutional settlement, rather than that government, that will begin to become vulnerable to separatist and anti-democratic forces.[90] An indication that the government's popularity may begin to decline sooner rather than later is that the much anticipated postelection inflow of Western investment has not materialized, perhaps because investors and hedge fund managers sensed from the Government of National Unity's incapacity to act that the real politics had yet to begin.[91]

We contend that the ANC should push hard to diminish the power-sharing dimensions in the constitution, but not in ways that stifle the organized and effective expression of opposition to its policies. In return for a more majoritarian system, however, its leaders should be prepared to give up the parliamentary rules that tie backbenchers to party leaderships. True, this will mean coping with more fractious and disagreeable backbenchers, and some groups will likely hive off and form new parties. But if the ANC leaders want the NP to give up the predictability that comes with power sharing, they must themselves be prepared to compete for grass roots support with the power of their

[88]Ibid., pp. 221–31.

[89]Horowitz, *Democratic South Africa?* pp. 142–43.

[90]By February 1995 the IFP was already testing these waters by storming out of talks in the Constitutional Assembly on the new constitution on the grounds that the ANC and the NP were conspiring to exclude them from the real decisions; see *This Week in South Africa*, February 21–27, 1995, p. 1.

[91]One indicator is the performance of South Africa's closed-end mutual funds since the elections. A look at the weekly reports in *Barrons* at the end of 1995 reveals that both the New South Africa Fund and the Southern Africa Fund have been trading at substantial discounts since May 1994 and, poignantly, that the drift has been to increasingly substantial discounts. The Southern Africa Fund last traded at a (small) premium in March 1994. By May 1994 it had drifted to a discount in the −15 percent range; by July it reached ≥20 percent for the first time, where it remained for the rest of the year. The average for the period March 7, 1994, to December 18, 1995, was a discount of ≥18.07. The New South Africa Fund exhibits a similar pattern, trading at an average discount of ≥17.52 percent for the period and reaching ≥23.4 percent for the first time at the end of 1995. Despite considerable movement of short-term speculative capital into the country, there was little evidence, in mid-1996, of substantial foreign industrial investment.

ideas rather than rely on coercive institutional devices. Tedious as meaningful opposition might often be to deal with, it gives rise to the complex competition that is the lifeblood of democratic politics.

The NP leaders should also think about their interests in a less myopic fashion. They should look not only at the present distribution of parties and the next election but also at South Africa's underlying political dynamics. Caution on the part of NP leaders is understandable, but they also need to understand that the way to step over a crevasse is not to tiptoe into the middle of it. They need to realize that divergent political forces cannot be held together artificially and that attempts to so will likely destroy the mechanisms that proponents hope will do the holding. With the best of intentions their negotiators are fighting the wrong battle by seeking to entrench power sharing in the permanent constitution.[92] Instead they should be thinking about ways to make the political system genuinely competitive, so that power sharing will no longer appear to be necessary.

The answer lies in getting rid of the mechanisms that currently prevent the breakup of the ANC into several parties. If the rules tying backbenchers to their party leaderships are discarded, it is hard to see how this could not happen to what is, after all, an umbrella organization consisting of a great diversity of groups that were held together principally by their shared opposition to apartheid. This has been the result with other liberation movements that have come to power, and once the strains of governing bring the latent divisions within the ANC to the fore, there is no reason to think the South African experience will be different. Indeed, if Rae is right that proportional representation with a combination of low thresholds and large constituencies promotes party fragmentation, this outcome is all the more likely in South Africa, which has both.[93] Bearing this in mind, the NP should be prepared to trade entrenched power sharing for the rules that permit the ANC leadership to hold their party together artificially. In the medium term this course of action holds out the possibility of voluntary coalition politics of the sort that is routine in Israel and much of Europe, where governments and oppositions can form and reform, as politics changes on the ground.[94]

[92]This view was still being pressed in the Constitutional Assembly on the NP's behalf by former cabinet minister Andre Foure in late January 1995; see *Southern Africa Report*, January 27, 1995, pp. 1–2.

[93]Rae, "Using District Magnitude."

[94]The discussion draft of the final constitution released by the government in November 1995 contained some encouraging proposed changes. Sections 41 and 66 (2) substantially deconstitutionalize the electoral system, stipulating that it be "prescribed by national legislation" and requiring only that it be based on proportional representation. Section 46 (2) provides a mechanism for the dissolution of Parliament before the end of its fixed term if the Constitutional

Of course there are no guarantees, but that, as we have noted, is in the nature of what makes democracy survive. The "guarantee" of power sharing is only a guarantee of one thing: that real democratic politics cannot get started and that those who do not perceive their interests as being served by the government of national unity will have no incentive to remain committed to the new constitutional order. The NP would do better to worry less about worthless paper guarantees, see institutionalized unpredictability as an opportunity, and focus on building new nonwhite grass roots constituencies so that they will be better placed to take advantage of a fluid and unpredictable future. Opening local offices in Soweto and working on people's rent problems will do more for their electoral prospects in 1999 and beyond than insisting on power sharing now.

That the power-sharing arrangement embedded in the interim constitution is so extreme might turn out to be an advantage by revealing that this "enforced coalition between thoroughly incompatible partners"[95] does not provide a viable basis for democracy in the longer term. The first indication of the unworkablity of the new system became clear as early as July 1994. Finance Minister Derek Keys resigned and President Mandela decided to replace him with Chris Liebenberg, a political independent. To achieve this without upsetting the power-sharing formula for the distribution of cabinet portfolios, it was necessary for Parliament to amend the constitution and for Mandela to give the National Party an additional cabinet portfolio.[96] Perhaps this was an early indication that the system will prove so unworkable that there will be no alternative but to refashion it. Once the political honeymoon for the new government is over, the difficulties of governing by constitutional amendment should become manifest. It is to be hoped that when this occurs both the will and the capacity will be found in Parliament to create a system that is at once more workable and democratic.

Assembly passes a vote of no confidence in the cabinet, thereby perhaps strengthening the hand of backbenchers. The president remains institutionally weak, elected and dismissable by the National Assembly (sec. 82). The president is required by section 78 (2) to operate "in consulation with other members of the cabinet," who remain bound by the doctrine of collective responsibility [sec. 89 (2)]. The president may appoint and dismiss cabinet ministers and deputy ministers [sec. 78 (3)(a), 86], although he or she will presumably remain constrained by the requirements of proportionality. It is not possible to tell from this document what will be the fate of the sections in the 1993 constitution that provide for leadership party control of membership lists and parliamentary seats, interim power-sharing requirements, or the current electoral system. See *Working Draft of the New Constiution*, released by the Government of National Unity on November 22, 1995. Source: www.constitution.org.za/drafts/3wd20115.html.

[95]Tim Cohen, "The Government of National Unity: Will It Survive the Five Years?" *South Africa Foundation Review* (January/February 1995), p. 4.

[96]*New York Times*, July 6, 1994, p. A4.

Elements of Democratic Justice

Democratic movements derive much of their moral authority from the hope they hold out of displacing unjust social arrangements. This reflects the fact that the promise of democracy and that of social justice are intimately linked in the modern political imagination. The great democratic movements of the nineteenth century were less concerned to implement an abstract democratic ideal, than, as John Dewey observed, "to remedy evils experienced in consequence of prior political institutions."[1]   One only has to think of the ways in which the lack of democracy and the presence of social injustice were fused in the ideologies of opposition to communism in the Soviet bloc and apartheid in South Africa to see that, in the twentieth century no less than in the nineteenth, many people blame social injustice on the lack of democracy and assume that democracy is an important weapon in replacing unjust social relations with just ones.

Yet this popular expectation is at variance with much academic orthodoxy, which correctly recognizes that achieving political democracy guarantees nothing about the attainment of social justice.[2] In countries where the basic democratic institutions of popularly elected governments based on universal franchise prevail, wealth may or may not be

[1]John Dewey, *The Public and Its Problems* (New York: Holt, 1927), pp. 84–85.

[2]See, e.g., Guiseppe Di Palma, *To Craft Democracies: An Essay on Democratic Transitions* (Berkeley: University of California Press, 1990), p. 23, for defense of the view that the democratic ideal should be disengaged "from the idea of social progress" if it is to endure, and Samuel P. Huntington, *The Third Wave: Democratization in the Late Twentieth Century* (Norman: University of Oklahoma Press, 1991), pp. 165–69, for the argument that political leaders who sell out on their constituents' demands for social justice are more likely to succeed in consolidating democratic institutions than those who do not.

redistributed, minorities may or may not be respected, opportunities may or may not be open to all, and religious dissent may or may not be tolerated. Far from necessarily promoting social justice, then, democracy can actually undermine whatever it might be thought to require, and partly for this reason, bills of rights and other constitutional restraints on democratic politics are argued to be worthwhile. They limit the possibility of social injustice by constraining what can be done by those who wield state power in democracy's name.

Once it is held that democracy should be constrained by the requirements of social justice, a difficulty arises however. There are many competing theories of social justice and no evident way to choose among them. Elsewhere I have argued that the standard attempts to resolve this difficulty fail and that the apparent tensions between democracy and justice need to be rethought along lines that have more in common with popular expectations than with academic orthodoxy. In my opinion, although democracy is not sufficient for social justice, arguments about democracy and social justice are more deeply entwined with one another than the conventional opposition suggests. The mutual dependence of these two ideals is signaled by the fact that, on the one hand, most arguments for democracy rest at bottom on intuitions about what is just, and on the other, if we dig deeply enough into arguments about social justice we frequently discover that they rest on appeals to democratic moral intuitions. This is not to say that commitments to democracy and to social justice entail one another; it is to say, however, that no account of one which undermines one's moral intuitions about the other is likely to be judged satisfactory.[3]

Drawing out the implications of this observation, I have sought to develop a view of social justice in which democratic considerations play a three-part foundational role: in the definition of social goods, in the determination of principles by which conflicts over goods should be resolved, and in the appropriate stance toward implementing principles of justice in the actual world of day-to-day politics.[4] These three ways to be a democrat set the basic terms of the view that I characterize as "democratic justice," in contrast to liberal, socialist, conservative, and communitarian views granted wide academic currency today. Although my view is conceived of as an alternative to these, I mean to make it attractive to many of their proponents because it depends less

[3]See Chapter 5.

[4]I should say at the outset that by using the term *foundational* I do not mean to take up a position here in debates about the nature of knowledge and existence. In describing a commitment to democracy as "foundational," I mean only to suggest that no prior or more basic political commitment rightly commands our common allegiance.

on alternative sets of assumptions about social justice and more on making explicit the implications of democratic moral intuitions to which many of them, on reflection, will find themselves committed. My earlier defenses of democratic justice have been ground clearing and programmatic, amounting to a down payment, at best, on a positive argument. My aim here is to deliver on the first installment of the constructive account.

Three preliminary points: First, democracy as I defend it is a subordinate good. By this I mean that although democracy is necessary for ordering social relations justly, we should resist every suggestion that it is sufficient, that it is the highest human good, that it is the only human good, or that it should dominate the activities in which we engage. Democracy operates best when it sets the terms for our civil interactions without thereby determining their course. Our lives require much else as well to be satisfactory, and it is wrongheaded to expect democracy to deliver those other things. This conception follows from the thought that because power relations form part—but not all—of most collective activities, democracy appropriately conditions those activities but does not appropriately displace them. Although we should aspire to get on with our collective lives in democratic ways, we should nonetheless aspire to get on with them. The creative political challenge is to devise mechanisms of institutional governance that can make this possible.

Second, my argument for democratic justice is semicontextual in that it varies partly, but only partly, with time and circumstance. Aspects of what democratic justice might reasonably be thought to require may change over time and vary both across the domains of civil society and from culture to culture. This means that a satisfying elaboration of the argument can only be developed as its injunctions are explored through a variety of contexts. Shouldering that burden is the central task of the larger project in which I am engaged. In this book's last chapter my attention is confined to exploring aspects of the argument for democratic justice which can be defended in general terms.

Third, in making the case for democratic justice my central focus is on the procedural and institutional level of analysis, not on matters concerning higher-order human interests and questions of ultimate justification. In this regard my approach is similar to Rawls's in his "political, not metaphysical" mode, although Rawls seems to me to press implausibly far the claim that a political conception of justice can be developed independently of controversial philosophic commitments.[5]

---

[5]John Rawls, "Fairness to Goodness," *Philosophical Review* 82 (1973), p. 228, and "Justice as Fairness: Political Not Metaphysical," *Philosophy and Public Affairs* 14, no. 3 (1985), pp. 223–51, 223–26.

The account developed here rests on skepticism toward the absolutist epistemologies and ontologies that a Platonist or a classical Marxist might embrace, but this skepticism is political rather than metaphysical; I take no position on whether or not the accounts are true, only on whether or not it is wise to allow our lives to be governed by their injunctions. This is not the same thing as philosophical neutrality, however, because partisans of such absolutist views are likely to find their political aspirations frustrated by the politics I am advocating in ways that many philosophical fallibilists, pragmatists, empiricists, realists, and philosophical antifoundationalists will not. My claim is that given the impossibility of neutrality among ultimate philosophical commitments, the democratic conception of social justice that I describe is the most appropriate foundational political commitment.

It might be said that, having conceded that neutrality about questions of higher-order interests and ultimate justification is not possible, one is not free to turn to the institutional and procedural level of analysis without first defending the higher-order assumptions on which a given analysis rests. This conclusion seems unwarranted for three related reasons. It is true, first, that every political theory rests on higher-order assumptions, but it is also true that all such assumptions are controversial. Consequently, if we put off the questions of institutional design until the higher-order questions are settled, we will get to them at the time of Godot's arrival. In the meantime, however, life goes on and we need grounds for preferring some institutional arrangements over others. Second, although it is common to think that we should start with general matters because people are more likely to agree on them and then move to more specific and divisive matters—to the details wherein the devil is thought to lurk—exactly the opposite is often true, as Cass Sunstein has usefully noted. A faculty may be able to reach agreement that a particular person should be granted tenure even though its members could never agree on the reasons why. By extension, in arguing about the merits of different political arrangements, it is often wise to avoid—or at least minimize—attention to controversial questions of higher-order interests and ultimate justification.[6] That is the assumption behind the present discussion. Last, because no one can do everything, it behooves practitioners in different disciplines to reflect on where they are most likely to make a useful contribution. In my view, normative political theorists best devote attention to analyzing how to structure the power dimensions of human interaction, leaving to

---

[6]See Cass Sunstein, "On Legal Theory and Legal Practice," in *NOMOS XXXVII: Theory and Practice*, ed. Ian Shapiro and Judith Wagner DeCew (New York: New York University Press, 1995), pp. 267–87.

psychologists, moral philosophers, and metaphysicians full analysis of higher-order interests and issues of ultimate justification. Although every intellectual division of labor will be unsatisfactory from some defensible point of view, choices inevitably have to be made in this regard. The reader must judge whether I have made the right ones here.

I. Two Dimensions of Democratic Justice

Democrats are committed to rule by the people. They insist that no aristocrat, monarch, bureaucrat, expert, or religious leader has the right, in virtue of such status, to force people to accept a particular conception of their proper common life. People should decide for themselves, by appropriate procedures of collective decision, what their collective business should be. They may reasonably be required to consult and take account of one another, and of others affected by their actions; but beyond this, no one may legitimately tell them what to do. The people are sovereign; in all matters of collective life they rule over themselves.

Although this is less often commented on in the academic literature, democracy is as much about opposition to the arbitrary exercise of power as it is about collective self-government. In this connection Barrington Moore remarks that, historically, democracy has been a weapon "of the poor and the many against the few and the well-to-do." Those who have actively sought democracy in organized political movements "have wanted it as a device to increase their share in political rule and weaken the power and authority of those who actually rule."[7] In the modern world at least, democratic movements have derived much of their energy and purpose from opposition to socioeconomic, legal, and political hierarchies that seemed capricious from a democratic point of view. Rooted in the remnants of feudal and absolutist regimes and shaped by the vicissitudes of conquest and chance, the political orders of eighteenth- and nineteenth-century Europe and North America seemed to the dispossessed to personify arbitrary hierarchy and domination. This reality, as much as anything else, motivated working-class and other democratic movements. The English philosophic radicals, the French and American revolutionaries, the nineteenth-century Chartists, and the anticolonial movements in the Third World after World War II all wanted to free themselves from hierarchical orders for which they could see no rationale or justification. It was to this opposi-

[7]Barrington Moore, Jr., *Liberal Prospects under Soviet Socialism: A Comparative Historical Perspective* (New York: Averell Harriman Institute, 1989), p. 25.

tional dimension of the democratic ideal that Nelson Mandela appealed at his sentencing for treason by a South African court in 1961. Conceding that he had disobeyed the law by inciting resistance to the government, he nonetheless wondered whether "the responsibility does not lie on the shoulders of the government which promulgated that law, knowing that my people, who constitute the majority of the population of this country, were opposed to that law, and knowing further that every legal means of demonstrating that opposition had been closed to them by prior legislation, and by government administrative action."[8]

Mandela's formulation might be taken to embody the conventional view that democracy is primarily about collective self-government and only secondarily about opposition. Part of his claim, after all, is that he should not be bound by "a law which neither I nor any of my people had any say in preparing."[9] But he insists also that the law lacks legitimacy because every avenue of legal opposition to it has been sealed off. In a world of ideal political institutions a derivative view of the place of opposition in democratic politics might be sustainable. But in the actual world, where social orders come to be what they are in morally arbitrary ways, and where all procedures of government turn out on close inspection to be flawed, opposition must enjoy a more independent and exalted status in a persuasive account of just democratic politics. Or so I argue; but first let us attend to the governance side of the equation.

Collective Self-government

If democracy is understood to require that the people be sovereign over their collective goals, it exhibits considerable overlap with liberalism as a political ideology. Both are rooted in antivanguardist conceptions of the good; their proponents resist the idea that values should be imposed on people against their wishes in the name of some greater social good. The reasons for affirming this antivanguardist stance vary: they can range from commitments to variants of philosophic skepticism, pragmatism, and antifoundationalism, to beliefs in the psychological value of critical reflection and contested authority, to the conviction that a degree of pluralism about values is sociologically or politically desirable. Liberals and democrats do not divide predictably over these

---

[8]Nelson Mandela, "Address to Court before Sentencing," in *Ideologies of Liberation in Black Africa, 1856–1970*, ed. J. Ayo Langley (London: Collings, 1979), p. 665. On the Chartists, see Dorothy Thompson, *The Chartists* (London: Temple Smith, 1984). Generally, see Elie Halevy, *The Growth of Philosophic Radicalism* (Clifton, N.J.: Kelley, 1972).

[9]Langley, *Ideologies of Liberation*, p. 664.

foundational matters; but for most of both, some combination of them issues in a principled resistance to moral vanguardism.[10]

Liberals and democrats do divide predictably, however, over the institutional implications they draw from their moral antivanguardism. Liberals, who typically regard individual freedom as the greatest good, characteristically focus on devices to protect the individual from the realm of collective action. Democrats, by contrast, try to structure collective action appropriately to embody the preferences of the governed. Liberals resist this logic on the grounds that no procedure can fairly embody the preferences of all the governed. For liberals, democratic decision rules all too readily become devices by which phantom majorities—sometimes even manipulative minorities—tyrannize over individuals.[11]

Although there is merit to the liberal argument, it rests on flawed assumptions about the nature of politics and about the limits of collective action. Concerning the first, the characteristic liberal mistake is to focus on the forms of tyranny performed by and through government as the only—certainly the principal—kind of tyranny that should worry political theorists. Liberal commitments to negative freedom, conventional constructions of public/private dichotomies, and arguments for limited government are all shaped by this governmentalist view of politics. Governmental power is one potential site of domination, but there are many others that permeate the domains of "private" life. Government can be an instrument for mitigating domination as well as a source of its generation. As a result, the choices and trade-offs that can minimize domination throughout society will likely defy such simplifying formulas as "The government that governs least governs best."

The liberal view is flawed also because its proponents tend to think that whether or not our lives should be governed by collective institu-

---

[10]Nor do all liberals agree with one another, any more than all democrats do, over which of these, combinations of these, or combinations of these and other, reasons they invoke for adhering to antivanguardist conceptions of the good.

[11]For one conventional statement of this view, see William H. Riker, *Liberalism against Populism: A Confrontation between the Theory of Democracy and the Theory of Social Choice* (San Francisco: W. H. Freeman Press, 1982). It might be objected that the depiction of liberalism in the text is something of a caricature in that it deals with academic rather than popular conceptions, and only a subset of academic conceptions of liberalism at that. This is conceded, though I would contend that it is an expansive subset, ranging at least from the fears of majority tyranny expressed through the state which can be found in John Stuart Mill, *On Liberty* (Indianapolis: Hackett, 1978) and Alexis de Tocqueville, *Democracy in America* (New York: Doubleday, Anchor, 1969); through the libertarian liberalisms of Riker, Nozick, and Buchanan and Tullock discussed in the text; and to the nonlibertarian anti-statism embraced by Shklar, *Ordinary Vices* (Cambridge: Harvard University Press, 1984).

tions is an intelligible question about politics. Hence Robert Nozick's remark that the fundamental question of political theory "is whether there should be any state at all."[12] This view is misleading because the institutions of private property, contract, and public monopoly of coercive force which its proponents characteristically favor were created and are sustained by the state, partly financed by implicit taxes on those who would prefer an alternative system. In the modern world, Nozick's assertion makes as much sense as would a claim that the fundamental question of astronomy is whether or not there ought to be planets. A characteristic liberal sleight of hand involves trying to naturalize or otherwise obscure liberal institutional arrangements in order to disguise this reality. Such subterfuges have received more attention than they deserve in the recent history of political theory; they cannot any longer detain us.[13]

This is not to say that the liberal fear of majority rule is groundless. It is to say that we need a different response to it than the conventional liberal one. We can begin to develop this response by noting, first, that there is no reason to think that there is one best rule of collective decision. Different rules will be appropriate in different domains of social life, depending on the nature of the domain in question, the importance of the decision to participants, the potential costs of decisions to third parties, and related contingent factors. Such a plural attitude about decision rules flows naturally out of the view that civil society is made up of domains of social action which differ qualitatively from one another.[14]

Few liberals would deny this last claim, but they usually regard unanimity rule as the best default option, the decision rule most likely to protect individuals against violations of their rights. This is at least partly why liberals so often find markets attractive. Markets embody unanimity rule in the sense that every transaction requires the consent of both parties. In the liberal view, classically advocated in *The Calculus of Consent*, it is always *departures* from unanimity that stand in presumptive need of justification, whether on efficiency or other grounds.[15] This story is intuitively plausible only if we take the contractualist metaphor

[12]Robert Nozick, *Anarchy, State, and Utopia* (New York: Basic Books, 1974), p. 4.

[13]For extensive discussion, see my *The Evolution of Rights in Liberal Theory* (Cambridge: Cambridge University Press, 1986), chaps. 4–6, and Chapter 2 of this volume.

[14]See Michael Walzer, *Spheres of Justice: A Defense of Pluralism and Equality* (New York: Basic Books, 1983), pp. 3–20, and Alasdair MacIntyre, *After Virtue*, 2d ed. (Notre Dame, Ind.: University of Notre Dame Press, 1984), pp. 181–203.

[15]James Buchanan and Gordon Tullock, *The Calculus of Consent: Logical Foundations of Constitutional Democracy* (Ann Arbor: University of Michigan Press, 1962), pp. 73–77; for further discussion, see Chapter 2 of this volume.

on which it rests seriously, assuming a prepolitical status quo where there is no collective action and then a series of consensual moves which leads to the creation of what we know of as political society. But, as Brian Barry, Douglas Rae, and others have pointed out, once this assumption is jettisoned there is no particular reason to regard unanimity rule as the most appropriate default decision rule.[16] In the real world of ongoing politics, if I assume that I am as likely to oppose a given policy as to support it regardless of whether it is the status quo, then majority rule or something close to it is the logical rule to prefer. Once we move from majority toward unanimity rule, we begin to privilege the status quo. This will rightly seem arbitrary in a world that has not evolved cooperatively from a precollective condition. In short, other things being equal, tyranny of the majority is something that people should rationally fear, but not as much as they should fear tyranny of the minority.[17]

The preceding discussion reinforces the suggestion that there is no single best decision rule for democratic governance. In domains of social life where relations really do tend to approximate the contractualist story—in that they are both created ex nihilo by the participants and are basically cooperative in character—a presumptive commitment to unanimity rule is defensible. One might think of marriage in contemporary America as a paradigm. It is created consensually, usually with the expectation that in important matters, day-to-day governance will also be consensual. (Indeed, with the advent of no-fault divorce since the 1970s, we see an unusually strong form of the unanimity requirement at work. In most American states, either spouse can insist—subject to a brief waiting period—on a divorce unilaterally: the marriage continues only so long as both parties agree. Far from privileging the status quo, this variant of unanimity rule makes it perpetually vulnerable, because the rule is not defined by reference to the status quo but by, in effect, recreating the conditions antecedent to it at the wish of either party.)[18]

[16]Brian Barry, *Political Argument*, 2d ed. (Hertfordshire: Harvester Wheatsheaf, 1990), pp. 242–85, 312–16; Douglas W. Rae, "Decision-Rules and Individual Values in Constitutional Choice," *American Political Science Review* 63, no. 1 (1969), pp. 40–56, 51; Michael Taylor, "Proof of a Theorem on Majority Rule," *Behavioral Science* 14 (May 1969), pp. 228–31. When the number of voters is odd, the optimal decision rule is majority rule, *n* over two, plus one-half; when *n* is even, the optimal decision rule is either majority-rule (n over two, plus one), or majority rule minus one (simply *n* over two). Generally see Dennis Mueller, *Public Choice: II* (New York: Cambridge University Press, 1989), pp. 96–111.

[17]Even if we accept the contractualist metaphor, the logic of Buchanan's and Tullock's defense of unanimity rule can be shown to break down once time and externalities are taken into account. See Douglas W. Rae, "The Limits of Consensual Decision," *American Political Science Review* 69, no. 4 (1975), pp. 1270–94.

[18]It might appear that no-fault divorce destroys the marriage contract *qua* contract entirely,

Many social relationships do not approximate the contractualist ideal; they are not created ex nihilo in the sense that contemporary American marriages usually are, and they are to a high degree struc-tured by forces other than the wills of the participants. Even childless marriages involve the generation of reliances and externalities that can undermine their exclusively consensual character. These are questions of degree, however. Social relations are often not contractualist to any-thing like the extent that marriage is, even when such reliances are taken into account; most obviously, think of parent-child relations. Con-stitutional political arrangements are often pointed to as presumptively contractualist because of their foundational character and their place in the social contract tradition. Such arrangements might once have been consented to by the relevant parties, although even in the American founding, a narrowly circumscribed class agreed in fact—and then not unanimously. Generations later, whatever contractualist element these arrangements once exhibited has receded into the mists of time. In such circumstances (and no doubt there are others) there is no evident reason to regard unanimity rule as best on the grounds that it embodies the consent of the governed.

Nor are there good reasons to think that some alternative decision rule should appropriately govern all relations where a contractualist element is either missing or overdetermined by other factors. As the examples just mentioned indicate, this is a heterogeneous class. In some domains, the sort Rae evidently has in mind, majority rule is prima facie the best decision rule. These include relations typically characterized by arms-length transactions, where substantial aspects of the collective action in question are competitive rather than cooperative and where there are no obvious reasons to countenance paternalistic decision mak-ing. They are also often circumstances in which people either are born into structural relations that cannot easily be escaped or, if there is a contractualist element to their participation, it is accompanied by a good deal of what Marxists like to think of as "structural coercion." Whatever the surface appearances, the relations in question are not substantially voluntary. Arguments for workplace democracy in which

---

given that it is terminable at the will of either party. But such a conclusion (1) ignores the fact that conventional unanimity rule operates in marriages unless and until the parties reach the point of dissolution and (2) conflates the *grounds* for divorce with the *terms* of divorce (and in particular the distribution of the costs courts will impose on divorcing parties). In fact many countries, and some American states, that embrace some form of no-fault divorce do not go all the way with it. Instead they insist that the court find that "irretrievable breakdown" has occurred, for which purpose the judge may take various factors including the wishes of both parties into account. See Mary Ann Glendon, *Abortion and Divorce in Western Law* (Cambridge: Harvard University Press, 1987), pp. 64–81.

majority rule plays a substantial role generally appeal to some combination of these characteristics in justifying their appeal; Rae's logic supplies us with reasons for accepting them.[19]

Not every noncontractualist or minimally contractualist form of association should be governed by majority rule, however. Both Buchanan and Tullock's and Rae's reasoning take it for granted that, ceteris paribus, decision-making costs should be minimized, for which they have sometimes been criticized by participatory democrats.[20] Rather than follow the participatory democrat's reasoning (which creates difficulties of its own),[21] the argument here is that participation must itself be thought about in a context-sensitive way. In some circumstances participation is no more than a cost to be minimized, subject to achieving or preventing a particular outcome. Anyone who has sat through enough faculty meetings will know what at least one of those circumstances is. In other situations, institutions may reasonably be structured to maximize participation. Juries are an obvious example. Unanimity is generally required just because it forces discussion and joint deliberation, which, in turn, are believed most likely to lead to discovery of the truth in trial courts, and that is the point of the exercise. Parent-child relations are also noncontractualist relations (for the child does not ask to be born, let alone born to the parent in question) that do not lend themselves to governance by majority rule, at least not on many questions. In these relations, more flexibility is necessary in delineating the appropriate scope for participation by the parties, because those relations encompass the total dependence of young children on their parents, interactions among more-or-less equal adults, and transactions between adults and their aging parents. And because human beings are developmental creatures for whom decision making has to be learned over time, there has to be space for regimes of domestic governance to adapt to peoples' changing capacities and dependencies. To be appropriate, the decision rules governing domestic relations must be able to respond to this complex reality.

Taking note of such complexities lends credence to the suggestion that when they can be discovered and made to work, local solutions to local problems are to be preferred. The kinds of knowledge pertinent to democratizing an activity will often be disproportionately available to insiders because of their hands-on experience and their participants' understanding of the activity in question. In this respect, the argument

[19]See Robert A. Dahl, *A Preface to Economic Democracy* (Berkeley: University of California Press, 1985), pp. 111–35.
[20]See Elaine Spitz, *Majority Rule* (Chatham, N.J.: Chatham House, 1984), pp. 135–215.
[21]See Chapter 5.

of democratic justice is compatible with the aspirations of many who think of themselves as communitarians. Notice, however, that there will be circumstances in which no local decision rule can be made to work effectively from the standpoint of democratic self-government, the most obvious being when the obstacles to exit are insuperable for some yet easily overcome for others. The American history of white flight from inner-city school districts since the 1960s stands as eloquent testimony to that fact. Whether the substantially white middle-class population opts out of the public school system, moves out of the inner city (or both, to avoid both using and paying for the inner-city schools), its ability to leave undermines democracy in educational provision. Local majority rule promotes white flight, but local unanimity rule gives disaffected individuals veto power, which enables them to avoid contributing to the provision of public education. In this type of circumstance, the presence of collective action problems suggests that constraints other than choosing one local decision rule over another should come into play.

The decision rules appropriate to various walks of life vary, then, with the activity in question and the purposes around which it is organized. Yet to say this is to solve one problem by raising another, because these activities and purposes are never fixed and there is usually, perhaps endemically, disagreement about them.[22] How can we say that the nature of the activity in question makes one decision rule more appropriate than another, having conceded that those purposes and activities are inevitably in contention? Whereas most liberals would say that all social relations should be redesigned to approximate the contractualist ideal as much as possible (regardless of how they are currently organized), the subordinate character of the democratic commitment in the argument for democratic justice precludes my defending an analogous claim. Instead it recommends a more pragmatic approach that is antivanguardist in method as well as substance, because we should neither accept things as they have evolved nor aspire to redesign them *tabula rasa*. Rather, the goal should be to take social relations as we find them and discover ways to democratize them as we reproduce them. Democratic justice thus has a Burkean dimension, but one tempered by the aspiration to create a more democratic world over time. Prevailing ways of doing things reasonably make a partial claim on our allegiance, but this claim is conditional and always subject to revision in democratic ways; the inertial legitimacy of existing modes of governance can

[22]This issue is discussed at length in my *Political Criticism* (Berkeley: University of California Press, 1990), pp. 252–61.

never achieve a status greater than that of a rebuttable presumption. The creative challenge is to devise methods of governance that both condition existing ways of doing things democratically and open the way to their reevaluation over time.

Although there is no best decision rule for the governance of different domains of civil society, a general constraint for thinking about decision rules follows from what has been said so far: everyone affected by the operation of a particular domain of civil society should be presumed to have a say in its governance. This presumption follows from the root democratic idea that the people appropriately rule over themselves. To require that everyone affected have a say is not to require that this presumption be conclusive or that every say should necessarily be of equal weight. There are often—but not always—good reasons for granting outsiders to a domain (who may be subject to its external effects) less of a say than insiders concerning its governance, and even within a domain there may be compelling reasons to distribute governing authority unequally and perhaps even to disenfranchise some participants in some circumstances. What these circumstances are cannot be specified in general, but we can say that we begin with a presumption of universal inclusion.

We can also say that proposals to undermine universal inclusion reasonably prompt suspicion, whatever their source. In the limiting case, if someone sells herself into slavery, her agreement should be regarded as void *ab initio*. Most incursions on inclusion are considerably less radical than selling oneself into slavery is. As a consequence, evaluating policies and practices that limit the nature and extent of the governed's participation in decisions that affect them is more difficult (and controversial) from the standpoint of democratic justice. In the ongoing world of everyday politics there will often be circumstances in which inclusion is reasonably traded off against other imperatives. But the general argument counsels suspicion of these trade-offs; the burden of persuasion lies with those who advocate them.

Although the requirements of the principle of universal inclusion will vary with circumstances, it is possible to defend at least one constraint on it in general terms that goes beyond the limiting case of slavery: participation by one individual or group in ways that render the participation of other legitimate participants meaningless is unacceptable. For instance, it is estimated that in the United States the health care and medical insurance industries spent upward of fifty million dollars in 1993–94 on advertising and lobbying to kill the Clinton administration's proposed health care reform legislation and that they would have spent whatever was necessary to achieve this result.[23] Granting, *arguendo*, this account of the facts, we can say that an understanding of participation which permits such a result goes too far. It gives one set of interests affected by the proposal the power to obliterate the participation of others and to determine the result more or less unilaterally. To be sure, this principle does not tell us which types of limitations on lobbying and political speech are appropriate, but it does set an outer constraint on the debate.

The account of collective self-government defended here is causally based. The right to participate comes from one's having an interest that can be expected to be affected by the particular collective action in question. In this respect, the argument for democratic justice differs from liberal and communitarian views, both of which tend to regard membership in the relevant community as a trump (liberals by assumption, communitarians by express argument).[24] Once the contractualist way of thinking has been dethroned, it is difficult to see any principled basis for regarding membership as primary. The structure of decision rules should follow the contours of power relations, not those of political memberships. Adopting the causally based view has implications for a host of issues relating to intergenerational justice and the handling of externalities. In a world in which international military and environmental questions increasingly dominate political agendas, whether or not one adopts this view can be expected to be consequential over an expanding portion of the political landscape.

It will be objected that serious difficulties arise in determining who is affected by a particular decision and who is to determine whose claims about being affected should be accepted. To provide a full defense of the causally based view here would take us too far afield, but two points should be noted. First, although who is affected by a decision is bound to be controversial, this fact scarcely distinguishes causally based from membership-based arguments about social justice. Who is to decide,

---

[23]The $50 million figure is reported by Tim Rinne, "The Rise and Fall of Single-Payer Health Care in Nebraska," *Action for Universal Health Care* 3, no. 10 (May 1995), pp. 4–5. See also Tom Hamburger and Theodore Marmor, "Dead on Arrival: Why Washington's Power Elites Won't Consider Single Payer Health Reform," *Washington Monthly,* September 1993, pp. 27–32.

[24]Liberals take the basic unit of the nation-state for granted, treating it as a kind of Lockean voluntary association writ large, as has often been pointed out in criticism of Rawls; see John Rawls, *A Theory of Justice* (Cambridge: Harvard University Press, 1971), pp. 371–82, and his "The Law of Peoples," *Critical Inquiry* 20 (autumn 1993), pp. 36–68. No doubt this assumption is often a consequence of the liberal proclivity for thinking in contractualist terms. For an illustration of the communitarian view of membership as the basic trumping good, see Walzer, *Spheres of Justice*, pp. 29, 31–63.

and by what authority, who is to be a member is as fraught with conceptual and ideological baggage as who is to decide, and by what authority,
who is causally affected by a particular collective decision. These
difficulties should not therefore count as decisive against the causally
based view if the membership-based view is seen as the alternative.
Second, there is considerable experience with causally based arguments
in tort law. Although tort actions are often concerned with the causal
effects of individual rather than collective decisions, in dealing with
them courts have developed mechanisms for determining whose
claims should be heard, for sorting genuine claims from frivolous ones,
and for distinguishing weaker from stronger claims to have been adversely affected by an action and shaping remedies accordingly. This is
not an argument for turning politics into tort law; the point of the
comparison is, rather, to illustrate that in other areas of social life, institutional mechanisms have been developed to assess and manage
conflicting claims of being causally affected by actions. They may be
imperfect mechanisms, but they should be evaluated by reference to the
other imperfect mechanisms of collective decision making that actually
prevail in the world, not by comparison with an ideal that prevails
nowhere.[25]

Institutionalizing Opposition

Barrington Moore contends that "the existence of a legitimate and, to
some extent effective, opposition" is the defining criterion of
democracy. One need not go all the way with him to be persuaded that
institutions fostering "loyal" opposition are essential to democratic
life.[26] First, opposition institutions perform the functional role of providing sites for potential alternative leaderships to organize themselves, making possible the periodic turnovers of power necessary—
though not sufficient—for democratic governance. Second, opposition
institutions help legitimate democracy by attracting social dissent toward antigovernment forces within the regime rather than directing it

[25]My contention that the causally based view is more defensible than the going alternatives is
compatible with some other arguments whose purpose is to decenter membership-based sovereignty as the decisive determinant of participation and to replace it with systems of overlapping jurisdiction in which different groups of persons are seen as sovereign over different
classes of decisions; see Thomas Pogge, "Cosmopolitanism and Sovereignty," Ethics 103 (October 1992), pp. 48–75; Alexander Wendt, "Collective Identity Formation and the International
State," American Political Science Review 88, no. 2 (June 1994), pp. 384–96; and William Antholis,
"Liberal Democratic Theory and the Transformation of Sovereignty" (Ph.D. diss., Yale University, 1993).

[26]Moore, Liberal Prospects, p. 8. See also Archibald S. Foord, His Majesty's Opposition, 1714–
1830 (London: Oxford University Press, 1964).

at the regime's foundations. Anger and disaffection can thus be directed at particular power holders without endangering the democratic order's legitimacy. Third, opposition institutions serve the public interest by ensuring that there are groups and individuals who have incentives to ask awkward questions, shine light in dark corners, and expose abuses of power. The importance of these considerations should not be minimized, but there is a more basic reason why the possibility of effective opposition is an essential requirement of democratic justice. Unless people can challenge prevailing norms and rules with the realistic hope of altering them, the requirement that the inherited past not bind us unalterably would be empty. The Burkean dimension of democratic justice could not be tempered in the ways that democratic justice requires.

Below I argue that the imperative to make effective opposition possible leads to three conditioning constraints on the exercise of power. Procedurally, it suggests that rules of governance should be deemed unacceptable if they render revision of the status quo impossible. Mechanisms should always exist, therefore, through which opposition can be articulated. Procedural guarantees need to be backed up by permissive freedoms of speech, petition, and association if they are to be effective, but even then they may often be insufficient to ensure meaningful opposition. Some have suggested that "substantive" democracy is the appropriate remedy for this malady, and although I resist this conclusion, I do defend a quasi-substantive constraint on the exercise of power: that hierarchies should generally be presumed suspect because of their propensity to atrophy into systems of domination. The presumption against hierarchy should be rebutted in many circumstances, some of which I explore with a series of queries that democratic justice bids us to direct at hierarchical arrangements. But the burden of justification appropriately falls on defenders of particular hierarchies.

Because there are no perfect decision rules, the products of even the best democratic procedures will leave some justifiably aggrieved. Libertarian writers draw from this the implication that it is better to have as little collective action as possible, but in a world of ubiquitous power relations, I argued earlier, that option is neither satisfying nor plausible. To point this out is not to deny that democratic decision rules can lead to the imposition of outcomes on one group by another or that the justification for those impositions classical democratic theorists believed available is not.[27] Rather, it leads to the suggestion that procedures for

---

[27]Even before the advent of the modern literature on public choice, Schumpeter had exposed the logical flaws in the Rousseauist idea of a general will, concluding that "though a common

expressing opposition should be thought valuable no matter what the prevailing mechanisms of collective decision. Recognizing that life goes on and decisions have to be made, we should seek the most appropriate rules of democratic governance for every circumstance. But people should nonetheless remain free to oppose what has been decided and to try to change it.

To require that meaningful opposition be tolerated is frequently to require more than dominant groups want to accept; for it can weaken their control of collective values and purposes. Accordingly, they often seek to oppose opposition or render it ineffective. Part of the challenge of democratic justice is to institutionalize ways to stop them, and it seems safe to assume that, on their own, procedural guarantees of the freedom to oppose will not secure this goal. Democratic theorists who value effective opposition, such as Huntington, have long recognized that unless procedural guarantees are backed up by permissive civil and political freedoms of speech, press, assembly, and organization, they are all too easily rendered meaningless.[28] The history of sham democracies during the communist era illustrates what can happen when permissive freedoms are not honored. Democrats would be unwise ever to think them dispensable.

Although permissive freedoms are often essential to securing the space for opposition and fostering it, it would be a mistake to conclude that in general they will be sufficient. To see why this is so, notice that permissive freedoms can actually undermine the possibility of challenging the status quo, as my earlier discussion of the proposed Clinton health care reform indicated. Inequalities in control over the resources needed to transform permissive freedoms into the service of effective opposition can mean that strategically powerful groups, when committed to prevailing arrangements, may be able to block all attempts to alter them. Thus, although permissive freedoms are reasonably deemed valuable for their propensity to permit and even foster opposition, they are not a panacea. When those committed to the status quo have unmatched access to information, wealth, and organizational resources, they may actually be able to use permissive freedoms to cement their advantages in place.

---

will or public opinion of some sort may still be said to emerge from the infinitely complex jumble of individual and group-wise situations, volitions, influences, actions and reactions of the 'democratic process,' the result lacks not only rational unity but also rational sanction." Joseph Schumpeter, *Capitalism, Socialism, and Democracy* (New York: Harper, 1942), p. 253.

[28]Huntington regards at least two turnovers of power following elections as necessary for a country's being democratic; see *Third Wave*, pp. 6–7. See also Robert A. Dahl, *Polyarchy: Participation and Opposition* (New Haven: Yale University Press, 1971).

Awareness of the combined impact of imperfect decision rules and differential control over political resources has led some commentators to defend "substantive" conceptions of democracy over "procedural" ones, usually by appeal to some variant of Justice Harlan Stone's celebrated fourth footnote in *United States v. Carolene Products Co.* Noting that well-functioning democratic processes might lead to the domination of "discrete and insular minorities," Stone countenanced the possibility that their operation might reasonably be limited when this occurs. Stone dealt with a circumscribed class of cases. But his point is a general one, and others have employed his reasoning more expansively.[29] For instance, John Hart Ely defended much of the judicial activism of the Warren Court by reference to *Carolene Products* reasoning.[30] Likewise, Charles Beitz has pressed the same considerations into a contention that the quantitative fairness of equal voting power will never ensure substantively democratic outcomes.[31] In Beitz's view, a truly democratic system of "qualitative fairness" requires a prior system of "just legislation," inasmuch as mere equal voting power can never be relied on to produce fair outcomes.[32]

Substantively democratic views merely have to be stated for the difficulty with them to be plain: How can Ely know what democratic processes ought to have achieved had they not been corrupted by the *Carolene* problem? Whence the theory of just legislation against which Beitz will evaluate the results of voting procedures? Writers such as Ely and Beitz have little to say to those who are unpersuaded by their respective conceptions of "equal concern and respect" and "qualitative fairness." If , as I maintain, there is no criterion for justice that is anterior

[29]Stone focused his attention on "statutes directed at particular religious . . . or racial minorities" and circumstances that tend "seriously to curtail the operation of those political processes ordinarily to be relied upon to protect minorities." *United States v. Carolene Products Co.*, 304 US 144 152 n. 4, (1938).

[30]John Hart Ely, *Democracy and Distrust: A Theory of Judicial Review* (Cambridge: Harvard University Press, 1980). Ely described his argument as purely procedural, designed to repair defects of democratic process. But as critics have pointed out and the discussion below makes clear, it is obviously substantive; see Rogers M. Smith, *Liberalism and American Constitutional Law* (Cambridge: Harvard University Press, 1985), pp. 89–91, 170–74.

[31]Charles Beitz, "Equal Opportunity in Political Representation," in *Equal Opportunity*, ed. Norman E. Bowie (Boulder: Westview, 1988), pp. 155–74. It should not be thought that *Carolene Products* logic is the exclusive preserve of the political left. For instance, Riker and Weingast employ it to criticize taxation of property: "What protection is there against members of today's majority from providing private, redistributive benefits to themselves under the guise of public purposes and at the expense of some minority of owners and the efficiency of production? Why is the abridgement of a minority's economic rights less troubling than an abridgement of the same minority's political rights?" William H. Riker and Barry R. Weingast, "Constitutional Regulation of Legislative Choice: The Political Consequences of Judicial Deference to Legislatures," Hoover Institution Working Paper Series, (Stanford, December 1986), p. 6.

[32]Beitz, "Equal Opportunity," p. 168.

to what democracy generates, this should not be surprising. To say this is not, however, to respond to the difficulty that motivates *Carolene*-type reasoning: there are no perfect decision rules, and those who are better placed to translate permissive freedoms into political power should be expected, ceteris paribus, to get their way. The problem is real but the proffered solutions overreach, suggesting the desirability of finding a middle ground. More than process, less than substance might be an appropriate slogan.

My suggestion is that we stake out the middle ground with the proposition that hierarchies should be presumed suspect. The reason is that although hierarchies can exist for many legitimate purposes, by definition they contain both power inequalities and truncated opportunities for opposition. Power, as Lord Acton said, tends to corrupt. Even, and perhaps especially, when they acquire it legitimately, power holders all too easily convince themselves that their authority should expand in space and time, that critics are ignorant or irresponsible, and that subordinates lack the requisite ability to ascend from inferior roles. The allure of power can thus divert power holders within hierarchies from their legitimate goals, leading to the reduction of hierarchies to their power dimensions. The comparatively limited scope for opposition within hierarchies makes it difficult to block or check their atrophy into systems of domination; indeed as atrophy advances, the possibilities for opposition are likely to be increasingly constrained. It is for this reason that democrats should keep a skeptical eye on all hierarchical arrangements, placing the burden of justification on their defenders. Power need not be abused but it often is, and it is wise for democrats to guard against that possibility.

The preceding observations do not imply that all hierarchies should be eliminated, even if abolition could be achieved.[33] Rather, they suggest that there are good grounds for prima facie suspicion of hierarchies, even when they result from democratic collective decisions. Avoidable hierarchies too often masquerade as unavoidable ones; involuntary subordination is shrouded in the language of agreement; unnecessary hierarchies are held to be essential to the pursuit of common goals; and fixed hierarchies are cloaked in myths about their fluid-

---

[33]The quixotic political commitments that follow from the injunction to overthrow all hierarchy everywhere have been explored in Roberto Unger's multivolume *Politics* (Cambridge: Cambridge University Press, 1987). For criticism of his argument, see my "Constructing Politics," *Political Theory* 17, no. 3 (August 1989), pp. 475–82. For a more helpful and nuanced discussion of the relations between hierarchy and domination than Unger's, see Iris Marion Young, *Justice and the Politics of Difference* (Princeton: Princeton University Press, 1990), especially chaps. 2 and 4.

ity. Democratic justice suggests mistrust of prevailing hierarchies; it invites us to look for institutional and other structuring devices to limit them and to mitigate their unnecessary and corrosive effects. Such devices may be thought of as contributing to the evolving frameworks of democratic constraints within which people should be free to negotiate and renegotiate the terms of their cooperation and conflict.

To say that hierarchies are suspect is not to say anything about what is to count as sufficient to rebut the presumption. Nor is it to say anything about what kinds of constraints on hierarchies should be employed in various circumstances or about how these constraints should be enforced. By itself, the general argument cannot answer these questions. But it does generate a series of appropriate queries about hierarchies—ways of probing them in the name of democratic justice.

The first concerns the degree to which a given hierarchy is inevitable. Consider the differences between adult domestic relations and parent-child relations. Both have taken a multiplicity of forms, even in the recent history of the West; yet almost all of these have been explicitly hierarchical. It is evident, however, that parent-child relations are inevitably hierarchical in ways that adult domestic relations are not. If a relationship is not inevitably hierarchical, the first question that arises is why should it be hierarchical at all? There may be justifiable reasons for a particular inessential hierarchy (that it is comparatively efficient, that it has been chosen, that the relevant people like it, or some other), but from the standpoint of democratic justice the presumption is against hierarchy and the proponent of such a reason should adopt the burden of persuasion.

When relations are inevitably hierarchical a different class of considerations becomes relevant. We begin by asking Is it necessary that the relations in question be maintained at all? Parent-child relations of some kind must exist, but not all inevitably hierarchical relations are of this sort. To consider a limiting case once again, history has shown that the institution of slavery need not exist. If an inescapably hierarchical relationship is unnecessary, it immediately becomes suspect—a kind of surplus hierarchy—from the standpoint of democratic justice. Slavery thus fares badly from this standpoint quite apart from its incompatibility with the presumption of universal inclusion.

A second class of appropriate inquiries about hierarchies concerns their pertinence to the activity at hand: Are the hierarchical relations that exist appropriately hierarchical? Parent-child relations, for example, may be more hierarchical than they need to be in many instances, and they may include unnecessary kinds of hierarchical authority. They may also be maintained for reasons ranging from the convenience of parents to desires to dominate which have nothing to do with the interests of their charges. Of alterable hierarchies we should thus always inquire In whose interests are they sustained? Those who would sustain a hierarchy of a particular kind, or sustain it for longer than necessary, take on the burden of establishing that sustaining it operates in the interests of those subjected to it. For this reason one would be unmoved by the argument advanced by Amish parents in the *Wisconsin v. Yoder* litigation, namely that they should be free not to send their teenaged children to school because experience had taught them that school attendance induced in the teenagers the desire to leave the Amish community, a desire that interfered with the parents' rights of free religious exercise.[34]

Democratic justice also bids us to attend to the degree to which hierarchies are ossified or fluid. We should distinguish self-liquidating hierarchies, as when children become adults or students graduate, from non–self-liquidating hierarchies such as caste systems and hierarchies constituted by hereditary transmissions of wealth and power. We should also distinguish hierarchical orders in which anyone can in principle ascend to the top from those in which that is not so. No woman can aspire to become pope, a fact that makes the Catholic religion less attractive than some others from the standpoint of democratic justice on this score. In general the argument tells us to prefer fluid hierarchies over ossified ones, other things being equal. Fluid hierarchies may not create permanently subordinated classes whereas ossified hierarchies will. Of course other things seldom are equal; nonetheless the requirement is a useful starting point. It tells us what the presumption is and by whom the burden of persuasion should be carried.

Similarly, asymmetrical hierarchies are questionable whereas symmetrical ones are not necessarily so. Polygamous marriages are generally asymmetrical, for example, and as such suspect from the standpoint of democratic justice: a husband can have many wives but a wife cannot have many husbands.[35] If these polygamous regimes were sym-

[34]*Wisconsin v. Yoder*, 406 US 205 (1972). From the standpoint of democratic justice, *Yoder* was thus wrongly decided, although it would have been a more difficult case had the parents pressed their best understandings of their children's interests rather than their own. See Chap. 6.

[35]This is not to say that all polygamous regimes fare equally poorly from the standpoint of democratic justice. Polygamous regimes from which there is no realistic chance of escape (as when they are enshrined in a country's legal system as the only available form of marriage) fare worse than polygamous regimes that are tolerated, but not obligatory, and from which escape is legally possible and not prohibitively expensive. Even in these circumstances there is always the possibility that voluntary adherents have been brainwashed, of course, and arguments to this

metrical, or had their members practiced "complex marriage," as did the nineteenth-century Oneida Perfectionist community (in which any number of men could marry any number of women), they would not be questionable by reference to this aspect of the argument for democratic justice. Again, there may be other reasons rooted in democratic justice for objecting to such arrangements, but their symmetry would count in their favor.[36]

Closely related to questions about the relative fluidity and symmetry of hierarchies are questions about the degree to which they are imposed. Did the people subjected to them elect to be thus subjected? What were their other realistic options at the time? Whether or not they chose to enter, what degree of freedom to exit now exists? Generally, nonimposed hierarchies fare better than imposed ones, and less imposed hierarchies fare better than more imposed ones. If someone elected to participate at the bottom of an hierarchical relationship when she had alternative nonhierarchical (or less hierarchical) options in front of her, the fact of her choice confers some presumptive legitimacy on the state of affairs. Analogously, if someone remains in an hierarchical order when we are fairly confident that he has the resources to leave, we have less reason to be troubled from the standpoint of democratic justice than when this is not the case.

Finally, the general argument for democratic justice directs us to attend to the relative insularity of hierarchies. To what extent do they consist of self-contained groups of people minding their own business who want to be left alone by outsiders? Withdrawing sects such as the Old Order Amish or migrating groups such as the Mormons who went to Utah in the nineteenth century to escape persecution in the East have at least prima facie valid claims that they should be able to set the terms of their association unimpeded. Such groups do not proselytize or seek

---

effect cannot be dismissed out of hand. But their proponents will have to come to grips with the eloquently reasoned denials of this put forward by some Mormon women. It has been argued, for instance, that polygamous marriage makes it possible for women to have both a career and a family so that polygamy "is good for feminism"; see Elizabeth Joseph, "My Husband's Nine Wives," *New York Times*, April 9, 1991, p. A22.

[36]The Oneida Perfectionists, founded in 1848 in Oneida, New York, by John Henry Noyes, rejected all forms of private property and extended their belief in community property to community property in persons. Like the Mormon polygamists they were persecuted by the state, eventually abandoning their commitment to complex marriage in 1879; see Carol Weisbrod, "On the Breakup of Oneida," *Connecticut Law Review* 14, no. 4 (summer 1982), pp. 717–32. In fact the community was run in an authoritarian manner by Noyes, who decided unilaterally who could marry, suggesting that the community would have been suspect on a number of grounds from the standpoint of democratic justice; see Spenser Klaw, *Without Sin* (New York: Penguin, Allen Lane, 1993).

to shape the world outside their communities (as religious fundamentalists, for example, often do). Hierarchical and undemocratic as these groups might be in their internal organization, they are of little consequence to the outside world. By contrast, an hierarchical established church whose influence on outsiders could not be escaped without substantial cost would not enjoy the same prima facie claim to be left alone. Relatively insular groups might be objectionable from the standpoint of democratic justice on some of the other grounds just discussed, but the fact of their insularity diminishes any externality based claim by outsiders to restructure or abolish them.

II. Some Difficulties Considered

The preceding elaboration of the two central dimensions of democratic justice is a first installment; it raises many questions that it fails to answer. In the space that remains I address those that seem to me to be the most important: those having to do with the complex character of democratic justice, tensions between it and other goods, and the appropriate role for the state which is implied by the general argument.

Conflicts Internal to Democratic Justice

Any argument for an internally complex set of principles must confront the possibility that they cannot be satisfied simultaneously. The question then arises How are conflicts among the different injunctions to be resolved? One response to this question is to come up with a system of metarules for resolving conflicts when they occur. For instance Rawls's theory of justice consists of principles that, he argues, should be lexically ranked: in the case of conflicts, the principles that are higher in his lexical ordering trump those that are lower.[37]

It is evident that democratic justice exhibits an analogous potential for internal conflict. What the general argument recommends as the appropriate system of governance in a domain may conflict with the presumptive suspicion of hierarchy. People might choose to create a hierarchy by voluntary action or majority rule. Likewise, the various injunctions against hierarchy might produce contradictory prescriptions as far as a particular practice is concerned. The insular character of withdrawing sects, such as Mormons and the Amish, counsels leaving them alone, yet their internally hierarchical practices prompt suspicion

[37]Rawls, *Theory of Justice*, pp. 42–45, 61–65, 82–89, 151–61.

from the standpoint of democratic justice. How should conflicts of this kind be resolved?

The two alternatives here are either to try to come up with a system of metaprinciples analogous to Rawls's lexical rules or to supply a principled defense of a more underdetermined view. To try to come up with a complete system of metaprinciples which would resolve every possible tension that could arise out of the complexities of the general argument seems to me to be so demanding a task that it would almost certainly fail.[38] The range of circumstances that can arise is exceedingly large, if not infinite, and the complexity of the social world is such that there will always be challenges to the logic internal to democratic justice. This is less troubling than might at first appear to be the case. For one thing, the lack of a complete system of metaprinciples does not silence democratic justice in every circumstance. We can still say, for example, that a practice that runs up against a great many of democratic justice's presumptions is correspondingly more suspect for that reason. Slavery is an easy case for democratic justice just because this is so. It violates basic principles of collective self-governance and it is on the wrong side of every presumption about hierarchy which I discussed: it is unnecessary, it is not usually entered into voluntarily, it is hard or impossible to escape, it is both asymmetrical and non–self-liquidating, and it has external effects that permeate the social world. By the same token, a practice that turns out to be on the right side of every presumption will be equally easy to deal with.

The more difficult and interesting cases are those that are less clear-cut. In many it may be possible to find accommodations among conflicting injunctions. For instance, in the case of the Amish one might take the view that the withdrawing character of the group and the absence of a threat posed by it to the rest of society counsels against any attempt to interfere with its existence but that the state should nonetheless insist that Amish children be educated so that they have the capacities to function outside the Amish community in the event they should decide to leave. Thus while on this view one would not tolerate all Amish educational practices, in other respects they would be left alone.[39] Likewise, although the ossified and non–self-liquidating hierarchies in the Catholic Church contravene some of the presumptions of democratic

---

[38]It is not difficult, for example, to demonstrate the existence of contradictory imperatives flowing from Rawls's lexical rankings; see T. M. Scanlon, "Rawls's Theory of Justice," in *Reading Rawls*, ed. Norman Daniels (Oxford: Blackwell, 1975), pp. 169–205; H. L. A. Hart, "Rawls on Liberty and Its Priority," in ibid., pp. 230–52; and Benjamin Barber, "Justifying Justice: Problems of Psychology, Politics, and Measurement in Rawls," in ibid., pp. 292–318.

[39]This is the view defended in Chapter 6.

justice, the history of domination that has accompanied established churches might counsel that there is wisdom in an especially wide latitude of tolerance as far as religious matters are concerned. A government guided by the principles of democratic justice might nonetheless attach some costs to religions that contravene them, such as denying tax-exempt status to those in which some offices are reserved for men, persons of a particular race, or any other group defined in a morally arbitrary way. The governing body of the religion in question would then be free to decide whether to live with the sanctions in question or to adjust its practices to avoid them.[40]

These examples indicate that once we recognize that there is a range of possible sanctions and of feasible responses to them, apparently conflicting imperatives can be managed in a variety of ways that can, over time, be expected to encourage civil institutions to evolve in comparatively democratic directions. To some, even this approach will sound like opening the way for dangerously radical interference with freedom of religious worship. But reflection on our current laws concerning racially exclusionary organizations, and on the distinctions we comfortably draw between religions and cults and between education and brainwashing, should reveal that we routinely make many judgments of this kind, however implicitly. These examples also underline the fact that when we value more than one commitment we sometimes have either to live with tensions among them or to come up with creative solutions to the tensions. This is no less true of the world in which we actually live than it would be in a world in which democratic justice furnished the basic principles of governance. The imperatives that follow from the constituent parts of the United States constitution and its amendments generate many tensions, and just as courts and legislatures have to order, rank, and accommodate them in particular contexts, so the same would have to be done in a world governed by considerations derived from the general argument for democratic justice. Admittedly, to say this is not to resolve any specific tensions, but it does perhaps indicate the limits of what it is reasonable to expect from a general statement of principles.

A different objection to the internally complex character of democratic justice is that it is unnecessarily complex. My claim that freedom to oppose collective outcomes is not derivative of rights to inclusive participation might be granted, but, if this freedom is valued regardless of

[40]From the standpoint of democratic justice, the Supreme Court thus reached the right result in *Bob Jones University v. United States,* when it held that the federal government may legitimately deny tax-exempt status to institutions that would otherwise qualify but which engage in racial discrimination; 461 US 574 (1983).

whether decisions were made democratically, then why value democratic decision making? Is not democracy, by my account, reducible to opposition? My answer is that although inclusive participation and freedom to oppose are of independent value, the ways in which they are exercised are not without implications for one another. In particular, I propose the following injunction: the more democratically those who win in battles over collective decisions conduct themselves in victory, the stronger is the obligation on the defeated to ensure that their opposition is loyal rather than disloyal—and vice versa. Processes of inclusive consultation, meaningful hearings, good-faith consideration of how to mitigate external effects of decisions, and willingness to consider alternatives all build legitimacy for democratic decision making, and they should. No less appropriately, their opposites breed cynicism and mistrust on the part of losers, which erode democracy's legitimacy in predictable ways. By linking the obligation to make opposition loyal to how democratically those in power conduct themselves, protagonists on all sides are reminded of the imperfection of the rules that give present winners their victories and losers their losses. In addition, if the two are linked, both winners and losers have incentives to search for mechanisms that can diminish the distances that divide them.

Trade-offs between Democratic Justice and Other Goods

Additional sources of tension arise from my argument being premised on the notion that democracy is a conditioning good—subordinate to the activities whose pursuit it regulates. This means that there can and most likely will be tensions between the requirements of democratic justice and the activities it is intended to condition. In the limiting case, there will be activities that operate in flat contradiction to the principles I have described. Apart from the case of parent-child relations, to which some attention has already been devoted, there are football teams, armies, and many other organizational forms whose purposes seem to defy democratic governance. No doubt one can always challenge the proposition that such organizational forms must necessarily be undemocratic, and as the rich literature on the governance of the firm indicates, we should always be open to creative possibilities for the democratic management of institutions that seem inherently undemocratic.[41] Yet one has to confront the possibility that there will be circumstances in which there are inescapable trade-offs between

[41]For useful summaries of the literature, see Henry Hansman, "When Does Worker Ownership Work?" *Yale Law Journal* 99, no. 8 (June 1990), pp. 1749–1816, and Robin Archer, *Economic Democracy* (Oxford: Clarendon, 1995).

democratic control and the pursuit of a particular good, be it the gathering of military intelligence, the running of a professional sports team, or other valuable activity.

One response is to deal with trade-offs of this kind in the same way that tensions internal to democratic justice are handled, by recognizing that when there is more than one thing we value at times we will have to choose among them. But this should be the last response, not the first. Although there is never a guarantee that trade-offs between democratic justice and other goods can be avoided, the argument for democratic justice bids us to try to find ways to avoid them. Consider the two examples just mentioned. Congress has devised oversight mechanisms that, however imperfectly, ensure some democratic accountability of intelligence agencies consistent with their secret purposes. No doubt we pay a price for them and they could be improved upon, but the outcome of the Cold War scarcely suggests that our system fared worse than the Soviet system, in which there was virtually no democratic accountability of any sort, or indeed that it fared less well than other systems in the West which until recently have had little or no democratic oversight.[42] As far as professional sports are concerned, there too the situation is less clear-cut than it might at first appear to be. Although one would not want everyone on the team calling plays, there are many areas in professional sports where a measure of democratic control can be achieved without compromise of athletic purpose. Pay and working conditions are the most obvious areas; no doubt there are others. To reiterate, the general point is that the presumption is against undemocratic ways of doing things. It is only a presumption and it can be overcome, but reasons should be demanded and the burden of persuasion should always lie with those who would limit democracy's operation.

Competing Demands of Different Domains

Yet other potential tensions arise, for democratic justice, out of the fact that it is simultaneously concerned with many domains of civil society. It may be that pursuing democratic justice in one domain makes it more difficult, perhaps even impossible, to pursue it in other domains. For instance, participating in governance is part of what

---

[42]Robert A. Dahl has argued that analogous skepticism is in order toward claims that democratic control of nuclear arsenals and development interferes with their efficient deployment; see his *Controlling Nuclear Weapons: Democracy versus Guardianship* (Syracuse: Syracuse University Press, 1985), pp. 33–51.

democratic justice requires. Yet there are limits to how much time people have available, so that increased participatory involvement in one domain may mean diminished participation in others. This is what Carmen Sirianni has characterized as the "paradox of participatory pluralism." It arises for anyone who both values democratic participation and embraces a view of politics that ranges throughout civil society. We cannot simultaneously maximize participation over all domains.[43]

The paradox is inescapable for participatory democrats like Sirianni (who offers no solution to it), but the argument for democratic justice suggests avenues for dealing with it. Participation is not valuable for its own sake in my view; rather, it is valuable only as it is pursued in conjunction with the goods that it conditions. Collective self-governance is important in every domain of civil society but it is never the most important thing; adherents of democratic justice should thus always be open to time saving and other novel devices to conserve participatory resources. For instance, since the 1970s some writers have explored the use of so-called citizen juries, randomly selected groups paid to debate public issues from the selection of presidential candidates to the governance of school districts.[44] Experience with citizen juries suggests that they may provide useful mechanisms for both exerting democratic control and solving the difficulty, pointed to by Sartori and others, that "knowledge—cognitive competence and control—becomes more and more the problem as politics becomes more and more complicated."[45] Randomly selected lay groups with no particular vested interest in the outcome in a given area can invest the time and energy needed to make informed decisions. Such groups can gather data and listen to expert witnesses, making use of esoteric knowledge without being held hostage to it. The decisions they render could be advisory or even binding, at least for certain matters. From the standpoint of democratic justice the possibilities offered by citizen juries are worth exploring because they provide a potential way out of Sirianni's paradox: they combine citizen control with the possibility of sophisticated decision making in a complex world, and they do it in a way that takes account of the economy of time.[46]

[43]Carmen Sirianni, "Learning Pluralism: Democracy and Diversity in Feminist Organizations," in *NOMOS XXXV: Democratic Community*, ed. John Chapman and Ian Shapiro (New York: New York University Press, 1993), pp. 283–312.

[44]See James Fishkin, *Democracy and Deliberation: New Directions for Democratic Reform* (New Haven: Yale University Press, 1991).

[45]Giovanni Sartori, *The Theory of Democracy Revisited* (Chatham, N.J.: Chatham House, 1987), 1:119–20.

[46]Citizen juries must confront the difficulty that whoever sets the agenda may exert disproportionate influence on the outcome, but this is a difficulty that every decision-making

Earlier I suggested that, from the standpoint of democratic justice, participation should be seen neither in purely instrumental terms nor as the point of the exercise in politics. Such devices as the citizen jury are attractive because they are an example of a creative institutional response to the goal of trying to occupy a middle ground between these two views. Everyone might be expected to participate in some citizen juries, just as everyone is expected to sit on some conventional juries. Everyone would know that, in the juries they are not involved in, other randomly selected juries were sitting with no particular agendas or interests of their own that were being advanced. Everyone would also know that no matter how complex and technical decisions were becoming, a meaningful element of lay control would nonetheless be present in all collective decision making. This is essential for democratic justice.

III. THE ROLE OF THE STATE

Apart from the extremes of limiting cases such as slavery, the general argument for democratic justice does not provide conclusive assessments of particular decision rules or mechanisms of opposition. Instead, as we have seen, it generates presumptions and distributes burdens of persuasion in various ways. That is as it should be. Because the general argument is semicontextual, particularities of context are needed to decide when burdens have been appropriately carried and when presumptions have been rebutted. Democratic justice generates determinate conclusions in particular contexts only.

To say this is not, however, to deliver on everything that should reasonably be expected of the general argument. Invoking the language of presumptions and burdens of persuasion immediately raises the question Who is to judge when burdens have been carried and presumptions rebutted? Since the evidence will often be inconclusive and opinion about it must be expected often to be divided, just where decision-making authority should be located is, and is bound to remain, an important general question. The answer is also partly contextual; different authorities are appropriate in different kinds of circumstances. But the answer is only partly contextual; from the standpoint of democratic justice, some general considerations apply.

---

procedure must confront. It is not the weakness in democratic theory that they are intended to resolve, though proponents of citizen juries, like proponents of other decision-making mechanisms, need to be concerned about it.

Antivanguardism and Its Limits

Whenever anyone claims to know how to get to democracy un-democratically, skepticism is in order for two reasons, one practical and one normative. The practical reason is that it is doubtful that she can know that she is right. Just because democratic reforms are typically reactive responses to particular evils and chart a new course into the future, it is usually difficult to know what their full consequences will be or what new problems they will create. For instance, the changes in American family law mentioned in Chapter 5—making marriage more of a contract and less of a status—were motivated by a desire to under-mine the patriarchal family. But it has since become evident that one of the net effects of these changes has been to render women increasingly vulnerable to the greater economic power of men in marriage. As this becomes evident, creative democratic responses will be sought and new experiments will be tried, which will give rise to new difficulties. So the process will continue. Likewise with the debate on democracy in the workplace, where there is now considerable disagreement on which are more effective in undermining alienating hierarchy: strategies of worker self-management, plans for employee ownership or part own-ership that leave the structure of management comparatively un-touched, or various other devices. Different possibilities have been ex-plored in different industries. It seems certain that no single model will turn out to be generally applicable and that new possibilities are yet to be tried.[47]

To take an example from the realm of institutional governance, dur-ing the nineteenth century reasonable salaries and working conditions for politicians were rightly seen as essential to undermining a system in which government was a part-time activity for the wealthy. But these improvements have brought with them new brands of ossified power in the form of professional politicians with lifetime career aspirations in government. In the United States, electoral politics have become depen-dent on money to such a degree that political elites often manage to maintain themselves in positions of power for life in ways that are at odds with democracy's hostility toward entrenched hierarchy.[48] In re-sponse, new democratic reforms are being called for, geared toward

[47]See Charles Sabel and Jonathan Zeitlin, "Historical Alternatives to Mass Production," *Past and Present*, no. 108 (1986), pp. 133–76; Hansman, "When Does Worker Ownership Work?" and Archer, *Economic Democracy*.

[48]See Herbert Alexander, *Financing Politics: Money, Elections, and Political Reform* (Washington, D.C.: Congressional Quarterly Press, 1976), and Frank J. Sorauf, *Inside Campaign Finance* (New Haven: Yale University Press, 1992).

limiting the number of terms politicians can serve and better regulating the role of money in electoral politics.[49]

It defies credulity to suppose that in these instances democratic reformers could have understood social processes profoundly enough, or seen sufficiently far into the future, to have anticipated all the problems and possibilities ahead. Yet these cases are not exceptional; life has more imagination than we do, and it will often defeat our best efforts and present unexpected obstacles and opportunities. The fabric of social life and the dynamics of historical change are complex and little understood; that is the reality with which we have to live. Designing democratic institutional constraints is thus bound to be a pragmatic business, best pursued in context-sensitive and incremental ways. New activities come into being; technological change, experience, and the evolution of other causally linked activities all present fresh problems and generate novel possibilities for democratic governance. There are good reasons to be skeptical of anyone who denies this, whether he harbors a hidden agenda obscured by his vanguardist pretensions or is acting out of misplaced faith in his own prescient abilities.

Means/ends dichotomies are suspect, also, for the normative reason that they undermine the spirit of democratic justice. Although I have argued that we should resist the participatory democrat's contention that participation is valuable for its own sake, we should be no less wary of purely instrumental conceptions of democracy. Democratic means are never the point of the exercise, but they are usually of more than mere instrumental value. There is value to doing things democratically, and there is value to struggling with how to do things democratically while still achieving one's other goals. Democratic habits of self-restraint and attention to the needs and aspirations of others have to be learned through democratic practice; succumbing to the authoritarianism inherent in means/ends dichotomies should be expected to undermine democratic practice. In this connection, Dewey penned the right maxim for democratic justice in 1939: "Our first defense is to realize that democracy can be served only by the slow day

[49]In this connection a small but not insignificant victory was achieved for democracy in March 1990 in *Austin v. Michigan State Chamber of Commerce*, 110 S Ct 1391, when the Supreme Court cut back on the *Buckley v. Valeo*, 424 US 1 (1976) rule, which had held that although contributions to political campaigns may be limited by legislation, limiting expenditures constitutes a violation of the free speech clause of the First Amendment. In *Austin* the Court held that some corporate expenditures on political speech may be regulated. As far as term limits are concerned, there is considerable scholarly debate as to how bad the incumbency problem is and whether term limits would be a solution to the ossification of power in professional hands. They might, for example, lead to a net transfer of power from politicians to bureaucrats, as Morris Fiorina suggests in *Divided Government* (London: Macmillan, 1992), pp. 53–59.

by day adoption and contagious diffusion in every phase of our common life of methods that are identical with the ends to be reached."[50]

The principled refusal to impose solutions from above can provoke the argument that without imposition they will not be implemented at all, and there are, indeed, at least three important classes of exceptions to the initial presumption against vanguardism. The first concerns the provision of public goods. As my earlier discussion of education revealed, when the provision of public goods is at issue and there are differential capacities for exit, no local decision rule is likely to be effective in diminishing injustice. This amounts to saying that effective policies will have to be imposed from above.[51] Proponents of "shock therapy" in the transition from communism to capitalism seem often to take an analogous view. Adam Przeworski argues, for example, that during transitions from authoritarianism to democracy, unless economic reforms are rammed through from above, those who are adversely affected by them will mobilize their opposition to them through the democratic process, scuttling the reforms. Consequently, fledgling democratic governments "face the choice of either involving a broad range of political forces in the shaping of reforms, thus compromising their economic soundness, or trying to undermine all opposition to the [reform] program." In Przeworski's view, any government "that is resolute must proceed in spite of the clamor of voices that call for softening or slowing down the reform program." Because reformers "know what is good," all political conflicts become no more than a waste of time. Przeworski goes on to point out that every instance of successful market reform during democratic transitions on record was implemented by executive decree, remarking, "This potential is inherent in the very conception of market reforms."[52]

From the standpoint of democratic justice, the critical question is whether the reformers really do "know what is good" and pursue it in

[50]John Dewey, "Democratic Ends Need Democratic Methods for Their Realization," *New Leader*, October 21, 1939, reprinted in John Dewey, *The Political Writings*, ed. Debra Morris and Ian Shapiro (Indianapolis: Hackett, 1993), p. 206.

[51]For elaboration, see Jennifer Hochschild, *The New American Dilemma: Liberal Democracy and School Desegregation* (New Haven: Yale University Press, 1984).

[52]Adam Przeworski, *Democracy and the Market* (New York: Cambridge University Press, 1991), pp. 183–84. See also Janos Kornai, *The Road to a Free Economy: Shifting from a Socialist System* (New York: Norton, 1990); Jeffrey Sachs, "The Transformation of Eastern Europe: The Case of Poland" (the Frank E. Seidman Lecture, Rhodes College, Memphis, September 26, 1991); and Boris Pleskovic and Jeffrey Sachs, "Political Independence and Economic Reform in Slovenia," in *The Transition in Eastern Europe*, ed. Oliver Blanchard, Kenneth Foot, and Jeffrey Sachs (Chicago: University of Chicago Press, 1994), 1:191–220. For a competing view, see Mitchell Orenstein, "Out of the Red: Building Capitalism and Democracy in Post-Communist Europe," Ph.D. diss., Yale University, 1996.

fact. Much of what is presented by economic reformers as uncontroversially "good" might in fact be controversial, and many economic reforms described as "public goods" do not meet the technical criteria that require both joint supply and nonexcludability.[53] Whether the sorts of privatization and stabilization policies that such political economists as Przeworski, Janos Kornai, Jeffrey Sachs, and others advocate lead to the supply of public goods in this sense is debatable. No doubt parts of what is provided are public goods, but other aspects of these policies may amount to little more than mechanisms for the raiding of public treasuries by strategically well-placed groups, generating little or no benefit for anyone else. In such instances, the pursuit of private benefit may be cloaked in the language of public goods, and opposition that is really a reflection of zero-sum distributive conflict will masquerade as a collective action problem. What are billed as solutions to it will actually be partisan policies that help some sectors and hurt others. Democrats who suspect this to be the case with substantial parts of postcommunist privatizations are bound to find themselves ambivalent, at least, about the "bitter pill" strategies that depend on "initial brutality, on proceeding as quickly as possible with the most radical measures," and implementing reforms either by administrative fiat or by ramming them through legislatures.[54]

In circumstances where one does not doubt that a public good is being supplied, one's democratic moral intuitions are not troubled by decisive action from above. For instance in the South African constitutional negotiations that led up to the April 1994 elections, it gradually became clear that—desirable as multiparty round-table negotiations sounded— they were not going to produce an agreement on a democratic constitution. Too many groups had too many incentives to pursue private agendas at the expense of ensuring that the public good was provided. Consequently, it became evident that, if a democratic political order was to be put in place, it would have to be hammered out as an elite pact and then imposed on the society. This is what in fact transpired, and the reason that democrats the world over applauded as opponents to the transition were so effectively either marginalized or co-opted was that almost no one doubted that what the elites proposed to impose—a democratic constitutional order—was in fact a public good.[55]

---

[53]"A pure public good has two salient characteristics: jointness of supply and the impossibility or inefficiency of excluding others from its consumption, once it has been supplied by some members of the community"; Mueller, *Public Choice: II*, p. 11.

[54]Przeworski, *Democracy and the Market*, pp. 183–84.

[55]On the collapse of the roundtable negotiations and the emergence of an elite pact between the National Party and ANC leaderships, see Chapter 7, pp. 193–205 and 213–19.

Distinguishing the provision of genuine public goods from spurious ones is a difficult and controversial business. Often the two will be mixed, making the task even more difficult, as is almost certainly the case with most privatization plans. Even in the case of the South African constitution it seems clear that the elites who committed themselves to providing the public good in question sprinkled in a few benefits for themselves, notably a system of electoral and parliamentary rules which greatly weakens backbenchers vis-à-vis leaderships, as well as bribes to particular interest groups to insulate them from the new political order.[56]

From the standpoint of democratic justice, the extent to which policies may legitimately be imposed from above varies with the degree to which genuine public goods are being provided. As the preceding remarks indicate, this will often be hotly disputed and ideologically charged, not least because there will be those who have an interest in obscuring the matter. It may also be genuinely unclear in certain circumstances. In either case, what we are witnessing is not a failure in the argument for democratic justice. Rather, it is a failure in understanding of, or agreement about, whether something constitutes a public good. This is not to diminish the normative importance of the matter; it is only to say that it would be to expect the wrong kind of thing from any political theory to ask of it that it resolve contentious empirical questions of political economy. The argument for democratic justice can be expected to counsel what to do when a certain fact pattern obtains; it cannot be expected to tell us whether or not the fact pattern really does obtain. The general argument does, however, counsel us to regard claims to be providing public goods with suspicion and to subject them to what lawyers think of as "strict scrutiny." American courts typically subject legislative action to this most demanding level of constitutional scrutiny when the proposed action interferes with a "fundamental" liberty, usually a freedom protected by the Bill of Rights. Strict scrutiny requires a showing that the governmental objective is unusually important—that a "compelling" state interest is at stake—and that it

---

[56]As far as political elites sprinkling in benefits for themselves is concerned, the 1993 constitution requires that any member of Parliament who ceases to be a member of his or her political party will also cease to be a member of Parliament, being replaced by someone else from the party's parliamentary list. This provision obviously greatly strengthens the hands of party leaderships. As for bribes, all civil service jobs and salaries were guaranteed for at least five years after the transition, and in the last weeks before the election President De Klerk transferred some three million acres of land to Zulu king Goodwill Zwelitini in order to prevent their falling under the control of the new national government after the elections. *New York Times*, May 24, 1994, p. A6.

cannot be accomplished in a less intrusive way.[57] By analogy we might say that the undemocratic imposition of a public good is justified only when the good in question is essential to the operation of a democratic order and cannot be attained in any other way. Because those who claim to provide public goods may have ulterior motives, and because private goods can often masquerade as public goods, the strong presumption should always be against their imposition from above.

A second class of exceptions to the general presumption against vanguardism arises when illegitimate hierarchies have been maintained by the state. For example, in the West the disadvantaged status of women in family life was for centuries sustained by the common law and other active state policies. One dramatic legacy of this history is that as recently as the 1950s throughout the United States a husband could not be prosecuted for raping his wife. By the mid-1990s spousal rape was a prosecutable felony during an ongoing marriage in well over a third of American jurisdictions as a result of a concerted feminist campaign in state legislatures and courts.[58] It would have been impossible for such changes to have come about without the state's active involvement because it is the policies of the state that were at the root of the injustice in question. Likewise, it took the passage of the married women's property acts (the first wave of which began in the 1840s) to destroy the common law rule that had given the husband control over, and sometimes title to, the wife's property and possessions during marriage.[59]

In such circumstances it will be necessary, and justifiable from the standpoint of democratic justice, for the state to be centrally involved in dismantling the unjust system it has created. Women would have been morally misguided as well as politically shortsighted had they not sought to enlist public institutions in this struggle to refashion the terms of their domestic association. As the unjust hierarchies to which they had been subjected were direct products of state policies and sustained by the legal order, it was reasonable to require the state to play an active role in dismantling the injustices in question. Likewise, the effects of the

[57]See Laurence H. Tribe, *American Constitutional Law,* 2d ed. (Mineola, N.Y.: Foundation Press, 1988), pp. 251–75.

[58]On the changing law of marital rape in the United States, see Michael Freeman, "If You Can't Rape Your Wife, Who[m] Can You Rape? The Marital Rape Exception Re-examined," *Family Law Quarterly* 15, no. 1 (spring 1981), pp. 1–29; Deborah Rhode, *Justice and Gender* (Cambridge: Harvard University Press, 1989), pp. 249–51; Rene I. Augustine, "Marriage: The Safe Haven for Rapists," *Journal of Family Law* 29, no. 3 (1990/91), pp. 559–90; and Sandra Ryder and Sheryl Kuzmenka, "Legal Rape: The Marital Exception," *John Marshall Law Review* 24 (1992), pp. 393–421. On the English evolution of the exception, see P. M. Bromley and N. V. Lowe, *Family Law,* 7th ed. (Stoneham, Mass.: Butterworth, 1987), pp. 109–12.

[59]See H. H. Clark, *The Law of Domestic Relations in the United States,* 2d ed. (St. Paul, Minn.: West, 1988), p. 589.

Group Areas Act in South Africa, which led to the forced removals of millions of blacks from viable communities to desolate deserts, are properly responded to by remedial action from a democratic South African state.[60] The general point here is that the more that anti-democratic practices have been underwritten by the state, the more powerful is the case for the involvement of state institutions in remedying the unjust status quo.[61]

A third class of exceptions arises when domination within a domain is not a direct product of state action but is nonetheless sustained by forces external to that domain and removable only by state action. This is what Walzer has described as "dominance," the transfer of power in a domain of social life where it may be legitimate into another where it is not. Walzer contends, for instance, that economic inequality is not objectionable as such and that it may be justified in the sphere of production for its incentive and other efficiency effects. What is objectionable is that disparities in income and wealth are all too easily translatable into disparities in the political domain, the domestic domain, the educational domain, and other areas where they have no evident rationale.[62] This transfer happens because the resources necessary to exercise power tend to be fungible across domains, and Walzer sees it as one of the appropriate tasks of a democratic state to limit this fungibility. Thus laws against buying and selling votes for money can be defended, for example, even though such laws are inefficient in the economist's sense. Similarly, refusals by courts to enforce antenuptial agreements that leave divorcing spouses destitute amount to a refusal by the state to allow economic disparities that may be justifiable outside the domestic domain to set the terms of life within it.

From the standpoint of democratic justice Walzer's intuition about this class of cases is defensible, if for different reasons than those that he supplies. For Walzer the reason for trying to prevent domination within a sphere by those who control goods external to it is rooted in shared meanings about which goods are appropriate in which domains, whereas from the democratic justice standpoint the justification is rooted in considerations drawn from the political economy of power.[63] I said earlier that the shape of decision rules should follow the contours

---

[60]For an account of the extent and effects of these policies, see Helen Suzman, *In No Uncertain Terms* (New York: Knopf, 1993), pp. 65–212.

[61]On which state institutions are most appropriate for the purpose, whether courts, legislatures, or executive agencies, see below.

[62]Walzer, *Spheres of Justice*, pp. 3–30.

[63]I have argued elsewhere that the appeal to shared meanings fails because these are invariably in contention; see my *Political Criticism* (Berkeley: University of California Press, 1990), chap. 3.

of power relations, not those of memberships. It follows that when obstacles to democracy within a domain are externally sustained, it is an appropriate use of state power that it be used to remove such obstacles. To deny this would amount to abandoning democratic justice in particular domains to those who have imperial control of fungible resources. In short—pace Walzer—because causal effects rather than shared membership within a domain are decisive in legitimating a right to democratic control, it follows that state action that crosses the boundaries of domains can be justified when necessary to achieve democratic justice within a domain.[64]

Action from above to advance democratic reform can be justified, then, but not as part of any missionary quest on democratic justice's behalf. There is no secular analogue to "Christianizing the infidels" to justify such action, whether by courts, legislatures, or invading armies. Rather, external involvement can be justified by three principal classes of reasons: First, when provision of a public good is at stake, imposed solutions may be justifiable, subject to the caveats I have mentioned. This we might think of as a market-failure justification. Second, the state may often have an affirmative obligation to help foster democracy, flowing from its historical culpability in creating and sustaining injustice. Last, when external sources of domination within a domain can be removed only by state action, this can be justified by reference to the argument from causal legitimacy.

Legislatures versus Courts

The aspiration to avoid imposed solutions suggests that the presumption should generally be in favor of doing things through representative institutions rather than courts or other agencies, for the conventional reason that legislatures are comparatively more democratically accountable. There will be exceptions, but it is the exceptions that stand in need of justification. In this connection the argument for democratic justice exhibits an elective affinity with the approaches to constitutional adjudication defended by Ruth Bader Ginsburg and Robert Burt, so it will be useful to end with some discussion of their views.

Burt conceives of a constitutional democracy as inescapably committed to two principles—majority rule and equal self-determination—that have the potential to conflict with one another. If majoritarian

---

[64]It should be evident from my earlier discussion of public goods and state culpability that I also think Walzer is mistaken in thinking that preventing dominance is the only legitimate basis for the imposition of solutions by the state.

processes are employed to promote domination of some by others, the contradiction latent in democratic politics becomes manifest. In such circumstances democracy goes to war with itself and an institutional mechanism is needed to resolve the conflict. This is supplied, according to Burt, by judicial review, understood as "a coercive instrument extrinsic to the disputants" in a political struggle. Burt sees judicial review as a "logical response to an internal contradiction between majority rule and equal self-determination. It is not a deviation from that theory."[65]

If the court's legitimate role in a democracy is rooted in this logic of preventing domination through democratic process, then it follows in Burt's view that the court's activities should be limited to dealing with the consequences of the democratic contradiction. And inasmuch as preventing domination is the goal, it also follows that courts should not take up sides in disputes that are by-products of the democratic contradiction (effectively imposing the wishes of one group on another). Rather, they should declare the domination that has emerged from the democratic process unacceptable and insist that the parties try anew to find an accommodation. Thus, in contrast to what many have seen as the altogether too timid approach taken by the Supreme Court in the school desegregation cases of the 1950s and after, Burt's view is that the Court took the right stand. In *Brown v. Board of Education* the Justices declared the doctrine of "separate but equal" to be an unconstitutional violation of the equal protection clause, but they did not describe schooling conditions that would be acceptable.[66] Instead, they turned the problem back to Southern state legislatures, requiring them to fashion acceptable remedies themselves.[67] These remedies came before the court as a result of subsequent litigation, were evaluated when they did, and were often found to be wanting.[68] But the Court avoided designing the remedy itself—and thus the charge that it was usurping the legislative function.

Ginsburg, too, has made the case that when courts try to step beyond a reactive role they undermine their legitimacy in a democracy. Although she thinks that it is sometimes necessary for courts to step "ahead" of the political process to achieve reforms that the Constitution requires, if they get too far ahead the result can be a backlash with charges that the courts are overreaching their appropriate place in a democratic constitutional order.[69] She and Burt both think that the sort

[65]Robert A. Burt, *The Constitution in Conflict* (Cambridge: Harvard University Press, 1992), p. 29.
[66]*Brown v. Board of Education I*, 347 US 483 (1954).
[67]*Brown v. Board of Education II*, 349 US 294 (1955).
[68]Burt, *Constitution in Conflict*, pp. 271–310.
[69]Ruth Bader Ginsburg, "Speaking in a Judicial Voice" (Madison Lecture, New York Univer-

of approach adopted by Justice Blackmun in *Roe v. Wade* exemplifies this danger.[70] In contrast to the *Brown* approach, in *Roe* the Court did a good deal more than strike down a Texas abortion statute. The majority opinion laid out a detailed test to determine the conditions under which any abortion statute could be expected to pass muster. In effect, Justice Blackmun authored a federal abortion statute of his own. As Ginsburg put it, the court "invited no dialogue with legislators. Instead, it seemed entirely to remove the ball from the legislators' court" by wiping out virtually every form of abortion regulation then in existence.[71]

On the Ginsburg-Burt view, the sweeping holding in *Roe* diminished the Court's democratic legitimacy at the same time as it polarized opinion about abortion and put an end to various schemes to liberalize abortion laws which were underway in different states. Between 1967 and 1973, statutes were passed in nineteen states liberalizing the permissible grounds for abortion. Many feminists had been dissatisfied with the pace and extent of this reform, which is why they mounted the campaign that resulted in *Roe*. Burt concedes that in 1973 it was "not clear whether the recently enacted state laws signified the beginning of a national trend toward abolishing all abortion restrictions or even whether in the so-called liberalized states, the new enactments would significantly increase access to abortion for anyone." Nonetheless, he points out that "the abortion issue was openly, avidly, controverted in a substantial number of public forums, and unlike the regimen extant as recently as 1967, it was no longer clear who was winning the battle."[72] Following the *Brown* model, the Court might have struck down the Texas abortion statute in *Roe* and remanded the matter for further action at the state level, thereby setting limits on what legislatures might do in the matter of regulating abortion without involving the Court directly in designing that regulation. As Ginsburg and Burt believe, this would have left space for democratic resolution of the conflict, ensuring the survival of the right to abortion while at the same time preserving the legitimacy of the Court's role in a democracy.[73]

---

sity Law School, March 9, 1993), mimeo., pp. 30–38. See also "Nomination of Ruth Bader Ginsburg to be an Associate Justice of the United States Supreme Court: Report together with Additional Views," *Executive Report* 103, U.S. Senate, June 1, 1993.

[70]*Roe v. Wade*, 410 US 113 (1973).

[71]Ginsburg, "Speaking in a Judicial Voice," p. 32.

[72]Burt, *Constitution in Conflict*, p. 348.

[73]Ibid., pp. 349–52. The Ginsburg-Burt approach was finally adopted by the Supreme Court in *Planned Parenthood of Pennsylvania v. Casey*, 112 S Ct 2791 (1992). By affirming the existence of a woman's fundamental constitutional right to an abortion, recognizing the legitimacy of the state's interest in potential life, and insisting that states may not pursue the vindication of that interest in a manner that is unduly burdensome to women, the Court set some basic limits

Although the tensions that arise within democratic justice differ from those that motivate Burt and Ginsburg, in three important respects their view of the appropriate role for courts in a democratic order fits comfortably within the general argument developed here. First, they articulate an appropriate institutional response to the injunction that, rather than impose democracy on collective activities, the goal should be to try to structure circumstances so that people will find ways to democratize practices for themselves. By placing courts in a naysaying stance of ruling out practices as unacceptable when they violate the strictures of democratic justice, courts can force legislatures and the conflicting parties they represent to seek creative solutions to their conflicts which can pass constitutional muster. Second, the Ginsburg-Burt view is attractive because it is reactive but directed; it exemplifies the creative pragmatism that motivates democratic justice. It involves accepting that there is an important—if circumscribed—role for courts in a democracy, yet it does not make the unmanageable administrative demands on courts which accompany more proactive views of adjudication. A court might reasonably hold that a given policy should be rejected without stating (indeed perhaps without having decided) what policy would pass muster. "This is unacceptable for reasons $a, b, c \ldots$; find a better way" is seen as an appropriate stance for a constitutional court. Finally, by recognizing the relatively greater legitimacy of legislatures and treating courts as institutional mechanisms for coping with legislative failure, the Ginsburg-Burt view takes account of the fact that no decision-making mechanism is flawless. Yet it does so in a way that is rooted in the idea that democratic procedures should be made to operate as well as possible, and that, when they fail, remedies should be no more intrusive on the democratic process than is necessary to repair them.

Some will object that this as too minimal a role for reviewing courts, but democrats have to concern themselves not only with courts that aspire to advance the cause of democratic justice, as they might reasonably be thought to have done in *Brown* and *Roe*, but also with courts that

---

within which legislatures must now fashion regulations that govern abortion. The *Casey* dissenters are right to point out that there will be a degree of unpredictability and confusion as various regulatory regimes are enacted in states and tested through the courts; see 112 S Ct 2791, at p. 2866 (1992). According to views of adjudication which encourage efficiency and clarity above all else, this will appear to be a reprehensible invitation to further litigation. By the Ginsburg-Burt view, however, that *Casey* invites litigation may be a cost worth paying. It places the burden of coming up with modes of regulating abortion that are not unduly burdensome on democratically elected legislatures and forces them to do this in the knowledge that the statutes they enact will be tested through the courts and thrown out if they are found wanting. These issues are taken up further in my introduction to *Abortion: The Supreme Court Decisions* (Indianapolis: Hackett, 1995), pp. 1–23.

do not, as was the case in *Dred Scott*, the *Civil Rights Cases*, and *Lochner v. New York*.[74] Insulated from any further review and lacking, at least in the American context, in democratic accountability, courts can put decisions of this kind in place which may not be reversed for decades or even generations. Although it may thus be wise from the standpoint of democratic justice to embrace an activist role for a constitutional court, it is equally wise to limit courts to a circumscribed and negationist activism.

I have sought here to render plausible the case for a democratic conception of social justice by building on the popular view in which considerations of democracy and justice are intimately linked, rather than on conventional academic views of them as fundamentally distinct and mutually antagonistic. My account rests on the twin commitments to government and opposition in democratic theory, suggesting that there should always be opportunities for those affected by the operation of a collective practice both to participate in its governance and to oppose its results when they are so inclined. These two injunctions should reasonably be expected to have different implications in different cultures and, within the same culture, to evolve over time and play themselves out differently in various domains. They are best thought of as conditioning constraints, designed to democratize social relations as they are reproduced, not as blueprints for social justice.

This view contains internal tensions, to be sure, but I have tried to show that they come with the territory in reflecting about the justness of social arrangements and to indicate something about how these tensions might best be coped with consistent with the spirit of the general argument. Beyond this, I have sought to indicate the main outlines of a view of the state that follows from my view and to develop some of its implications for the provision of public goods and for the state's appropriate role in advancing democratic justice more generally. I have sketched the basic principles that should guide state action, as well as the fitting nature and place for judicial review in the argument for democratic justice. No doubt these arguments raise as many questions as they settle, but I hope, nonetheless, that I have characterized the central argument and its motivation sufficiently fully to cast it in an attractive light.

In 1918, Dewey remarked that any philosophy animated by the striving to achieve democracy "will construe liberty as meaning a universe

---

[74]*Dred Scott v. Sandford*, 60 US 393 (1856); *In re Civil Rights Cases*, 109 US 3 (1883); *Lochner v. New York*, 198 US 45 (1905).

in which there is real uncertainty and contingency, a world which is not all in, and never will be, a world which in some respects is incomplete and in the making, and which in these respects may be made this way or that according as men judge, prize, love and labor. To such a philosophy any notion of a perfect or complete reality, finished, existing always the same without regard to the vicissitudes of time, will be abhorrent."[75]   Democratic justice is conceived of in a similar contingent and pragmatic spirit. Just as there are no blueprints, there are no final destinations. Social practices evolve, as do technologies of government and opposition, often presenting fresh injustices and novel possibilities for dealing with them. The challenge is to confront the injustices and take advantage of the possibilities in a principled and satisfying way. Democratic justice is intended to help in that endeavor. Exploring its implications more fully, in a variety of contexts, is the task that lies ahead.

[75]From an address to the Philosophical Union of the University of California in November 1918, reprinted in Dewey, *Political Writings*, p. 44.

Index

Condorcet, Jean-Antoine-Nicolas de Caritat, Marquis de, 32, 42
Consensus, 116–22, 127, 181, 186, 223, 228–29
Conservative Party (U.K.), 47
Consociationalism, 14, 100–105, 176–77, 180–84, 205, 212–14, 216–17, 219
Constitutionalist fallacy, 8, 30–42, 51
Contractarianism, 28, 29, 225–30, 233
Courts, role of, 30–31, 34, 36–39
  limiting democratic institutions, 8, 15
  remedying defects of majority rule, 30, 37
Cover, Robert, 42
Critical reason, 158, 162–65, 167–71, 173, 174; as essential for democracy, 13, 146–49
Culture, contribution to democracy, 84, 89, 90, 92, 96, 99, 107–8
Cutright, Phillips, 95
Czechoslovakia, 93, 207

Dahl, Robert A., 8, 42–43, 47–48, 49, 80, 100, 101, 102, 178
De Klerk, F. W., 88, 91, 185, 193, 194, 198–204
"Democratic justice," 220–61
  conflicts within, 242–45
  method, 127–34, 135
  metric, 111–22, 124, 135
  principle, 112, 122–27, 135
  See also Justice
"Democratic relativism," 40
Democratic Russia coalition of parties, 88–89
Democracy:
  appeal to idiom of, 3, 109
  and capitalism, 109, 227
  citizenship in, 139, 145–49, 165, 171
  as collective self-government, 225–34, 247, 260
  democratic path to democracy, 13, 14, 15, 213, 249
  as foundational good, 121, 127, 134–36, 222
  within groups and institutions, 10, 81, 106–7, 120, 137, 143–45
  institutions of opposition, 12, 15, 179–82, 205, 214, 219, 223, 234–36, 239
  legitimacy of regime, 3, 234–35, 245, 257
  "loyal" opposition, 11, 13, 14, 15, 92–93, 177, 179, 182, 234
  loyalty to, 84–85, 89
  nonoptional character, 3
  as opposition, 7, 13, 51, 93, 126, 127, 175–219, 224–25, 234–42, 244–45, 260
  opposition to injustice, 6, 108, 109, 126, 220–21

and quality of outcomes, 41, 123–24
representing interests, 9, 10, 32, 33, 48, 49, 80–81, 180–82
and social justice, 10, 80, 82, 109–36, 220–61; *see also* Justice
as subordinate good, 15, 111, 126, 132–34, 222, 231, 236, 245–48, 260
two-turnover test, 1–2, 14, 82, 84, 179
as "will of the people," 80
See also Participation; Proceduralist democracy; Substantive democracy
Determinism, 74–75
Dewey, John, 5, 126–27, 128–29, 220, 250–51, 260–61
Di Palma, Giuseppe, 80–81, 82, 84, 90–93, 220
Direct democracy, 21, 230
Distributive justice, 7, 25, 54, 55, 59, 64, 69–75, 110. *See also* Justice
Divorce, 153, 159
  and property, 66, 67, 133, 255
  See also Family relations; Marriage
Domination, 11, 124–25, 127, 132–33, 135, 144, 172, 226, 238–39, 243–44, 254–56, 257; among "spheres," 116–17, 119–20, 255–56
Dunn, John, 110–11
Dutch Reformed Church, 89
Dworkin, Ronald, 9, 38, 54, 67–75

Economic models of preferences, 7, 10, 17, 80–81
Education, 13, 137–74, 240, 243–44, 257
  mandatory age of, 13, 138, 159
  purpose of, 141–43, 145–49, 158, 162, 166
  quality of, 159–60
Egypt, 83–84, 96
El Salvador, 207
Elite democracy, 10, 15, 81, 106, 181, 251, 254
Elites, 187–93, 217–18
  dominance of, 47–48,
  internal group dynamics of, 88, 102–3, 105
  relations with grass roots, 93, 102–3, 187, 189, 190–92
Elster, Jon, 159
Ely, John Hart, 16, 41, 42, 51, 124, 237
Employment:
  democracy in, 246, 249
  politics in, 52
Environmental threats, 2
Equality, 59–60, 64, 68–69
Equilibrium, 42–45
Ethnic identity, 83, 102
Expertise, 128–30
Exploitation, 60, 61, 63, 66
Externalities, 22–26, 29, 46, 129, 132–33, 148, 229, 232